SON OF A

ISBN 978-1-9161464-1-9

Trickett and Holland

SON OF A DOG

IMMERSED IN INDIA

JACQUES TRICKETT

Trickett and Holland

Introduction

This book is not a dramatised or romanticised collection of events, all that is written here is more than a geographical journey. It describes behaviours, apparent social mores, emotions, misunderstandings and their consequences, as well as activities. It all happened and it could also happen to you!

You will enjoy a glance at a colourful land, and take in descriptive elements in India, i.e., sea, countryside, roads, wandering cattle, smoke fumes, accidents, events and meetings with individuals and local Indian groups, plus an Indian wedding and much more.

You could easily say this book is also about pie in the sky, a dream maybe, an idea, an experiment, a kind of DIY event. However, there is more to this venture than that! There is a hope and energy, the hope that it should be possible for people from radically different cultures to assist each other in order to achieve their practical goals — the avoidance of poverty — without the assistance of distant bureaucratic, charitable institutions.

The idea was to finance, to physically assist to build and renovate, suitable premises for independent tourists to stay whilst on holiday, in a coconut grove near Kovalam, a seaside resort in India, and thereby contribute to the income of the family who already owned the property, as well as helping the micro economy i.e. the local village near the hut cum holiday home to be. And in return provide myself, the author, with the owner's good will and consent, and an occasional off-season holiday venue.

The main events took place during a prolonged stay in Kerala, South India, from 1998 to 1999, sparked off by a brief and previous holiday visit and encounter in 1997. Although this writing is finished twenty years after the events took place and India as a nation has progressed greatly since then, I expect many down to earth every day circumstances, situations and personalities are still there in various forms to be encountered to this day, such is the wide variation of development in India amongst the many.

We, that is myself Jack, and my companion for the project Queenie, a good friend, describe living in a village house with an Indian family. As people who started our lives pretty near the bottom of the social hierarchy, myself as an apprentice bricklayer and later reaching the dizzying heights of community care worker. Queenie as a betting shop counter assistant and later primary school teacher. Both brought up in the far north of England, we know the pain of hard work and poverty, we empathise, we agree to help the family to achieve their goals.

We show how relatively uneducated Brits, because that's what we know we are, both from very working class beginnings, with all our prejudices and imperfections and blindness, become seriously and easily "confused" when we attempt to cross cultural and geographical boundaries, and realize that humanity is a disparate, complex species indeed. You the reader may laugh or cry as you see we were plainly out of our depth.

Things do not go to plan. Conflict arises as cultures and family dynamics clash and misunderstandings spiral out of control. Nonetheless, the project was completed to the satisfaction of the home-owner and her husband, at least that is what was written in a letter I received some months after our returning home to the UK all those years ago.

Prologue

Things in India don't work as they are meant to...
Bottle tops won't come off.
Unbroken seals leak.
Things in India don't work as they are meant to.
Glass splinters.
Gas seeps from soda bottles.
Finished, fine woodwork splinters.
Carpentry is butchery by mistake.
Finished articles born broken.
Paintwork, not started, not completed,
Runs and smears,
Brown meets green and runs to black.
There is no safety in numbers.
Electrical items give shocks at no extra charge.
Screws holding electric sockets to walls, give shocks.
Electric plugs don't fit sockets and vice versa.
Main power cables drop from pole to ground, and up to tree, and down to roof, from roof to you and trip you up.
You, me, unearthed to earth.
Toilet flush tanks lean over, fall off, walls.

So do cisterns, and buildings,
People get killed,
Lots of them. Often.
There is no safety in numbers.
Cows so slowly walk in clouds of flies, while crows place themselves on strategic thighs.
Bulls sit amongst buses, cars, bikes, rickshaws, shops, roads, libraries, and temples, walk the wrong way around crowded roundabouts and drop.
And so do people.
There is no safety in numbers.
Politicians scandalise and slander.
Governments fall but never fail.
Wife of assassinated prime minister takes over dynasty.
Sonya, Non-Hindu, English-speaking Italian, runs for prime minister
Against her will.
Communists go to church, contribute to temple funds,
Pray to cobras, monkeys and elephants,
Won't touch untouchables,
But agree drugs are a social evil.
Unstirred government dissolves
Chief Minister colludes with gun runners,
Home troops killed,
Fellow diplomats confused.
There is no safety in numbers.
Temples explode
Hindus cook beef parrota and serve chicken curry
Crackers CRACK

Drums clatter walls wail shake and rattle.
Wake up the GODS
BANG CRASH CRACK.
The gods left long ago.
THERE IS NO SAFETY IN NUMBERS.

Chapter 1

It was 1999, early October when I, "Jack" your main narrator, and Queenie my accomplice and past partner in crime, had already decided it was time to return to Kerala, South India, as we had for the past twelve months planned to do. It wasn't a difficult decision, we had a mission to complete, a commitment to our Indian friends of a year ago, Once finalised, goodbyes said, bags packed, we were off.

We were on the plane and several short meals and eighteen and a half hours later we had finally emerged from the usual cold, icy, wet grey winter of the UK that we all know and love, to this exceedingly hot, exotic place.

Although we had travelled this path to India twelve months ago, the hours waiting here, there, time spent on coaches, in airports, pacing the aisles, into and out of cafes bars and shops, all this was telling badly on us both. The combined excitement and anticipation mixed with the doubts and fear of the unfamiliar touched our nerves and shot us through from time to time with adrenaline, heightened awareness, followed by the deeper inner shakiness of uncertainty and apprehension.

Over the snow-capped alps, the beautiful sunset reflecting off the white mists of cloud. A bump, a swerve, we had landed. The air-tight sealed doors were released, and hissed good bye to us, their expectant cargo. Condensation formed and ran. The sugary polite cabin staff smiled widely, curtsied, and officially thanked us as per script, "Good afternoon, and thank you for travelling Kuwait Airways. We wish you a beautiful and happy holiday, thank you, thank you." Their hands formed a prayer-like posture, heads bowed. We returned a smile a compliment.

The first steps onto the rickety stairway leading down toward the tarmac were as if stepping into the direct thrust of the jet's hot engines. Then a sudden cooler wetness emerged, of perspiration, a momentary reprieve. Then the final reality, the total immersion into the steaming heat of this tropical sub-continent.

Uncertainty and discomfort were compounded at the sight of a nearby truck full of unkempt unshaven soldiers shouting at and over each other incomprehensibly above the sound of the dying whine of engines. It seemed that they were excited by our arrival. The heavy looking old battered British Lee-Enfield rifles grasped from the rear of the open backed truck were tossed casually from hand to hand. The muzzles waving away from us more by accident than design it seemed, and then waving ad hoc but in our direction. An accident waiting to happen, so it felt to me.

As the first of our number reached the tarmac, we were herded, sheep-like, into the distorting heat haze and throat-retching engine fumes. Three hundred and five people, mainly in family groups, stepped warily forwards down the wobbling and corroded open topped metal stairway, into the mirage of the shimmering but real enough airstrip. The sun burning fierce on the back of every head and neck. We were all escorted now militaristically toward the large rust red, black mould stained semi-functional looking building.

In fact this was the nerve centre of "Trivandrum Military Airport." Several hours later we stepped out again, into what we hoped would be a freedom of some kind, having been checked over, questioned, re-checked, and checked again. Shuffled, pushed from one queue to another, desperately trying to shelter beneath an occasional small wall-mounted fan. We were accepting the constant flow of sweat running in rivulets underneath our clothing. It brought back memories of our first holiday visit here. The taste of salt in our own facial sweat was no longer unusual. We were out. "Free," into the relatively unknown. After all this was not a package holiday, we were not used to going it alone so far from home in such an alien country. At least that is how it felt for me and Queenie at the time.

We were able to bypass the Foreign Exchange Desk in the airport exit having left this country some twelve months previously with quite a bit of local money left over i.e. rupees, thereby saving us the long queuing time some other passengers had to endure.

After struggling through the mass of waiting humanity around the luggage carousel, I spotted our four heavy rucksacks. Snatching, pulling and tugging, I finally lifted them clear and away. Together we scurried to a quieter corner in this great clattering hall, staggering as we were under the combined weight of hand and hold luggage. We assisted each other to lift up and adjust the heavy packs front and rear, located the vital rupees and allowed ourselves to be pushed, bounced and nudged outside into the shock of brilliant white sunlight.

The smells of tobacco, diesel smoke, sewer, two-stroke fumes, petrol, oil, spice and sweat hung in a visibly still, thick mist in the air. We walked slowly into a light fog of brown/black faces, each one, it appeared, with red-rimmed eyes and dripping betel juice from red stained teeth. Each one, it seemed, shouting, spitting into any available space, each person jockeyed for position, straining and craning to see or be seen by the new arrivals. I desperately scanned them all, looking for a familiar face. A single face amongst many faces. A familiar beard amongst many beards. Our Indian friend Kadhikan was nowhere to be seen.

"Queenie!" I shouted above the din.

"If he were here, he would have seen us by now, we are the only two white faces, and we are a bit obvious."

"Yes, you're right." She called back, as she was being pulled to one side by a rickshaw driver. Three more drivers stepped into my path now, halting my forward progress, each trying to out-scream the other and into my face.

"Teksee!" the nearest bellowed.

"Kovalam this way." shouted another.

"Rickshaw! Give me bag!" pleaded a third.

"Where you go?"

"Very cheap!" "Teksee!" The clamour increased.

"Go with yours! I'll follow!" I shouted, I saw Queenie's driver stumble at the unexpected weight of her packs. Finally extricating myself from the melee I got to them, and helped Queenie unravel herself from her tangled harness. She fell into the tiny rickshaw, heaving the clumsy packs onto her lap. I followed suit. The driver leapt in as I called to him,

"How much....?"

"Kovalam?" He interrupted brightly.

"No, no, Pachalloor." I corrected him. He paused.

"Pachalloor?" Doubt clouded his grinning face.

"Yes. How much?" I insisted. Calculating swiftly.

"One hundred rupees?

"Sixty?"

"OK," I agreed, "Sixty. Let's go!"

He reached down and pulled the mechanical starting handle upwards vigorously, three times. The small two-stroke engine, three-wheeled vehicle spluttered, banged and rattled itself into life. We lurched away into, and leaving behind, clouds of blue smoke. We were off! Negotiating objects, people and other vehicles. I asked myself, would we find our host to be Kadhikan, and where will we stay? "Of course we will. It's all OK, but why hadn't he turned up to meet us at the airport?"

The taxi finally left us at the start of our well-remembered red dust track leading to Kadhikan's house. Burdened with our heavy packs, feeling jet lagged and confused, we trudged wearily along in the steadily increasing heat of early morning.

We were surrounded by a forest of tall coconut palms with deep, broad, green leaves. The strong sunlight of a moment ago on the open road was now focused into beams, shafts of light permeating the darkness of the grove. The Craaw Craaaw louder than any crow I had ever heard before pierced the silence. Gargantuan, they swooped down to the ground from the tree tops to scavenge. The piles of coir here and there indicated a measure of industry. We were anticipating our first glimpse of what might become our home in our temporarily adopted country. Turning the final corner on the narrow track my personal fears were realised. The beautiful traditional palm leaved thatched roof, which we had envisaged as an integral part of the renovated structure, was no more. The house now appeared truncated. The soaring apex of palm leaf thatch was tragically reduced to an expanse of flat grey concrete. We approached in silence, neither of us willing to voice our dismay, our disappointment too deep for words. I felt betrayed. We had sacrificed so much, not just the thousands of pounds but the effort and the planning — for this! An absolute eyesore, an affront to the area.

Bracing ourselves, we knocked smartly on the door, hoping against hope that this was merely a bad dream and we would soon awake to find ourselves with cricked necks and sore eyes and on the plane. With a keen sense of unknown we waited. Again, as once before a year ago, on our first visit the bolt clacked, the door scraped, swung open. Kadhikan stood there. The shock, surprise, indeed, the look of naked fear, on his face, totally disarmed us. Smiling hopefully, we greeted him warmly. Visibly mastering himself, Kadhikan in his own way invited us inside. "Oh Jacky, Jacky- You are my God, please, please, come, come," he continued, "I send letter you get Jacky week ago? You like tea? Madam please come Jacky you are my god!"

We found ourselves apologising profusely for our early and obviously unexpected arrival. I carefully explained that perhaps his last letter asking us to re-arrange our date of arrival must have arrived after our departure. Consequently we were unable to re-confirm the date and time of our arrival. Reassured that we were not angry at his non-appearance at the airport and remembering his duty as a host, he made the tea. We accepted gratefully, and before he left us to supervise its preparation, he proudly switched on the lights and the fan, a clear demonstration that the electricity had indeed been connected, as he had promised in the last letter we had received from him. Left alone for a few minutes, we were able to take stock of our surroundings. How different was this room from when we had first seen it only one year ago. The small cramped rooms, gone. The black soot lined walls, gone. The worn hollowed-out earth floor, gone. We were beginning to feel all might not be lost. Most of the interior walls as agreed had been removed, creating, as we had envisaged, a large airy space. The remaining walls had been plastered, albeit rather roughly, but acceptable. Along with the high but flat ceiling, this accentuated the sense of space. The floor was now smooth with a red and black concrete finish. This room now, simply furnished with a desk, two wooden beds and the familiar wooden chairs served as reassuring contrast to the shock we had outside at the sight of the flat concrete roof and exterior walls. With effort on his part Kadhikan could prosper from the extra income stream this property could afford him. We had made this possible. That was a good thing. Feeling more positive by the moment about the project, but badly in need of a toilet, Queenie needed to avail herself and thoroughly inspect the modern facilities in the new bathroom. Opening the door to the windowless ante-room, she hurried through to the bathroom, and temporarily disappeared from sight.

Chapter 2

As Queenie went off in search of a toilet and possible reconnoitre, I wandered out through the open door, and stood musing for a while, reflecting on the days we had first met Kadhikan S. R. Surendran, and the events leading up to our present situation.

A year ago, give or take a week, I remembered quite vividly. The day had been, as one would expect in South India shortly after the end of the monsoon, hot and humid. We had embarked on one of those once in a lifetime opportunities, "a different package holiday", somewhere really interesting, new and unusual, different places to see, things to do. So after sleeping almost all day after this gruelling first flight here, we were settling down on the veranda of our package tour operated hotel, when Kadhikan made his first diffident approach. He said something about 'backwater trips' in uncertain and heavily accented broken English. As he spoke, he pushed photographs and a child's slightly battered red exercise book into my hand. This was only the first day of our first ever holiday in India, and we were a little wary as we were not seasoned travellers. The tour company's representative disingenuously warned us of the local people who will want to sell us everything from lengths of cloth to marijuana. Nonetheless I took the book from him, albeit a little reluctantly. He began to plead.

"Please sir, please sir! You look. See! Lots of peoples write good things. Please sir. You look!"

Sure enough, 'lots of peoples' had indeed written brief notes in the book, extolling the virtues of Kadhikan, his boat trips, and the backwaters. Most added that Kadhikan was trustworthy, and gave excellent value for money. I had heard about the backwaters, in the brochures and large pictures displayed and available in the hotel reception area. They showed beautiful palm lined canal ways, opening out from time to time into placid inland lagoons, and we had hoped to fit in a trip to them during our stay. This could be the opportunity. He continued to plead and beg, as I flipped through the book. "You will come, sir. Only small deposit sir. Please come, small deposit." So, after ascertaining the length, starting point and total cost of the trip, I and Queenie agreed to join his "Sunset cruise" on the following day. This fragile, almost skeletal man, heavily bearded, now went off into paroxysms of joy. Hands clasped, he bowed and bobbed, exclaiming all the while,

"Oh yes sir! You will not regret. I, Kadhikan, promise this. You will not regret. God will bless you sir! Thank you sir. Many peoples pleased, you also." And so on and on to the state of embarrassment. Queenie and I were sure that, had we not handed over the one hundred rupees deposit and excused ourselves very firmly, he would have continued to bob, bow and bless us for the rest of the evening. As it was, we felt we needed a cooling shower, so we hurried indoors, his final exclamations still ringing in our ears and finally fading away into the dusk beneath the palms as we closed the door of our room.

Next morning at breakfast, we mentioned our forthcoming backwater trip to the owner of the small hotel where we were staying; Indira assured us that Kadhikan was indeed a very good man, and that we had made the right decision. Little did she know that the recommendation she gave us was to have much longer lasting repercussions than one would normally expect from a mere four-hour boat trip.

Surprisingly for India, where things are said to be, "laid back" Kadhikan was on the ball, and appeared promptly at two thirty pm, as promised. Daylight confirmed Kadhikan to be a short man, cadaverous of face and body, the dark beard accentuating the thinness of his face. His soft brown eyes had the appealing look of a kicked dog. This was not a rich man, his European style clothes were clean and tidy, not traditional and not modern. Nonetheless he presented well enough for a working man. We both wondered and asked ourselves and each other what such a life was likely to be like, and how hard it might be for him to make a living relying solely on his capacity to plead his case day in day out and forever, my heart went out to him; he was not a man of charisma or charm.

He nervously shepherded us along the hot sandy beach, rounding up the other pre-booked tourists here and there as he went. By the time we reached the taxi which was to take us the eight kilometres or so to the backwaters, we were seven in number. Five large tourists, ourselves included, somehow levered and manipulated ourselves into the back of the ageing Ambassador taxi, while our guide and the one remaining tourist squeezed themselves in beside the driver.

The taxi, groaning under our combined weight, wheezed and clanked up the steep, narrow track from the beach. All view of the outside world was severely restricted to mere glimpses around an arm, a leg or a face. Sweaty and uncomfortable, we struggled to free ourselves from the confines of the elderly vehicle as it finally lurched to a halt. We tumbled out onto a hot, deserted road, the taxi sped off, vanishing in a cloud of dust and blue-black exhaust fumes, leaving us alone in the scorching sun with Kadhikan, our guide for the afternoon.

Smiling brightly, "K" gestured for us to follow him. Setting a fair pace, he led us down a steep, dusty, red sand path, which led off the road into the gloomy, mysterious but welcome shade of the coconut grove. I was fascinated — the echoing sounds, the darkness, the shafts of light — search lights sweeping with the movement of the large fan like leaves way above us.

We halted outside a crumbling, mud-brick walled house, into which Kadhikan disappeared. We waited outside, looking around us, feeling rather lost. He suddenly reappeared, burdened with a couple of wooden chairs and some dusty black umbrellas.

A small boy and two smiling young women also appeared from the gloomy confines of the same cottage, similarly burdened. Chairs and umbrellas were distributed amongst the tourists, and gesturing for us to follow him once more, our guide set off along an ever-narrowing track under and between the trees. "K" hurried us along, pointing out the various interesting flora and fauna along the way. He stopped and pointed to the ground where a calf-high fern-like plant grew amongst other plants. "K" clapped his hands loudly, the plant rolled its fern like leaves up and inwards in a defence-like posture. We were aghast, and then amazed as the leaves slowly but surely unrolled themselves to take on their original shape. "Name sensitive plant!" Khadikan called out, delighted by our response. Hampered as we were with chairs and umbrellas, we continued and could barely take in the passing scene. The afternoon was taking on the air of a small adventure, and we grinned cheerfully at each other around the cumbersome chairs and unravelling black umbrellas. When we finally halted, at the edge of a still, palm-fringed lagoon, we were ready for anything.

Moored close by was a long wooden traditional canoe-like boat, ancient and weathered, with pools of water lying in its dilapidated bottom. We were all delighted with the quaintness of the scene, a mood which rapidly descended into consternation as our guide indicated that we were to board the crumbling relic, thereby trusting our lives to it. We assumed that the cheery young man who appeared from nowhere was to be its motive power. He indicated that we tourists were to board the leaky vessel first. There was mutiny in the ranks.

"No way! I am not getting into that!" Queenie muttered fiercely to me, trying not to be overheard.

"Where's your sense of adventure?" I laughed.

"You go first, if you don't fall in I'll give it a go."

So as Queenie's personal test pilot, I felt professionally and duty-bound to follow her instruction. Similar disputes were obviously going on amongst our travelling companions. So, recognising that if no-one was going to be brave enough to make the first move, the afternoon's jaunt would never get under way, I made the decision to follow the instruction. Taking a breath, I stepped aboard. Seeing me safely in position, having easily assisted Queenie on board, there was a flurry of activity, and in no time at all, despite the rocking and rolling we tourists were safely set in a neat single row down the centre of the narrow craft. Apart from wet feet and increased heartbeats, we reassured each other of our comfort and safety, and the lean and muscular young man punted us off from the bank. Plying himself energetically to the pole, we glided silently into the middle of the lagoon, and were able at last to relax, look about us, and enjoy the tropical beauty sliding past. We were stunned to silence by it all. Green, blue and red feathered Kingfishers seemed as common as sparrows at home. Fish eagles soared high above, while every white egret stood guard over every water buffalo's bum. Bright colours flickered in the reflection beneath the coconut palms, red, violet, orange, livid green, pink, eventually revealing themselves as the colourful saris of the village women. Their dark skins blended perfectly into the shadows beneath the trees, so that when they smiled, a sudden flash of white appeared atop the glowing colour of the sari. We drifted gently past small waterside shrines, people bathing, children splashing and giggling, a fishing village. Boats coming in the opposite direction, so laden with sand that we wondered how they stayed afloat, passed heavily by, our canoe rolling gently from side to side in their wake.

We disembarked and were fed fresh coconut and pineapple at a small palm leaf shack, where Kadhikan introduced his parents and sisters, whose home the small shack was. Refreshed, we followed our guide through the coconut grove, to a busy main trunk road, which we crossed, nimbly dodging the roaring, beeping, fume-exuding crazy traffic, whilst of course desperately trying to keep our guide in view. We followed him to a large, mainly roofless building, which he proudly described as, "Most famous temple in whole of Kerala, and all India!"

To gain admittance to the temple women were required to cover their shoulders, men to remove shirts. Both were required to cover their legs. So, finally removing our shoes at the entrance, we walked in compliance and respectful silence into the cool stone shade of the temple grounds.

Priests lounged on the grey stone walls, and beggar women entreated us for alms. The temple was constructed of large grey blocks of stone that could have easily been concrete. The only colourful item we noted was the statue of the deity, axe raised, with a look of deep anger, guarding the entrance to the temple. However, we felt we were very privileged to enter here, as we were told most local Hindu temples prohibit entry to tourists. I could see why that might be.

As we walked about, our guide informed us that his first name, Kadhikan, pronounced cardigan, meant "storyteller."

"I tell stories and sing in the temple at festival time." He told us proudly. He asked us to guess the title of the village's favourite story that he would tell at these festivals. We assumed it to be one of the tales of gods and goddesses so beloved and so carefully handed down over the centuries. To our shame, we didn't know the names of any of these stories, and so were unable to make even the wildest guess. A wild guess would not have even come close. We were amazed when he told us triumphantly,

"It is Lady Chatterley's Lover! My friend translated it into Malayalam for me! It is very good story." He was understandably very proud of this, and we were suitably impressed. We tried to imagine what simple village folk in India would make of the story, and how it would sound accompanied by Indian music and song.

"Mind-boggling", was the only comment a fellow tourist made. The story of a gamekeeper having a relationship with the lady of the manor was, I thought, wholly appropriate here in the land of harems, eunuchs and the Raj .

Having finally divested ourselves of the requisite number of rupees in order to propitiate temple gods, committee and beggars we were coaxed out once more into the hot sun to retrieve our shoes and resume our cruise. Asking us to stand and wait a moment as we re-entered the village, Kadhikan disappeared into the throng, reappearing a few minutes later carrying garlands of sweet-scented jasmine flowers. We assumed that these were to be an offering for the temple, but we were proved wrong. "Follow me!" he cried, plunging into the chaotic traffic. We followed fearlessly, our confidence growing by the minute, and somehow between the screeches of tyres and blasting of horns we all ended up safe and sound back on the other and original side of the road. Kadhikan conducted us to his father's house, where his sister shyly pinned the jasmine garlands into the short grey European hair of the ladies in the group. We were instantly surrounded by the sweet smell of the flowers. Delighted with the gift, the women hugged Kadhikan's sister, and thanked our guide profusely. Meanwhile I passed the time and asked "K" about how many boat trips a week he did, and was it a good business? I stated that I thought he did a very good job. He was happy with my compliments, saying, "Business only good few weeks in year, monsoon no good — no visitors, only one flight per week from UK and Europe, so not many peoples."

"So what do you do then?" I asked.

"If I have money enough I make holiday tourist home so more people come stay. You can see if you want see. You see tomorrow morning, you come see eight in morning you see, I show." I admit I was fascinated.

"I will think, and tell you later at the end."

"OK, OK" he replied, smiling.

Making our way back slowly to the leaky vessel, we climbed aboard with a slight feeling of abandon, knowing that the boat had become more romantic and less dangerous as the afternoon progressed. We drifted lazily on to catch the sunset, and punted softly on to a beach-like sandbank.

We disembarked and could clearly hear the thunder of surf on the other side of the bank, so we trudged up through the soft white sand, gleaming and sparkling now in the waning light, toward the sound. At the top of the bank we were rewarded with the sight of a spectacular sunset as streaks of orange, gold and red flamed across the purple sky and set the heaving ocean surf alight. We watched, entranced, as the sun dipped below the horizon, to the thunderous accompaniment of the crashing tide. We finally left the deserted beach in bright moonlight, and climbed back aboard our craft to sail on beneath the coconut palms where dozens of tiny lamps had been lit, sparkling like fallen stars under the trees. The smell of wood smoke and incense filled the air as we moored up at our starting point. We carried our chairs and umbrellas back to the tiny tumbledown house, stumbling a little in the dark. Then we made our way silently back to the road, where the taxi was already waiting. We squeezed in, laughing quietly, agreeing that it had been a wonderful experience.

Like a photograph, a time frame, the finer details of the event could hardly be repeated in exactly the same way again. We finally thanked and congratulated our guide, I confirmed I would see him the next day at his house, added our written praises to his little book, which now took on a new respect and dimension, almost the aura of a sacred text, and then politely took our leave of him. Reaching Kovalam, we both ambled slowly back to our hotel, our heads full of ideas, chats and visions, nostrils full of the scent of jasmine. But only one of us really held the knowledge of future possibilities.

Chapter 3

"Queenie! Wake up! Come on, it's seven thirty. Let's go!"

"What, now? Where?" She exclaimed, in a manner that let me know just how much she appreciated being robbed of sleep and dreams. She was thoroughly alarmed and confused.

"There's nothing wrong, it's just that I have arranged to take you on a mystery tour."

"A what? Where?"

"Not telling. Anyway, it's supposed to be a surprise."

"Well if you wake me up at some ungodly hour, tell me we are going somewhere, and not tell me where, you can go on your own!" With that, she turned her back on me and prepared to go back to sleep.

"Oh, come on. It's meant to be a surprise, and you have actually been there before."

"WHERE?" She demanded, now thoroughly awake with all prospect of sleep abandoned.

"OK, OK, I'll tell you, if you'll just get up, I'll tell you." I could see she was beginning to concede.

"What do I need to wear?" she asked, resigned now to her fate.

"Same as yesterday." I replied encouragingly.

"Can't! It's dirty," she complained, "now, tell me where we are going?"

"To the lagoon, you know, same place, well nearly the same place as yesterday" I said, hastily.

"The lagoon again? Why?"

Now I was getting impatient.

"Come ON! Wear anything, I'll tell you on the way."

Muttering incoherently, she finally roused herself and dressed hastily, grumbling all the while. And still unhappy, but at least only with me, I finally loaded her into an auto-rickshaw.

"Laguna," I asked the driver, "how much?"

"Hundred rupees." He replied.

"Too much. Fifty." I returned. Learning to haggle saves a fortune, so fare agreed at fifty rupees, we set off in the usual cloud of smoke. "Why Laguna?" shouted Queenie.

Trying to explain any detail over the noise of the engine was not a task I relished. Taking a deep breath, I began with raised voice.

"You remember when I was talking to Kadhikan, on his own, you remember the guide on yesterday's tour? Well I was day dreaming, fantasising about how nice it would be to stay, you know, visit a beautiful place like this. On a regular basis. You know a break, a holiday for a month every year, OK a fortnight a year." Sensing no sign of a thaw on Queenie's part, I nevertheless plunged on.

"Well, he, Kadhikan, told me he had a spare house."
I began to mimic Kadhikan's quick fire, fractured
English. "I have spare house make tourist house. You
look". Queenie stared at me stonily. "So I made an arrangement to see him this morning, look at the house,
and meet his wife." I finished, somewhat lamely.

"What for, why?" Queenie exploded. "Surely you are
not ..."

"I'm not anything." I broke in, hastily. "I am just
looking. You know. You never know until you look."
This was one of Queenies favourite phrases, so she
could hardly argue with the concept. Could she? She
looked away. I don't know what she thought I was up
to. I didn't dare ask. Her expression was far from con-
ciliatory. It had all seemed such a good idea to me last
night, to look, see what the idea was, the possibilities.
I am a sucker for a good idea.

With nothing more said, we arrived on a slightly
down note, paid off the taxi driver, who wanted to
wait for us, then walked down the narrow dusty path
to Kadhikan's house. Water buffalo present, one
standing, one sitting, swinging their long tails against
the flies, while half a dozen or so white egrets perched
at strategic points on their bodies ready to snatch a
morsel.

The path led us, after just a few yards, into the refreshing coolness of the thick coconut grove, the same
one that we had started our trip from the day before.

The area was residential, to the extent that it had
four large houses constructed within a couple of acres
of a much larger coconut grove that then led down to

the lagoon. Two of these houses were constructed of mud brick, with large red tiled roofs, encasing a single storey living and working space. The whole dark area was illuminated by streaks and beams of harsh sunlight that had sought and cut passages through the canopy of palms. The light was further diffused and softened in clouds of wood smoke that seeped through the roofs of the other two thatched-roof houses. So large was the roof space in relation to the wall height, one could be forgiven for believing that they were no more than large smouldering compost heaps, lightly smoking on a traditional English garden allotment.

We walked the path straight to the closed door of the house, where yesterday chairs and umbrellas had been disgorged. The liquid chatter of several unseen females could be heard, sometimes punctuated with laughter, over the gentle whirring of the giant spinning wheels. The same wheels that sustain economic life in these parts. I knocked hard on the closed door, and waited. I knocked harder on the still closed door, and waited. A voice shouted something in Malayalam, the local language — a noise — scraping, like a chair on a hard floor. A door bolt clacked, the door scraped the floor as it opened, and there stood Kadhikan, bleary-eyed and confused.

This reminded me of my clumsiness with Queenie earlier this morning. I was, once again, an invader of sleep and dreams. This mental vision served to calm me a little. I said, in the softest tones I could muster,

"Hi, Kadhikan, sorry, I thought you said eight o'clock. It's now eight forty five, I think." Gathering his wits, and now beaming brightly, he exclaimed, "OK, OK, OK".

"Please, please, come in. Madam. Hello! Hello, Sir. Sit. Please sit. It is early. You like tea?" He enquired, all the while urging us to sit, come in, and generally fluttering haphazardly like one of the large black butterflies which abound here. I sat down on the hard wooden surface of the bed, while Queenie sat on the only other piece of furniture in the tiny, smoke-blackened room, which we recognised as one of the chairs from our boat trip.

"Yes, please. Tea would be lovely." She said gratefully. Kadhikan hurried into the room opposite. As our eyes became accustomed to the gloom, we looked around us. The tiny space was no more than ten feet square, with an earthen floor. As we looked up, we saw that the wall dividing this room from the next stopped at what would normally have been a low ceiling level just over the head, with an empty space between that and the inner roof probably another ten feet at least to the top of the apex. Looking higher, we realised that we were sitting inside the previously imagined palm roofed compost heap,

Smoke from the wood burning kitchen area poured over the tops of the low interior dividing walls, and filled the roof space, and edged increasingly downwards, adding to the dimness. Our guide returned, proudly brandishing two half-pint glasses of milky tea.

The house was not on fire, nor was the heat and smoke anything to do with any internal combustion. It was all simply the result of cooking, or in this case, boiling water for tea on a wood fire with no means of expelling or containing the fumes and smoke. This house, like the others we had seen now, and others we saw later, did not have a chimney. Smoke from cooking fires simply filled the roof space, drifted down to a level below the interior walls and slowly leaked out through the palm thatch high above. We realised that apart from the more obvious environmental reasons — diesel fumes and the like — that this design of house around India was probably a contributory factor for the extremely high incidence of respiratory decease. A choice then, bronchitis, cancer, or mosquitoes and malaria. The drifting smoke within the thatch we were told later is intended to deter the ever annoying and dangerous mosquitoes bites and malaria. Hobsons choice!

Kadhikan seemed pleased with his offering of tea, and beamed at us encouragingly.

"Tea very good, very sugar. You like?"

"Yes," we replied, not altogether very truthfully, "thank you, you are very kind."

It was Indian tea, that extraordinary, sickeningly sweet mixture of fiercely boiled milk, tea-leaves, cardamom and sugar; we did wonder about the scummy brown froth on top. Hovering over us as we drank, Kadhikan attempted to explain a little about the house.

"This good house. Very, very good house sir, madam." He exclaimed, in the face of all evidence to the contrary.

"My wife house. Not for me. Have tea!" He urged, "Then look."

At this point, a beautiful, five foot tall, oval-faced woman, with smiling brown eyes, entered the room. She held a tiny baby in her arms, while another child, a girl, clung to her mother's smock-covered lower legs. An older boy, aged about eight, appeared briefly in the doorway, glanced into the room, and then moved nervously back and out of sight.

"She my wife, Valsala," said Kadhikan proudly. Pointing to the little girl, he added "Surya, girl child. New baby — boy. Name Surjeen. Deepu other boy." Suddenly changing the subject, he went on, "Here we not live always. She stay with mother's sister's house." He said, pointing to his wife, who continued to smile brightly at her new baby and her unexpected guests.

"Where do the children stay?" I asked.

"Just here." He said pointing outside the house. "Mother's sister's house, all stay. Very big house."

"What about you?" Asked Queenie. "Where do you stay?"

"I not stay. Sometimes here, maybe father's house."

"So you don't all live together?" We exclaimed.

"No, madam, house not too good. Only maybe sometime." He replied, appearing to contradict his earlier statement about "this very good house."

Seeing that we had finally finished our tea, Kadhikan took back the glasses, saying, "Now you see house. Please, madam, sir, come. Kitchen." We followed him down the dim passageway and stopped at the small room on the right. For some reason the floor of this room was about eighteen inches lower, and a large boulder served as a step down into it. There was no electricity or even water on tap. The walls were black and soot-lined. The only visible means of cooking was what looked like a fire-blackened terracotta plant holder with a large hole in the side. This small earthenware container held the remains of burnt coconut husks and twigs that had provided the energy to boil the milk for our tea. Presumably it also provided the heat to cook the family meals. A sparkling clean aluminium pan lay beside it. An interestingly shaped water carrier, designed to rest on the hip, and a stone slab with a slightly concave centre, together with a stone roller cum pestle, adorned the floor. Valsala lay the baby down on a thin raffia mat, which was spread out on the floor in one corner. She continued to smile brightly. We were to discover that this was her natural expression. I asked if there was a toilet.

"No toilet sir. Only outside. Not good for you." Ignoring any possibility of my urgency.

He continued to show us the other rooms. In comparison with Western standards, all were completely unusable, and without any doubt would be deemed not fit for human habitation. Termites had almost eaten away the window frames in two of the rooms, and the inners hung drunkenly from their hinges. I doubted they were able to open or close.

Trying to remember the exact details of our broken conversation the previous day, and needing to understand, without a shadow of doubt, just what he had in mind for the house, I asked, "Do you want to sell the house?"

"Oh, no sir! Not sell. I make tourist home. You come live here also. Make your home." This added to my confusion, so I attempted to clarify the situation, going through the three main points as I saw them.

"So, you don't live here as a family?" I began.

"No sir, we live...." and he proceeded to repeat at even greater length, all that he had said before. Interrupting his flow with some difficulty, I asked my second question.

"You want to make money from this house, make it into a tourist home?"

"You can help me sir! Please. No boat trips in winter. I have no money to feed family, not nothing."

Trying to stick to the point, I persisted. "You want me to help you to build a tourist home here?'

This set him off again, with this addition,

"No problem sir. You live any time. You good man."

I tried again.

"If I made a tourist home here, when would I live here?"

"You live any time. You good man. You can be rich. Many tourist come." I was confused.

We seemed to be completely missing each other's point. This was a feeling we were to become very familiar with. How could I live here at the same time as tourists, and how would this make me rich? What was his idea? I tried again, trying to peer through my personal fog and spats of blindness I struggled. The best I could make of it at the time and what he confirmed was that he needed an extra income in order to sustain himself and his family when the tourist season ended. He would also be happy so long as he was able to comply with the local cultural mores and pass the house on to his daughter — a peculiarity of this matriarchal culture. Therefore, if I supported his cause, by designing and financing a Western style tourist home, I would be able to use it when the tourists were not here, presumably in the monsoon period.

I could feel myself awakening to this idea already. What a deal! He wins, I win, no charity, all honour intact. We prepared to leave, promising to return within a day or two with an answer and maybe some ideas.

We took our leave, perhaps a little shell-shocked at this unexpected turn of events. Probably by virtue that neither of us had dismissed Kadhikan, or his fantasy, as we interpreted it, within the first ten minutes of our departure from the 'compost heap', was a good omen for him. We had both, silently and individually, decided that we were prepared to discuss the possibilities.

An opportunity to do a bit of good for a fellow worker from a developing country was not easily dismissed, this family had the odds stacked against them, that was obvious, and so was the fact that Kardy worked as well as it was possible to do, chasing tourists and then providing a good service and holiday experience for them. These folk were a good cause and I felt it a privilege to be in a position to help if I could. However an offer of assistance from a friend and colleague in the form of Queenie would be a more of a need than a want.

Chapter 4

I can't remember who started or when or how the discussion began yet again, only that within an hour or so of reaching Kovalam, we were both immersed in a soup of speculation. What kind of man was Kadhikan? we asked ourselves. Sure he was poor, and appeared to be trying his best to provide for his family. The fact that he did not own even the rickety old boat he used for backwater trips had not discouraged him in his present venture. His motivation appeared to be good.

We estimated, or should that be guestimated, that he could possibly earn around two to three thousand rupees, say £30, per week, with his new plan. That is, if he were able to find enough guests to visit his envisaged holiday home each and every week. It would certainly provide him with a better living than most folks around here for at least three months of the year. An average monthly income at a lower management level in an up-market hotel, we were told by a head waiter, was around 800 to 1,000 R's per month so "K" could, if he worked at it, earn a year's salary in the short season described above. That seemed to us a great prospect.

An improvement, we thought, on his present situation.

Scribbling down our figures on bits of paper by candlelight (we were in the middle of one of India's nightly 2, 3, or 4-hour power-cuts), we were surprised to discover that at our best guestimate, presently fully fifty percent of his gross earnings could be swallowed up by expenses. Taxi fares, boat hire, advertising leaflets etc. This would leave him and his family, on my reckoning, the equivalent of twenty pence per day each. That is 100 R's for the whole family, a little over a dollar a day! Not good. The holiday home project was, as one says, a no-brainer. It had to happen!

We began to feel an unreserved respect for this man, and could empathise with him and his apparent no-win situation. We understood how, from his point of view, outside intervention i.e. finance at the very least, was possibly the only way forward for him. We concluded that he had good ideas, even if it sounded a little muddled, which may have been due to our combined language difficulties. He gave good value for money on the tours, we had asked more about him locally, the hotel owner and manager people liked him, and he came apparently well recommended by other small business people in his community.

Feeling that we now had some speculative measure of the man, his ideas and predicament, we felt that this was the time to put some personal principles to work and to help this family if we could. There was to be no hint of charity, or patronisation. To all intents and purposes, this would be a business style partnership. Our final thoughts, before each settling down for the night, were that we needed to revisit the site, examine the house in more detail, and then determine the viability and practicalities of the project, and could I afford the costs? We therefore decided to dedicate the whole of the next day to the Kardy project.

Nothing is easily accomplished in India, it seems. The very same taxi driver who took us to the lagoon the day before for fifty rupees, today demanded seventy rupees for the same journey. We protested, we won the argument, and were on our way. The driver dropped us off at our destination, he then wanted to wait for us rather than seek a fare elsewhere. Another argument ensued, with much hand waving and gesturing. We won that argument too. I expect I may tire of taking on the whole of India man by man, meanwhile he left us in peace at last, to explore the environment surrounding what we had affectionately come to call the compost heap.

Sure enough, other houses in the vicinity, but not in the village, had been dedicated to tourist homes, and were hidden here and there amongst the palm trees. This particular spot, where the backwaters and the sea met for the first time, did seem an obvious place for the development of an authentic Indian holiday experience to take place. Providing as it did the warm Arabian Sea and beautiful coastline, with the quiet serenity of the palm fringed fresh water lagoons close by.

The deafening CRAW CRAW CRAW of the crows could take a little getting used to, but of course this is a genuine experience, including the occasional discomfort. The whole essence of an authentic experience is, we thought, at least partially dependent on such realities. "Just get used to the birds!"

Finally arriving at Kadhikan's house, we were greeted by Valsala, who indicated that Kadhikan was not at home. By means of sign and gesture, we asked if we might see inside the house again. She understood perfectly, and smiling, opened the door and pointed the way into the gloomy interior.

Free from Kadhikan's excited chatter it was surprisingly easy to see what needed to be done to make the place into an acceptable tourist home. Space could easily be created by the removal of all interior walls to the left of the central passageway making the room at least three feet wider. The two rooms on the left could be made into one. None of the dividing walls were load or roof bearing and therefore safe to remove. This would then create a living/sleeping area of about eighteen feet by thirty. The kitchen would remain in its original position, but be upgraded, while the two smaller rooms on the right of the passageway would serve for the bathroom and anteroom. With growing excitement, we began to plan the details.

"Can you imagine it," I enthused, "with all the interior and exterior walls rendered with smooth cement and painted, and flat smooth concrete floors?"

"Yes I can," Queenie replied, "and what about a flush toilet and shower in a nicely tiled bathroom?" Queenie had a thing about toilets. I knew the lack of adequate sanitation was a source of worry for her.

"Of course." I agreed. "And what about that kitchen?" We both stood in the doorway, gazing speculatively around.

"It needs some kind of hood over the cooking area," I said, "and maybe gas or electricity instead of wood for fuel."

"It needs some sort of work surface." mused Queenie.

"How about brick pillars supporting a concrete slab, like the ones in the restaurant kitchens?" I suggested.

"Hmm. It could do with a bigger window, too."

"I agree. All the windows need to be bigger, and it needs to be connected to all services, water and electricity." We started to list our other priorities, fan, beds with proper mattresses, tables.

We envisaged cutlery and crockery neatly stored on shelves and in cupboards. With strip and/or soft lighting options in the main area. We liked the authentic compost heap shaped thatch appearance of the roof with its large apex covered in palm leaf and the surprising height and space it created within.

Having been offered shelter by a kind lady who saw us running past her house during a sudden downpour on our first day or so in the country, and in a similar house to Kardy's we became all too aware of the limitations of the palm roof structure as eventually the heavy rainfall began to drip through the thatched roof in several places until it began to pour into the house and on to the earthen floor of the passage where we were sheltered. This was a very useful experience presenting as it did not just the failings of a palm thatch roof, but an introduction to the intuitive kindness of the local people. This lady inviting two foreign strangers to shelter in her home. Remarkable. Not a likely prospect in the UK, methinks.

Taking the notebook from Queenie, I sketched out my ideas.

"Look," I said, "we could re-roof the structure using palm leaves and traditional techniques. We could then trap a waterproof membrane, either polythene or pitched coir, between the outer and the inner roof, the inner could be made of those woven palm leaf fence panels we see everywhere." Ethnic and waterproof.

"Great idea!" enthused Queenie, gazing up at the roof and sharing my vision of a clean dry inner to the soaring roof structure. From the outside it would retain the compost heap thatch look we liked so much, which is the main charm of the buildings in this hamlet, yet have a dry, attractive, interior. All this would enhance the sense of space, and inexplicably a certain cosiness.

Pleased with our progress so far, we took our leave of Valsala, and returned to our hotel. All thoughts of a conventional holiday were jettisoned at this point, and we spent the next few days drawing up plans, checking and confirming measurements, and writing up a schedule of works. All these, plus a list of estimated costs, were passed on to our new partner for consideration.

Oh yes reader, a once apprentice bricklayer in the 1960s and more lately care worker can do these things, such is the varied and disparate life of a working free spirit.

Kadhikan's enthusiasm knew no bounds, over-reaching even our own. He too, had made an estimate of costs, which was about twenty-five per cent over my own partially/clumsily researched estimate. I had some reservations, even nervousness about his pricing system, but eventually had to concede that he could have a better local knowledge of prices than I would, and so I agreed to his figures. Seven million rupees or about seven thousand pounds seemed a bargain price for a complete renovation, including all furnishing and fittings, complete and ready to go.

It took a further three days to draw up the contract I had insisted upon, which was merely a vehicle for stating the obvious, or so I thought at the time, i.e. a business venture, a contract to be respected.

The money I would supply would be spent I envisaged as per the discussed plan, with the stated intention that the project was to provide Kadhikan with extra income from letting the house to tourists. In return Queenie or one other person and I could live in the house when deemed to be appropriate and to be determined by Kardyy. There was to be no obligation for Kadhikan to repay the sum offered, nor would any charges be incurred. Kadhikan and his family would retain first call on the use of the house.

We conducted the final negotiations, and the signing of the contract. We agreed Kadhikan should receive the first instalment of cash from the UK within the next three months so that the works could begin, the amount was to be as near to half the agreed cost of the works as I could muster. I did not have the full amount at present but would work and do everything I could to provide the finances needed. Finally, we agreed a time limit of twelve months for the completion of works, promising to return one year later just before, or just at the back end of the rainy season, for myself and one other, hopefully my good friend Queenie, to use as a temporary base for our further exploration of this fascinating country. Kadhikan was over joyed with the proposition and agreed and signed up whole-heartedly.

Our first priority on returning home to the UK was to find some means of earning

and sending Kadhikan the promised finance. With details of his bank account, we found it was surprisingly easy to transfer, and within a couple of months of our return, my virtual life savings of two thousand eight hundred and eighty pounds was winging its way to him via the auspices of the Bank of India.

A very small amount of money to better heeled people, to me it was a fortune. Our real wealth is our capacity to willingly work at many things and at the same time. Our second priority was now to raise the second half of the sum we had agreed. It turned out both of us spent more than a few sleepless nights and some days debating such pertinent questions as "Are we mad?" and "Whatever had possessed us?" The fact was it was a once in a lifetime opportunity to help and change some people's lives for the better, and for the long term. It could well be a positive life changing event, it was a privilege to be part of such a thing. We both set to work with a will to launch this man and his family on to at least a possibility of a successful venture and a positive future. We could do it! Those next twelve months flew by in a flurry of frenzied activity. We completed the renovation of the semi-derelict cottage I had purchased some months earlier, and put this, along with a large flat belonging to me, on the market. We needed no crystal ball to see that the maintenance of these two ageing properties would be a considerable drain on my resources for the foreseeable future. Trawling the Yellow Pages for a suitable estate agent, I came across Crooke and Blight. Not a wholly positive name for such an enterprise. It appealed to my sense of the ridiculous, however, and happily, it has been a rewarding relationship. Everyone in the office seemed to take a keen interest in our projects, and in no time at all it seemed, I had sold both cottage and flat.

I moved into a spare bedroom in Queenie's terrace house in the small Welsh village of Tredegar, famous for its outstanding Labour P.M. Aneurin Bevan.

I had for some time been working in the probation service in a small town, Port Talbot, and living in a large town, Newport. Queenie, who I had also worked with at a county-wide community development charity, would not take any rent from me, which helped a great deal. This meant that spare money from property sales and work projects could be committed to our project "compost heap". In return for her kindness

I carried out a maintenance programme on her lovely little cottage.

In the meantime, I acquired a variety of jobs mostly through an national agency, from window salesman, to long distance gas meter reader, to care assistant, putting in too many hours a week swapping from job to job, often seven days a week. Sometimes for commission only payments, It was all good, I was young and enthusiastic, driven by a longer term goal. It was great, I loved it.

Queenie's part-time post gave her some time for the various decorating projects in the property renovations, which of course helped in the presentation for sales.

However, some bad luck seemed to stalk us. My ageing but beloved Ford Escort was stolen, and found abandoned as a burnt out wreck. In an attempt to cut costs, we relied solely on Queenie's even more elderly Vauxhall Nova, only to have it stolen. It was however returned intact, stolen again, returned again, only to be hit by a van while parked in the street. It was stolen for a third time, and suffered the same fate as the Escort.

An ex-girlfriend of mine was horribly murdered by her boyfriend drug dealer, close relatives of Queenie's became ill with life threatening diseases, her own health suffered — she was diagnosed as having fibromyalgia a difficult and complex ailment possibly brought about by extreme stress. In fact this alone could have scuppered Queenie's revisit to India in the future, as this is an unpredictable, depressive, painful and nasty ailment. But, we had our dream, and despite all this, were more and more determined to make it a reality. Queenie is a fighter, little did we know at that time, fighting as she did emotionally, was a major contributory factor to the disease.

Despite our efforts the cash needed was slow to accumulate so I sold my treasured Norton vintage motorbike, various old historical engravings, and my Great Western Railway antique clock. Consequently I was able to send the promised second half of the money six or so months after the first. We were in fact ahead of the game!

Imagine my distress and anger when Kadhikan wrote back complaining and whinging.

"I am a poor man, I am not son of a dog, I am not a thief," so on and so forth, merely because I had requested sight of invoices and receipts for the money I had sent him.

Some short time later, he wrote again, this time enclosing photographs of work in progress, and incredibly asking for more money over and above the original agreement. We wrote back with a refusal informing him that he must comply with our agreed contract. I also told him that we would see him in two months' time when we returned to India. He wrote back immediately, with more pictures, and asking what he had done to upset us. The photographs looked strange, and appeared to bear no resemblance to the house or site we had seen all those months ago. I was confused now, thoroughly alarmed, and thinking to myself, "What is he up to?"

I wrote back with a definite time and date of arrival, and a request that he meet us at the airport, and as always, wishing him and his family well. Subsequently we discovered later on our return to India his reply to this letter was sent to the address I had left some time before.

The final days before our departure are a blur in our memories, as we hastened to tidy up the loose ends of our separate lives in the UK. It was therefore with very mixed emotions that we finally boarded the plane at Gatwick and settled down for the long flight to India. Queenie's fibromyalgia had calmed, care would need to be taken however in order to prevent a fresh attack.

I find myself outside Kadhikan's house still waiting for Queenie, stumbling up the rubbish strewn newly constructed concrete outer stairway to try to gain access to the new uninspiring looking concrete roof, believing it may be cooler up there amongst the overhanging branches. Queenie has taken so long in the toilet area that I am beginning to worry that she may have simply fallen asleep in position on the toilet, but conveniently for us, has allowed me the time to update you the reader to a little of my and Queenie's history, our motivation and some of the events leading to this present time.

Chapter 5

Extracts From Queenie's Diary 1

As I left Jack to wander around the outside of the building I stepped through into the house and looked around again. My imagination painted large blue waves on the large open walls, I imagined simple light linen curtains at the now large airy looking windows. Simple Ikea style lamp shades, flowers, ornaments, large roomy king-size beds, electric cooker, white and chrome fridge freezer, all in the mind, but nice though, I could see it all! I went through to the bathroom, of course initially to use the facilities, I was totally unprepared for what I saw there.

Most certainly, there was a white ceramic, western style toilet, complete with black plastic seat. It was not, however, connected to a water supply, and lacked the necessary flush cistern. Perhaps Jack had assumed too much from one of Kadhikan's photographs of the toilet area, as had I. What appeared to be a perfectly well fitted white ceramic toilet was not. The water flush cistern was in fact lying on the floor behind the door, incidentally a door so badly fitted that it scraped the floor and jammed tight on opening and closing. The floor, walls and ceiling were of rough, dark grey cement. There was neither hand basin nor shower, and the room smelt strongly of urine and excrement. A pile of dirty clothes lay wet in one corner, and a large red plastic bucket, containing very dubious looking brown liquid, completed the scene. Quite desperate for relief, I made what use I could of the facilities, threw some scummy brown water into the pot, which had a coating of rich brown sediment around it, and left in search of Jack. There was no way I was prepared to stay here, I called loudly for Jack thinking, God knows what he will make of this space. I went outside, where I'd left him. I felt deeply disappointed, stressed and exhausted. I could feel the beginnings of a deep inner ache, one that I had experienced several times before in other worrying circumstances.

"JACK WHERE ARE YOU?"

ON THE ROOF

"No wonder he didn't meet us at the airport!" I was thinking, when Queenie's shout interrupted my musings. "Up here," I exclaimed, "You have been ages, did you fall asleep on the toilet?"

"OH, I see you." she replied, sounding tired. "Be very careful of the steps," I called down, "if you come up here. Be careful, they are steep and full of rubbish." I did feel I had some duty of care to Queenie after dragging her all this way, let's face it, it was now looking more like a nightmare again as the minutes ticked by. I looked around again at the unfinished roof I was standing on. Old, wet cement bags, piles of unused concrete that had been left to go hard. Sand of different shades, some looking more like red earth, littered the whole surface. Smashed pieces of balustrade, with twisted and corroded reinforcing rods, lay scattered all around, metal rods sticking up or twisted or bent like a bomb site standing dangerously amongst smashed glass soda water bottles, plastic water bottles, cigarette cartons, palm branches and coconut husks. Large pools of water lay on the indented and unfinished concrete surface. Bricks, blocks, tin bowls, piles of rusty steel chisels and broken trowels. More reinforcing bars peeped out of the already partially constructed balustrade; its concrete uprights already blown open by the expanding and corroding metal inside. These must be second hand or been around in someone's yard for years. It felt like a bomb site — and "HOW" and "WHY?" I asked myself, "WHY? Why is there human shit on the bloody ROOF!"

Queenie was standing at the bottom of the newly built and already crumbling stairway. The stairs had not one single flat step, nor could one place a foot completely on any step. This was surely the construction from hell, paid for by me. What had I done? "Another bloody cock-up!" I thought. I felt like a fool having been taken in by this man Kadhikan.

From the bottom of the steps Queenie, I could see, was reading my expression correctly, and by the look on her face, I could surmise there was more bad news to come. Kadhikan stood directly behind Queenie. "You stay tonight?" He shouted, his head bent slightly and cutely to one side in an incomplete head wave.

"You must be bloody joking." I shouted back at him. His head waved from side to side kind of enquiringly. In hindsight I can see that I was as unaware of his sensitivities as he was of mine. With an effort, I controlled any further outburst. Queenie's eyes met mine. "Let's get out of here." we said in unison. So, with what in hindsight was more than slight bewilderment on Kadhikan's behalf, he asked, in all seriousness, with his arms raised to the gods, "Why you go now?"

I became aware of a shaking sensation yet, holding out my hand, I could see no visible tremor. I felt an inner deep weakness, faintness, brought about by despair, tiredness and a total lack of sleep. "I really must sleep soon. I can't deal with all this in this state". With a forced politeness, I explained at some length that I would return in two days, at the same time of day. Queenie had to repeat this twice more to him, but we felt that he had not really fully understood. Or was he somehow trying to play safe by pretending he didn't understand the language? I couldn't tell. I needed to leave now.

Leaving one of our packs with Kadhikan in the house making our load lighter, we walked back up the narrow track to the main road, with Kadhikan walking slowly along behind. "I get rickshaw, you go Kovalam?"

I agreed, and as we climbed aboard, I said out loud to Queenie what I had been thinking. "I must be the only fifty-odd year old who still believes in Father Christmas." I muttered, bitterly. "And do you know, Queenie, for a moment, I thought Kadhikan was the bloody idiot."

Queenie tapped my knee affectionately, saying reassuringly, as she so often does, "It'll all look different
after a good sleep and a nice cup of tea."

I was about to remind her but didn't that the main
requirement for a good sleep was a comfortable bed,
and that a 'nice' cup of tea of an English variety, in India, was about as rare as hen's teeth, boiled milk, cardamom and a tea bag wouldn't do it. We needed to live
in hope a little longer. The bumpy, noisy, dusty trip to
Kovalam brought back memories of my previous trip,
the long walks. "What is your name?" "Where are you
going?" The cheap and very tasty food consumed in
broken down, rustic roadside shacks. I felt my spirits
lifting, and hardly had these memories flashed by
when we found ourselves driving down the steeply
winding track to the famous Kovalam beach. A new
energy seemed to rise in me, goodness knows where
from. We looked at each other and smiled and exclaimed "The sea!" in unison, pointing and grinning
like a couple of excited kids.

"Let's get a room, and then go for a swim." I suggested, as we scrambled out of the taxi. "If we try to stay
awake as long as we can, we might match up our body
clocks to Indian time." Strange but interesting idea?

Chapter 6

Needless to say we found a room or perhaps more truthfully the room found us, or the owner Sadinand did. We didn't argue about the cost because we were too tired. It was a pleasant enough large room with a connecting shower and toilet so we were happy with that. We awoke at about eleven thirty the following morning, or possibly the morning after, to the sound of whirring and clacking helicopter blades above us. No, we were not lost out at sea. The noise was that of the fan which must have spun continuously overhead since we had switched it on maybe some twenty hours or so previously. We were still fully dressed. We hadn't made it into the sea after all.

"Good God!" Exclaimed Queenie. "Look at the time! The door is still wide open as well. We must have fallen asleep immediately we came in!" She had fallen on to one of the two single beds, and me I hadn't made it that far. I must have simply sat on the floor for some reason, fallen to one side and slept. The pain in my neck was killing me.

"Don't worry about it." I replied sleepily, "lie back, and wake up slowly."

Fifteen minutes later we declared that we were starving. We showered, changed into shorts and t-shirts, and ventured out into the midday sun to find food.

"So, what's the plan?" asked Queenie, in a muffled, mouth-filled fashion.

"Don't forget to inhale through the nose." I said, laughing.

"NO! With Kardy and the house, I mean, you idiot." she replied, almost choking as the chilli omelette slid down her gullet.

"Well, it's a bit too early to tell, really. We need to go back again, have a proper look, and work it from there."

"I think he's done a pretty good job of "working it" himself." responded Queenie.

"Yes, of course you're right" I replied.

"He's certainly tried to squeeze a quart out of a pint pot financially, and failed. Instead of carrying out our agreed plan, he's used the money we sent him for his own ill-considered and badly planned ideas. It is his house, he can choose to do what he likes irrespective of any previously agreed commitments."

I had wanted to trust him.

"The reason he's spent so much money on that abomination of a roof, I guess is so that he can extend and build on top of it at a later stage."

"You're giving him a lot of credit for forethought Jack," Queenie chipped in. "The problem he has is that he cannot complete the downstairs area which he needs to do in order to earn further income for his add-on structure upstairs. Unless of course he gets another substantial pot of money from somewhere, he could have scuppered himself."

"You're right Queenie, he's miles off-piste but we shall see what we can do. Mind you I am not feeling very generous about all this. I guess that as soon as we left the country, he decided on his new plan, and continued to take my money without saying a word to me about it."

"I suppose it was brave of him to send the photographs," proffered Queenie.

"He plainly has no idea about the amount of effort, inconvenience and stress this project has caused us, or he doesn't care, to him we are just another tree to be stripped of its fruit."

"I don't suppose he thought we would ever put in an appearance again, either, hence the look of fear and amazement when we arrived."

"What he's done," she continued, "he's squared the circle his own way. If there is a mango on the tree you pick it even if it's not ripe and agreed not to."

"Hey, that is so clever Queenie!"

"It's not theft though Jack. Its acceptable practice here, you know that, if you are poor and an opportunity arises you take it"

"Another lemon tea, waiter please. Two please." I knew she was probably correct, to me it was an abuse of trust, to him however, it was using the situation to best advantage, he was probably unaware of what I thought about his abuse.

"The question is what do we do now?"

It was to be a difficult decision to make or think about. It felt that almost any decision would be the wrong one. I needed a little more time to think.

An exotic black and red butterfly fluttered largely past, in and out, and in between us.

"That's why we are here!" said Queenie, nodding toward the butterfly.

"Yes, of course it is." I touched her hand. "Thanks Queenie." Saved my life again!!

Before we had left "K" the previous day we had agreed to meet him at the house the following morning to look over the place in detail, and unbeknown to him let him know that he had been "sussed".

However, Queenie agreed we should not want to waste the effort and money already spent. I reckoned that he should, if he could, get the place in good enough condition at the very least, for us to move in and save us added accommodation expense. At least get the toilet and shower done.

It had just occurred to me — where would the water come from for the toilet and shower, when in fact the government water was at a standpipe useable only every other day, and then a hundred or so yards away from the house? He needed to sort that out. He said he would, he may have already, and then I remembered.

"The well. Yes, next to the house! OK now it's coming back to me". If he did all that, then we could probably do the rest of the work ourselves, make it good and ready for tourists.

"Let's see how much it is all going to cost." Suggested Queenie. "And let's put a limit on how much more we are prepared to spend." She suggested a further five hundred pounds — that was a lot of Rupees.

My over thinking self-talk continued, "I do not want to be responsible for any abandoned project." Why should this be any different? We walked back towards the concrete monolith.

We were getting to know this narrow red track, the water buffalo and attendant hangers on. Somehow, the house looked brighter that morning. To the uninitiated, I suppose the smoky haze seeping through the tops of the compost heaps, plus the gentle whirring of the cottage industry, could seem quite romantic, at least to the holiday maker. We hoped so. The door was already open. We called, "Hello Kadhikan, Valsala!" Kadhikan appeared, looking nervous, keeping several feet of space between us. A very unusual act of politeness for most locals, who, to our Western eyes, appeared to know nothing of our accepted "comfort zones" or "personal space". Maybe he was giving himself a head start in an anticipated chase.

After the usual bobbing shaking of head and enquiries about tea, and requests for us to be seated, I told him I would like to look into every room, and at all the work done so far.

"Yes sir, no problem, later, later." The first wave of the red flag to the not so distant bull.

Later, later is not what I had come here for. "Not later Kardy. Now. This is business."

With some show of astonishment, Kadhikan replied, "Not later? Why not later?"

I was in no mood to argue.

"Now please!" I retorted. "The only reason I have come here is to see how you have spent my money, also where is your copy of the agreement you signed?"

"Agreement sir? No agreement, house not finished sir."

I was beginning to feel defeat. Very slowly, and calmly but through gritted teeth, I said, "I can see the house isn't finished, where is your paper copy of the agreement?"

Hurriedly, Kadhikan replied, "At father house. I get?"

Suspecting that if I let him go, I would not see him again, I ignored this, saying instead, "Show me all the work." He was off the hook, I suspect he thought. He leapt forwards, showing me the lighting, as he had before. The well outside the back door, that was very good, the electricity meter around the other side of the house.

"Where exactly is the government water?" I asked.

"No, sir, no sir, well water only. Not good. Only for washing."

"Why no government water here, you said you could arrange it?" He attempted to divert my attention.

"Electric good. Look, sir."

He pointed at what looked to be a twisted five amp extension lead tied to the branch of a tree, and then to a coconut palm trunk that was plainly carrying the drooping electricity mains wires on little more than a fifteen amp extension lead.

"OK. But where is the government water?"

Kadhikan's brown eyes flicked worriedly from my face to Queenie's and back.

Addressing Queenie, he said, "Madam, government water in tap."

Good. Now we were getting somewhere. I distinctly remembered Kadhikan mentioning something about his connection to government water in one of his letters.

"Which tap?" I asked.

"Government tap." I looked around. I could see no tap. Queenie sensed my mounting confusion.

"Show us the government tap." She said encouragingly.

"Not here Madam." Now it was her turn to look stumped.

Glancing at each other, we said in unison, "Well, where is it then?"

Addressing Queenie once again, whether out of some sort of olde worlde courtesy or self-preservation, Kadhikan asked as his mental light dawned, "Madam, government water you want see?"

"Yes."

"No problem. You come. Up track, see. Standing pipe. Government water good water very clean not every day." He pointed into the gloomy distance under the trees, along a barely discernible track leading away at right angles from the house.

Queenie allowed herself to laugh, "At least there is clean water somewhere.

It's quite interesting how one can become thankful for small mercies."

"I don't know whether the future tourists would see it that way." I said. Surely they would expect water in the house near a sink and a toilet and shower.

Picking up on the only word he'd caught or understood, Kadhikan exclaimed, "Mercy, Madam? Oh, yes please. Mercy."

This sent Queenie off into fits of giggles. I was not, however, at all amused.

"This is bloody ridiculous," I muttered, "where's the shower and toilet, Kardy?" He heard.

He led us back inside the house, and through the anteroom, over cement bags and to the black hole of a bathroom. The floor was still of uneven earth, and all remained as Queenie had described it to me during our discussion of the previous day. The unconnected toilet was indeed next to a redundant putty drum, which in turn was full of what looked and smelt like pee.

"What's that?" I demanded of Kadhikan, pointing to the drum.

"No problem, sir. I can tip. No problem. Maybe you like more tea?"

We backed out of the stinking bathroom, glad to be free of his presence for a while. Leaving him to prepare the bloody tea.

We looked around at our own pace. The entire house had been reconstructed, all the mud brickwork removed and replaced with new baked bricks. Eight large concrete pillars had been constructed, in order to support the enormous weight of the roof, which was now accessed by the narrow, unfinished, outside stairway. None of the exterior of the building had anything approaching an acceptable finish, the whole of it requiring at least two coats of smooth cement render.

Concrete floors were still required everywhere except the main room. The window frames were new, but badly constructed, and apparently painted by a two-year-old, judging by the varying thicknesses of dried and run-patterned paint. The inadvertent spread of paint on the window panes further excluded the light. There was still a small gap at ceiling height between the main room and the kitchen. This, we speculated, was for the benefit of air circulation. In reality, it would circulate fumes from his newly constructed private area and separate kitchen into the tourist living area as it had previously, but perhaps less so?

I listed all the jobs to be done as I walked about, tea glass now in hand. We climbed up to the roof again. It had not been topped off, and was still full of rubbish as previously described. I listed this with the rest, and then called to Kadhikan to come up. He was lurking nervously, half-smiling, and pacing about down at the foot of the stairs.

I tried to explain very carefully to Kardy, in a manner I hoped he could understand, what I thought of the state of the work, the workmanship, and his lack of ethics when dealing with other people's money.

I accept that I had, in a rather childish way, asked him for the balance of the money so that I could complete the job properly myself. Of course, this brought an anticipated response, with the added revelation that he had pawned his wife's dowry, her gold, for twenty-four thousand rupees, in order to keep the job going. I was speechless.

I had played my little game, and he had trumped me again. Plainly I would never learn that I had met my match. This man was cleverer than me. I asked him to get the actual prices for the jobs I had listed, and to come and see me at eleven the following morning at the Pink Flowers restaurant, when I would decide which, if any, further work I would pay for.

"Oh yes, sir. Madam. Please. You make nice house. Tomorrow I come, tomorrow get money!" He had already decided I was going to pay up.

Chapter 7

I suppose by way of respite, Queenie and I walked into the gentle breeze whispering through the coconut palms, crossed the lagoon via the aged-looking ferry-man and his equally ancient boat, and on to the palm fringed beach beyond the fishermen's huts. The waves roared and crashed. The beautiful clear blue sea reminded us again of one of the reasons we were here. We walked along the beach, looking and listening to the waves. As the sun grew hotter, we ambled back into the coconut grove, which served as shelter and shade, not just to ourselves, but to the people living, working and playing in this idyllic looking setting.

The main occupation for the men and boys here is fishing. The nets, circular and about fifty feet across, were lying on the sand like great spider's webs. The boats reminded me of crudely constructed Viking ships. Thirty to forty feet long, with a wide beam, made of timber caulked to keep the sea out, with one and a half inch wide pitched rope, which seemed to be somehow stitched into the timber and over and through into the outside of the joints. A very cumbersome looking design, doubtless part of the local, probably quite ancient, boat building tradition, and by the look of the water in the bottom of the hulls, not all that effective, either. The launch of the vessels seemed to be a very dangerous affair, and appeared to rely as much on luck as on anticipation or skill. At least it seemed that way.

Such was the size of the waves crashing onto the beach that the boats, once pushed out onto an outgoing wave, left hardly any time for the eight to ten men to run, wade, scramble and pull themselves aboard, then sit, quickly catch an oar and row hard and deep, before the next wave crashed down and pushed them the same few feet back to the shore.

With good strength and management, the boat slid over the back of the wave and up, nearly vertical, in front of the oncoming swell, and back down. Thereafter, it seemed in perfect control, and out they pulled out into a safe and less violent swell.

Sat in amongst the trees and houses a few yards from the shore, were mainly women and children. Without exception they looked happy, shouting across and chatting to each other. Apart from some women tending the occasional open fires, heating the contents of bright aluminium cooking pots, most of them were working at the various processes of coir rope making.

The coconut delivered to the West in its raw state, does not have the large green or brown outer husk, just the kernel. It is this outer layer that produces the coir for rope, carpets, sleeping mats, brushes, firewood etc. This inside of the outer shell is compacted extremely tightly with a string-like, wiry material. After spending some time laying in the sun to dry, it is forced out of the shell, and again, left to dry. Later it is beaten with clubs and then light sticks, quite hard, which serves to release the compactness. After several hours of this treatment, the coir looks like a mountain of light brown wire wool. With the aid of two spinning wheels, it is turned into string and then into rope. It seems that not one piece of the coconut tree is wasted, including the trunk and leaves. An extremely efficient use of resources, we thought.

As we walked on, we came across a whitewashed, mud brick building. The door was wide open, and in the doorway sat an old man wearing his spotless white lungi, white hair neatly brushed, smiling cheerfully. After calling out the usual greeting , "Hellowhatisyoumame?" in a single word, he gestured for us to come closer, finally insisting that we go inside the tiny space. Except for three small chairs, the room was bare of furniture. A flimsy door, secured with an enormous padlock, was the only other item of interest in the room.

"This library." He told us, his once cheerful face assuming that sad, beseeching look we were beginning to recognise.

"No books," he continued sadly. "Please, ten rupees?"

Damn. Trapped again. Resigned to our fate, we handed over the money. I wonder if the 'library' has acquired any books yet?

It felt impossible to pass a local person without conceding to their repetitive, nagging demands for cash for one reason or another, it was wearing.

We reasoned that this could be the unfamiliarity of alien faces in a peasant culture. However unsophisticated they may appear to be, they do know that we carry money, and much more than they do. They also know that persistence pays.

We walked on until we could see the first of the now familiar beach side cafes. We had walked the few miles almost back to Kovalam, and we resolved to look up an acquaintance from our previous visit.

Prabu was an unusual man, intelligent and well educated, certainly much more than me, but poor. He worked as an Ayurvedic masseur, in one of the many palm leaf surgeries or massage parlours dotted around Kovalam, presumably for the benefit of tourists. These places were solely for remedial treatment. The practice is that each establishment has to have a registered and fully qualified Ayurvedic doctor in attendance.

Our friend Prabu was a young looking forty-year-old, who had undergone considerable personal trauma recently. Within a period of two years, due to illness and severe road accidents, his entire family had been wiped out, leaving him in a state of breakdown, which had in turn lost him his well paid job as an officer in a wildlife reserve. His easy politeness and friendliness sometimes slipped over into a nervous fussiness, the result, we speculated, of his not knowing what was going to happen to him next. Nevertheless, dear Prabu was recovering, indeed, had been saved from near death, through the care and kindness he was receiving at an Ashram located a few miles inland from Kovalam. We were drawn to him because of his openness and his willingness to deal with us as human beings, and not meal tickets.

We asked for him at the massage parlour, and were told that he was making his usual full moon visit to the Ashram, for prayer and meditation.

As we turned away, disappointed at not immediately finding our friend, a familiar, short, rotund figure appeared on the narrow trackway between the hotels, shops and parlours. I recognised at once the bright round smiling face of Sabu the Sadist, as I called him, a masseur with whom I'd had more than a passing acquaintance the previous year. He was one of three sons of a Salvation Army Commander, who as a respected charity worker, collected money for the poor of his parish around Kovalam. He executed his duties with the uprightness and politeness one would expect from a man of his devotion and status. Father/Commander had travelled to the Salvation Army Headquarters in London, an experience he was very proud to speak of.

Sabu and his brother Johnson had worked at the Green Valley Hotel, indeed the very one I had been based at as part of a package holiday the year before. I had spent a few riotous evenings drinking beer and joking with them and the rest of the staff. It was at one of these evenings that Sabu had cajoled me, against my better judgement, to visit his massage parlour for a 'Very relaxing massage". Relaxing? Nothing could have been further from the truth. After having been persuaded to part with two hundred rupees, I had trailed up the concrete steps leading to the roof of the hotel, where a singular small room sat, cabin-like. I was invited to lie down face first on a backless bench, covered in somewhat suspect bright orange PVC, not unlike a lorry tarpaulin. Sabu set about pummelling and twisting my limbs and torso, smothering me in oil which had the smell and consistency of gear oil. He worked very hard for an hour, stretching and pulling every joint and muscle. Face up, face down, he worked with a will, smiling reassuringly all the while. Finally he was done, and suggested that I go and lie down for a while, have a good sleep, before showering. With what I hope was not too unseemly haste I made my way down the stairs to my room, aching in every muscle and joint, and showered and soaped myself over and over until I was satisfied that I had finally rid myself of the oil slick, the sticky stench, the decaying, earthy smell of the lubricant that Sabu had applied to my flesh in order to facilitate the massage.

It was too early for sleep, so I had walked the short distance to the restaurant, and sat at an empty table. The light was fading. A waiter approached to light the stub of a candle, to combat the expected power cut. It was Johnson.

"Good evening sir. I see you have already met with my little brother Sabu," he laughed. Even in the dim light, he could see the difficulty I was having in making even the simplest of movements. "Tomorrow you will be very fit," he continued, as he handed me the menu. "Did you enjoy the massage?"

"I'll tell you tomorrow." I replied, with a smiley groan.

Now, twelve months later this familiar figure Sabu drew near, he too recognised us, and greeted us warmly.

"You remember me?" he asked, "You Jack" he said, laughing. "You must be Jill."

"No, Queenie."

"You sure you not Jill?"

"QUEENIE!"

"So sorry. You remember me Jack?"

"How could I forget the pain, the torture?" I replied.

"You want massage today?" he asked hopefully.

"No, absolutely not!" I instantly replied. In order to divert the conversation I asked, "Tell me, how is Johnson?"

"He is very good, earning one thousand rupees a month."

I remembered a good salary. "He still head waiter, Rockholme Hotel." This last was said with some reverence, the Rockholme being the local five star hotel.

We were suitably impressed, and said so. "Also, he marry two, three weeks time. You like to come wedding?"

"Maybe," I answered hesitantly.

"Please, you must. I will bring official invitation. Where do you stay?"

We sat and talked for a while as we had by now slowly walked to our favourite spot. We explained a little as to why we had returned, and where he could deliver the invitation. He was a pleasant young man, and it would be a privilege to attend an Indian wedding, we decided. He took his leave, and we spent the rest of the evening lounging, drinking lemon sodas (yes, really), and sitting in the soft candlelight, discussing how much it might cost and how long it might take to complete Kadhikan's house.

Chapter 8

It was nine-thirty next morning when we awoke to loud exclamations from outside.

"Sir! Jack, sir. Madam. Hello!"

Queenie sat bolt upright, startled out of a deep sleep.

"Who's that?" She called out.

"It'll be Kardy, I suppose," I said, as I tumbled out of my bed. Sure enough here he was bright and early, a good sign I thought.

"Hello Madam. Kadhikan here." He called brightly.

"Right, hang on. Wait a minute."

Silence. Queenie climbed out of her bed, and headed for the shower closet. I opened the door, and there he was, bright-eyed and buoyant with expectation.

"Yes," I reaffirmed. A good start, I thought.

"You in bed sir. Sorry. I think maybe come to see early." He was all enthusiasm.

"Fine. It is good you came. Look, I've got to have a shower, how did you find us, anyway?"

"Pink Flowers, Sir. Man say you come here. Same man has many rooms, Sadanand. He boss also restaurant here."

"I see, right. Well, I'll meet you at Pink Flowers shortly, if that is OK. Have you got the prices?" I added hopefully.

"Prices most good, yes sir. See you later."

Queenie emerged from the shower, quickly dressed and got ready to go. Now fully awake and buoyant-ish we quickly walked the short distance to the restaurant for breakfast and our meeting with Kadhikan. Wasting as little time as possible on the niceties, we got down to business. Between bites of chilli omelette and toast, I looked over the long lists that included every conceivable item needed to equip a tourist home, down to the toilet roll holder and the dishcloths. His costings, I thought at the time, were too much, at ninety-seven thousand rupees, equivalent to eight years' wages for a head waiter at the Rockholme hotel or similar. I was apprehensive. I really did not want to give him that much more of my money. Although I accepted now that it would definitely cost more than the five hundred pounds we had anticipated in extra spend. Dilemma! Dilemma!

"But how else am I going to get the job finished?" I asked myself. Grimacing, I looked at the papers spread out in front of me, trying to give myself time to think. I had not thought of all the possibilities, it was too early, and what should I do? I delayed.

I passed the papers to Queenie, who glanced at them, and exclaimed, "WHAT? This will mean we have spent over seven and a half hundred thousand rupees, more than seven and a half thousand pounds at least, in total!" Turning angrily to Kadhikan, she said, "You told us two hundred thousand rupees originally. This is more than three times as much again."

Nodding enthusiastically, Kadhikan asked innocently, "What is originally, please?"

"In the beginning, last year." I explained.

"Oh yes, sir. I make small, very small, mistake. But, make much better house!" He finished, triumphantly.

Kadhikan drank his cardamom flavoured sweet, milky tea. Queenie and I munched thoughtfully on the remainder of our omelettes, inwardly digesting this latest onslaught. Even when you do expect the worst it doesn't help when one is actually faced with it. Kadhikan busied himself with a rapid-fire conversation with Sadanand, the owner of the Pink Flowers. I would have loved to know what they were talking about. "Probably about what a gift horse I am," I thought.

I am aware that it could easily be argued that I should not have embarked on this project without knowledge of what the effect of my contributions and other expectations may have on all concerned.

After all it is usually the very wealthy, institutions and charities that do this kind of work, and usually with other peoples' money, tax relief and a sophisticated, well-researched knowledge base to rely on.

"OK" I said, "I can't practically afford all this, we need to compromise so I'll tick off the items I want you to get done, and I'll work myself and do the rest. How's that?"

"How's that is OK sir. Some we can leave as you choose, sir." I excused myself to use my Visa credit card at one of the local larger hotels that ran an exchange bureau, and got the extra money needed. At a miserly 70 rupees per pound. I had expected 100 Rs per pound. I'd worry about the consequences later. I re-joined the waiting group at the restaurant.

"How long to finish the floors, render the outside, and finish the toilet and shower?" I asked as I sat down.

"Day after tomorrow sir."

"Right. Remember, I need you to get the best possible prices to complete these jobs. I'll give you a whole week, I expect the place to be cleaned up as well. No cement droppings, floors, tiles clean and grouted, you know what grouting is?"

"Oh yes Jack, is in middle of tile. I get good men to do all it will be very much you like OK Jack."

"Don't forget that disgusting roof, clean it all off no dirt, no shit or rubbish, clean yes!"

"No problem, sir. As you wish, no shit, you are my god, sir. I go now, start job."

Hoping for, but not expecting the best, I reluctantly handed over the thirty-four thousand rupees. As he took the money from me, he fired one last shot.

"Please Sir. One more hundred rupees you give. Buy a little rice and fish for wife and children?"

I felt instantly anaesthetised. This guy is an artist. But is he REAL? Jaw slack, I numbly handed over the extra notes, enough to feed his family well for two to three days.

"Oh God, sir. You are my God sir. One week, all finish. Have a nice day."

With that, he vanished into the midday heat beneath the coconut palms.

Chapter 9

Sadanand was a large, burly, square headed man with a large moustache tweaked and styled at the ends with wax. He was apparently doing quite well for himself. Apart from the restaurant, he owned the well-kept six-roomed apartment house where we were staying. I had made contact with this man on my previous visit to South India in anticipation of this eventuality, and unusually the arrangements had gone almost to plan. We had in fact arrived three weeks early, he seemed accepting and pleased to see us.

The rooms had all the basic facilities that were in good working order. All passageways, small gardens and roof area were swept daily, and rubbish free. Located on the outer edge of the main activities on the beach, it was quiet and did not attract the unwelcome attentions of the local street sales force.

Sadanand's nineteen-year-old son, a polite and helpful young man, who spent a great deal of time at the Pink Flowers, generally slept overnight in the office, adding a sense of security. During the day, he ran errands for guests, cleaned and swept around the place, and also did the washing. So, with all these conveniences, we considered ourselves well served, especially as the room was priced at a modest tourist rate of one hundred rupees per night.

Having scurried away, thirty-four thousand and one hundred rupees the richer, K left space at our table which was promptly filled by Landlord Sadanand's large and jovial presence.

"You are liking your room, Mr Jack?" He enquired pleasantly, easing his bulk into the bending plastic chair so recently vacated by the slender wiry form of Kadhikan.

"Yes, we are very happy, thank you. It is nice, very clean and tidy."

"Thank you, thank you. You are so kind." He beamed, then proudly continued in his gravely voice; "I am Sergeant in Indian Army. I know to keep clean is good for health."

"That explains it." I answered. "Your rooms do have a well-ordered, military air about them, they are very good indeed."

"You know this man Kadhikan?" he asked, abruptly changing the subject.

"Yes, I met him last year."

"How long you stay my house?" A sudden change of subject. We were becoming accustomed to these spontaneous interrogations, and had learned to simply go along with them.

"Maybe ten days." I responded. He looked pleased.

"Ten days very good. Then where you go?" He demanded.

"To Kadikhan's house."

Affecting an air of nonchalance, he asked,

"You buy Kadikhan's house?"

"No, no, we help him make it into a tourist house." I explained. "We work to make it good, so that he can earn a better living. He has a big family, three children, elderly parents, and sisters to support.

"You help him?"

"Yes."

"You will help me?"

"We have no money to help anyone anymore." I said, rather firmly. "We are all spent up."

Undaunted, he went on persuasively, "You can tell your friends in England to come to my house, very good house."

He had not taken on board fully the anticipated guest house at Kadhikans and our interest in it.

"We know it's very good," we chorused, "but we can't promise anything."

"You will tell?" He insisted.

"If I know of anyone who is coming here, yes, I will tell them." It seemed easier to go along with his request than to restate our position with K.

"OK. Good. Is good. Thank you. You must visit my home," he urged. "It is near Kadhikan's house, we are neighbours." I glanced across at Queenie, who nodded, open mouthed, at me. I felt a rising sense of panic. What other project would he invite me to participate in?

"OK," I agreed, "When we've got settled in, we will visit you."

"Very good. Very good." He looked delighted. Shaking our hands warmly, he stood, then, saluting smartly, he excused himself. I pondered. I wondered why he thought we would support his cause, when he knew that we were committed to his poorer neighbour's. I looked up into Queenie's eyes, searching for wisdom, or a comment that might help unravel the tangled confusion of what appeared to me to be a totally illogical proposition,

"God knows, Jack!" She said, answering my unvoiced question. "I certainly don't."

Chapter 10

The following week was fairly relaxing. Swimming, walking, visiting the nearby villages I had not had time to explore on my previous two week holiday trip. We also continued to look for Prabu, the nearest to a genuine friend I thought we might have here, one of the world's good guys. He still wasn't around, but would turn up soon, the doctor at the massage parlour assured us. We renewed other acquaintances who expressed enthusiasm and pleasure to see us.

One thing we now knew with absolute certainty was that any smile, acknowledgement or enquiry as to our names, well-being, or country of origin, or voluntary disclosures of personal circumstances by a local to us would inevitably lead to an invitation to donate money to their own personal charity.

Each individual, by way of authenticating their credentials, would have a relative in London, Hull, Birmingham, or Hastings, and would brandish an exercise book, the double of that brandished by Kadhikan a year ago. In it would be written; in a variety of hands; eulogies extolling the salient virtues of the owner of the book.

Half-way through the week, being brought down by my usual bout of bronchitis that always attacked after any climactic change, I asked Queenie to visit Kadhikan in the role of Inspector of Works while I found a pharmacy who would sell me the appropriate inhaler and other medication, incidentally at a fraction of the cost in the UK.

Queenie's building inspector's assessment of the Kadhikan house situation was positive. Plumbing works were complete as far as she could tell, and cement works were well in progress.

This cheered me up to such an extent that I left my sick bed and went with Queenie to look up Smitha and her family, another person we had met the previous year. We had exchanged a few letters, Smitha seemed to have a genuine interest in us, our lives, the things we did at home, and life in general in the UK.

Our first meeting had taken place on one of our many singular walkabouts a year ago when we had passed her home where she lived with her extended family, in search of the temple I had seen sign-posted off the main road in the village. She had seen us as we debated with ourselves whether it would be the right thing to do to open the gate into the compound which housed the tiny shrines, and go through to have a closer look.

She had gestured for us to remove our shoes, and had opened the gate for us, offering to show us around and explain the various deities. Her English was difficult to understand, so her attempts at detailed explanation were wasted on me. However, her enthusiasm, beautiful manners and childlike inquisitiveness were not wasted, and had gone some way to compensate for more dubious encounters elsewhere.

We had been disarmed by her insistence that we should not leave until I had been inside her family home. This was a township house, a pretty bungalow set in a small courtyard garden, with a well in front, and a toilet out the back. The rooms were tiny and almost devoid of furniture, the walls were once white but now partly smoke-blackened, the floor swept clean. We were introduced to grandmother, aunties, sisters, and various other unspecified females. Mother and father were out at work.

A sudden monsoon downpour initially familiarised me with the thatch leaking roof issue and had also trapped me for another hour or so in Smitha's home, so she insisted that we must stay and eat a meal. It seemed a fantastic opportunity to gain insight into a family, and courtesy I thought demanded that we comply with this request.

We did, and at once all the available females piled into the kitchen. A furious sound of banging and chopping ensued, and glancing through the open door, I could see the women squatting on the floor and chopping an assortment of vegetables and spices, talking and laughing together excitedly. We sat down to wait, while the rain poured down outside.

After a few minutes the rain had found its way inside the bungalow by way of the leaking roof. Again an example of the failings of a palm thatched roof .

Smitha's sisters appeared with a cloth, and wiped up the growing puddles on the floor, smiling apologetically at me before scurrying away back to the kitchen. A faint spicy aroma, wafted on plumes of smoke, began to seep from the kitchen. It grew stronger and set my mouth watering. Suddenly, I felt terribly hungry, and could have eaten the proverbial horse.

Smitha appeared, sari still spotlessly clean. I wondered how she managed this, without emerging covered in flour or spice or something. Cool and unruffled despite the ferocity of the chopping, Smitha gestured for us to follow her outside, where she produced a jug of water, a bowl and a bar of soap. We washed our hands, dried them on the ragged but clean towel she provided, and headed back inside to join the family, as I thought, for a meal. Only two plates were set on the tiny table. One each for myself and Queenie.

The family were not to share the meal. Our value was in pure entertainment; in return for the meal, we had to endure the close scrutiny of the entire family as we ate every morsel.

I soon forgot my embarrassment, as the meal was so delicious, and was able to disregard the fascinated stares of my hosts. I ate until I could eat no more, to the delight of the assembled family.

We eventually took our leave, promising to return one day, and most certainly to write when we returned home. It was the memory of this happy day that persuaded me to enquire again after Smitha and her delightful family. Queenie was in ecstasy at the prospect of meeting the family again.

I was also keen to know whether she had received the pens, books and birthday present we had jointly sent her. The next day, being a Saturday, seemed a good time to go we thought, as we might then have a chance to meet mother and father too. So, early in the morning, we walked in the direction of Vizhinjam, with us trying to remember which of the maze of paths would lead to the cart track, which would lead to the main road, off which was Smitha's township house.

Surprisingly, we remembered the route quite well, give or take a deviation or two. Fortunately we had had the presence of mind to start early. At seven thirty am with the sun barely risen, it was cool, but by eight thirty it was hotter than a mid-July afternoon back home. We debated whether we might arrive at Smitha's house too early for anyone to be around, then agreed that most Indian households tended to use the coolest part of the day, early morning, to get household chores completed before it became unbearably hot. We could always stop for tea at a wayside shack, and walk slowly.

Although the monsoon had ended some weeks previously, the heat was very sticky and moist as the ground dried out. Apparently it would take another few months to dry out completely and vaporise the water which had fallen in the three-month rainy season.

"Here we are, this is the junction." I remembered the large hammer and sickle painted in white on the tarmac road. An obvious symbol of the state government political party that I believe were voted in after the abdication of the then-Maharajah of Travancore some decades ago.

What I couldn't remember was whether the house was to the left or right of this junction. We could see a tea stall some way off to our left, and in buoyant mood, singing as we went, "Cup of tea, cup of tea, cup of tee-ee!" to the tune of Onward Christian Soldiers, we headed for it. The elderly tea vendor was apparently not in such a buoyant mood. "Chai?" He muttered grumpily.

"Yes please." We replied politely, somewhat chastened by his surly manner. "Two?" he growled, holding up two fingers. We nodded silently, and watched in admiration as the boiling milk and water mix was tossed expertly from one grimy glass to another and back, to and fro without spilling a drop, until a suitable froth took up about one third of the glass. Satisfied, he slammed the glass down on the greasy wooden counter with a smart crack! Then proceeded to repeat the performance with a second glass.

"Six rupees!" he barked, holding up six fingers to clarify the cost. We offered a ten-rupee note.

"No change!" he barked happily. That's the way it goes. Just be glad it wasn't a hundred rupee note.

The township was a few hundred yards further along in the direction we were facing. The road was by now very busy, with motorcycles, buses and taxis weaving their way in between children playing and women in bright saris carrying baskets of fish, firewood, cooking utensils or fruit on their heads. A lorry and three yellow and black auto rickshaws were battling it out for precedence, taking up the whole width of the narrow strip of tarmac which served as a main road, and occasionally using the rough track normally used by pedestrians at the side of the road. No-one seemed willing to give way to anyone else, and amazingly, no-one was hurt. Lorry and rickshaws sped past in a swirl of dust and fumes. So, tea consumed, we were free to cross the road and continue our saunter into the township and Smitha.

We walked onto the large cleared open area of dust that lay immediately in front of the township. A group of boys and girls were playing cricket, which was immediately abandoned at the sight of us. They rushed at us, shouting questions as they ran.

"What is your name?" "What is your country?" "From?"

"My name is...." I began, but was interrupted by cries of "School penna, school penna!" endlessly screamed. It was impossible to answer an individual child, or even the group as a whole, as the questions were not asked in unison, each child was simply trying to outshout the other. So, surrounded by the shouting, giggling children, we made our way across the dusty stretch of open ground to the narrow dirt track that led to Smitha's house.

It looked like it had been gouged out of a dried riverbed that had been cut by a raging torrent. The children still followed, repeating the same questions, refusing to listen to any answers.

As we approached the end of the lane, we saw a tall, stout balding man in the garden of the house and I felt sure I recognised it as the one I had visited the previous year. The man saw our dilemma with the children, and sent them scurrying away with a quick fire blast in the local dialect. Turning to us with a pleasant smile, he asked, "Please Sir, you lost?"

Queenie answered him. "Smitha? Young lady, twenty-one years old, Smitha, does she live here?"

He looked puzzled for a moment, then "Wait!" he exclaimed, turned, and went into the house behind him. Seconds later a strained and puzzled looking Smitha appeared at the door. Seeing myself and Queenie, her expression changed, and with a laugh and a cheery "Hello," She skipped up to Queenie and gave her a big hug, which Queenie returned enthusiastically. Calling out to someone in the house, Smitha danced joyfully around us, clapping her hands with delight. Next moment, women of all ages and sizes poured out of the house, followed closely by the beaming balding gentleman who had first greeted us. He held out his hand and introduced himself.

"I am Nadh," he said smiling broadly, "Smitha father."

Hands reached for ours, and we were pulled into the house amidst much laughter and chatter. The room had not changed since the last time I had visited, except perhaps it was even more crowded, Smitha's parents and a few neighbours had increased the throng. Tea was produced, and once again we were invited to eat. How could we refuse? Smitha told us she had passed her exams. We congratulated her. She produced a pile of English text books. We flipped through them, astonished at the difficulty of the Victorian text. This was the way Smitha had learnt English, her book learnt knowledge was quite extensive, but her pronunciation was very poor. We guessed that she had rarely heard a native English speaker for any conversation. We could not help but feel humbled at the dedication of people, as they struggled to learn a language from such archaic text books.

Smitha asked if we had a camera. Of course we had, and so a photo shoot was organised. This took some time, as all combinations of Queenie with assorted relatives, me with assorted relatives, and everyone with everyone else, were worked out. Queenie was then drawn into a tiny bedroom off the main room, and to the accompaniment of much giggling, was dressed in Mrs Nadh's best sari. Mrs Nadh, being approximately a quarter of Queenie's size, had struggled manfully to squeeze Queenie into the glorious red, green and gold silk, with a black blouse piece. Finally satisfied, Queenie made her grand entrance, and was duly photographed with Smitha, who had changed from her simple house dress into her best sari for the occasion.

Then it was my turn. Mr Nadh, chuckling to himself, drew me into the same small room. An immaculate white shirt was produced, and a length of white cloth with a gold border. I was wrapped around in the lungi, and a new Kerala man was created! Mr Nadh was delighted, and posed proudly by my side for his photograph. The meal was finally ready, and again we became the object of everyone's attention as we tucked into the delicious fish curry, rice, and other curries too numerous to mention. We were completely stuffed, and could eat no more. But we were not to escape so lightly. A dessert had been made in our honour, a heavy, sweet, banana pancake, and somehow we managed to eat one each. We could barely move.

While we ate, Smitha told us that the pens I had sent had all been deliberately broken before she received them, but that the books had arrived safely. She had also received her birthday card, but sadly, the ten-pound note that was included was missing. We were particularly upset by this, as it was a twenty-first birthday present and therefore quite special.

The meal over, we were taken by Smitha into the little house next door, where her grandmother lay on a narrow, hard bed. She looked very ill. She had a colostomy bag attached with sellotape to a chair by the bed. I touched her hand, and said "Hello." She made a faint choking noise, as she attempted to smile up at me. Smitha spoke to her softly, genuine concern and kindness in every feature. Leading us out of the room, she said, "I am nurse. She will die soon."

I felt completely inadequate, and all I could say was, "I am sorry." Queenie was silent, visibly moved.

"She very old, she OK." Came the philosophical response.

We returned to the main room, and began to take our leave. Queenie gave me one of her knowing looks. I knew she was thinking the same as me. We couldn't leave without replacing Smitha's lost gift, which would mean so much to this lovely, lively family. A quick conference on the road outside confirmed that she was in agreement with me. We returned to the house, and called Smitha out. Queenie took her hand, and pressed a thousand rupee note into it, saying "Happy birthday!"

Tears filled her eyes, and she hugged Queenie tightly. Mrs Nadh appeared at the door, we waved our goodbyes once again, and walked away, leaving Smitha standing in the road, watching and waving until we were out of sight. We have not seen her since, though we called a few days later with copies of the photographs, which we left with her father, Mr Nadh. He appeared to be babysitting for the entire street that day, judging by the number of children playing in the garden. Smitha was at college, he said, as he thanked us for the photos, laughing as he looked through them. We didn't go in the house that time. We have been left with a lovely memory of a warm and welcoming family.

Chapter 11

We decided to return to Kadhikan's house as previously agreed, one week after handing over the cash. Taking into account Queenie's visit on the fourth day, and finding the plumbing complete, together with other work well in progress, it seemed reasonable to suppose that the latest agreed work should be completed. However, taking into account that Kadhikan had not been seen boasting progress, we resolved anything or nothing at all could have happened.

Unperturbed however, we packed our large rucksacks and found ourselves on the red dusty path under the shade of the coconut palms once again. We were greeted by the bubbling stream-like sound of children's voices, and the usual whirring of the spinning wheels. Across our path was a huge pile of prepared coconut coir, so high that we could not see over the top, all waiting to be spun into rope. We skirted around it, smiling a greeting to the ladies who were working happily chatting, and who were we hoped soon to be our nearest neighbours. We were rewarded with huge smiles and cheery "Allos!"

This time the large door of the house was open, the fan spinning, giving a gentle and welcome draught. We knocked, and stepped in to see Kadhikan washing the floor, using an old coat tied to the branch of a tree as a floor mop.

"Hi, Kardy, how are you? Where's Valsala and the kids?"

"You come now sir? All good, everything finish as you say, sir. Please, now can you stay here? Please sir I make good for you, you stay."

With great pride, shoulders back and smiling, he directed us to the bathroom, and sure enough, all appeared complete. Beautiful white tiles with a green leaf motif had been applied two-thirds of the way up the walls, and even the floor area was tiled. He showed us the fixed toilet and flush tank. The connection to the water pipe dribbled water out against the wall. The male/female threaded joint leaked at the flush tank water inlet. I flushed the toilet and water gushed from the pipe, which connected to the toilet pan. The water, instead of flushing into the pan, poured from the joint onto the floor.

I laughed.

"What's this?"

"No problem sir, I fix, later, later."

"Who will fix it?" I asked.

"I will sir; I am plumber — Saudi Arabia." — With a wobble of the head.

"OK, fine, no problem."

Queenie shouted through to the bathroom. "We will have to buy a mattress or two. I can't sleep on the bare plywood Jack!"

"Can you make tea, Kardy? Then after we have made a list, we will go shopping."

"Shopping sir? Why shopping?"

"For mattresses, plates, chairs, tables."

"As you like as you like." He responded, as if he really could not see the need.

"Can you come with us and show us the shops?"

"I come sir, first, tea."

"Great, I'll unpack. Let's put the gear on the base of the bed, then I can use the rucksack for shopping."

"I get taxi, sir?"

"First tea, Kardyy."

He stepped into the kitchen as Valsala came into the main room. Big, big smiles, as usual, and carrying her newest baby, which she passed to Queenie. We both later commented on her approach and how honest and confident she appeared. We sat on the edge of the bed and poked and made noises at the baby, while she returned to the kitchen.

The place certainly looked better. Light, wide and airy, with clean pale blue walls. Even the window frames had been re-gloss painted, the previous brown painted wood could still be seen underneath. The floor was a pitiful sight. Someone had made a very good and calculated attempt at a red and black patterned finish, then someone else — at least we hoped someone else, but you never knew — had mixed cement in piles all over it then left cement stains, completely ruining the original effort. Not to worry, we had stage one all but complete. A few modifications and a bit more care and we'd have it! This is progress I thought.

Valsala came back and took the near naked baby from Queenie, laying it on its back on the bare plywood bed base, where it lay kicking and squeaking. It is interesting how babies and children here did not have, and did not appear to need, toys. Almost everything around them is there to be played on, in and with. Copying adults is their full time occupation. Even two-year-olds will carry firewood on their heads, or try to emulate Mum as they struggle to carry an empty water vessel, which is as big as they are.

We had brought with us some gifts from my daughter for the children, who imagined, I expect, that all children are like Western children, and need lots of artificial stimulation. The truth is, they don't, and they are extremely tantrum free, and seem to chuckle their lives away very happily. Children of any age are never told not to play in puddles, that kind of activity is a birthright here. Lucky kids!

Valsala and Kadhikan arrived from the kitchen with several large stainless steel trays, each containing various items of hot and wonderful looking, appetising food. Chapattis, fried whole fish, crispy poppadoms, rice and two stainless steel bowls full of curry, plus four bananas. I hadn't the heart to ask where the tea was.

"First you eat, then you get rickshaw. Now eat!" Came the command.

"I have never tasted such wonderful food," said Queenie to Valsala, who did not speak English but understood the look of pleasure. She looked faintly embarrassed at the compliment. The curry was a symphony of varied flavours, each bursting out at a different taste. Whole ladies' fingers as big as small carrots, not mushy, but firm and tasty. Crisply fried fish, perfectly cooked rice.

Valsala went off into the kitchen, while Kadhikan took up what would become his usual apparition-like position, he sat and watched, leaving just enough of a distance to suggest a haunting presence. This habit of K's became oddly annoying, it was constant observation; we didn't have a choice, he was there, just in the distance looking on. I didn't get used to it but had to accept it. The smoke had rolled down from the kitchen area and into the room from the spaces above the walls and ceiling. It added to the ghostly illusion. I stood up and opened the windows.

"We are staying here then are we?" Asked Queenie, finally pausing for breath between mouthfuls of food.

"Of course, of course, you must. We go shop!" exclaimed Kadhikan.

"Where will YOU live?" Queenie asked.

"No problem is up to you. We go to father-mother house. Is good, like normal all time, no problem."

"Kardy, we are not having you with no home!" I didn't like the feeling of kicking him out of his own home.

"OK. Good sir, then we will have private room in there." He said, pointing to the separate kitchen area.

"What about the smoke and the baby?" Queenie replied.

"Cook outside, no problem, really, madam. If you prefer, as you please, we can go."

"No, no." We both insisted.

"Very good sir, you are good, madam, sir!"

Queenie responded. "First of all, it is YOUR home."

I didn't quite see why Queenie had to state the obvious.

"Yes madam, it is my home. This I know. I am very happy you stay here."

"OK", I said, getting bored with the kicked dog expression, "that's fine, Kardy, you stay mate."

I could hear Valsala's voice outside the kitchen door. I got up to thank her, and to assess the practicalities of the private room. The kitchen was 18 feet by 8. I've lived in half that space myself before now. It was clean and dry with good surfaces, and a lot better than it was a year ago. In fact this room didn't exist at all. So although not feeling totally happy about their accommodation, I put it to the back of my mind. After all it was not beyond the wit of man to build a palm leaf building on the flat roof, I convinced myself if I could do it which I could, he should be able to for sure.

"I must remember to do something about the air vent, the one from the kitchen into our room, because they will probably cook and smoke will pour into our area." I told myself.

So now that was registered in my mind as an urgent task, along with the toilet repair, I returned to the main room.

Ten minutes later we were in the usual rickety rickshaw, and off to the capital, complete with list of possible purchases. Maybe once Kadhikan had shown us around the town, we would work out a more comprehensive list of items for another day; now, we would see what we would see. The drive was the usual rattling banging chariot race, totally devoid of discipline, courtesy or respect for life. The air was blue with diesel and two-stroke engine fumes. We travelled the twelve kilometres in fear of our lives.

We left the rickshaw, and Kadhikan led us through narrow, stinking streets, not quaint or picturesque as in brochures of "Incredible India." The sides of the streets were piled to shoulder height with saturated, rotting rubbish. The stench of urine, excrement, the heat, the mud, and cow shit sprayed a yard high as motorcycles sped through the slush, soon began to tell on both of us. After only 10 minutes of trudging ankle deep in sludge I needed reassurance.

"How far?" I shouted over the racket of horns and engines.

"Here!" Kadhikan pointed to a knee-high water tap that was open and wasting its precious contents into the sludge.

"Wash feet here then we go up steps." He said pointing to three steps, leading up to an open fronted building. I washed my legs and feet, as did Queenie. We looked at each other. "This is madness!"

"Let's get it done and get out of here!" I said.

Inside the open front revealed a large store, with every possible household furniture item stacked, leant and balanced haphazardly on top of each other not quite to ceiling height. We had made it! So far so good.

"We will get a taxi back, a big one, for the mattresses."

"I expect so, Queenie. Maybe it'll take a couple of trips; I'll ask Kadhikan to get the store owner to ring for one."

Kadhikan had overheard, "Yes I will ask, as you please sir." He volunteered.

The store owner was a short round man wearing square framed spectacles. Glasses are an unusual addition to an Indian's ensemble. I expect this is due to the cost, which may be prohibitive for all but the middle class, as this shop proprietor plainly was. His two male teenage employees stood suddenly to attention at what seemed to be a command of his high-pitched voice. At the sight of us, a burst of native language ensued between himself and Kadhikan, and a pussycat smile slid across his face. The two young helpers merely looked terrified, and, as it transpired, spoke no English. Queenie spoke up as she edged her way through the piles of stacked items.

"Double mattresses. How much?"

In spite of the large selection of available mattresses of different thicknesses, the store proprietor could not resist his apparently genetically implanted impulse to completely ignore Queenie's request, and pull out a plastic chair in front of her, obstructing her passage. Pointing to it, he said, rather unnecessarily,

"Nice chair."

I spoke up. "Do you speak English, sir?"

"Oh, yes. What is your name?" He volunteered.

"Great" I muttered. "I'm Jack and we need you to show us and then tell us the price of different mattresses. Doubles."

He looked around at the nearby, unusually neatly stacked mattresses of different colours and sizes, and dismissed them all with, "Mattresses here," — pointing to them — "all no good."

"No good!" I repeated, perplexed, "Why no good?" I couldn't think what could go wrong with a brand-new, unwrapped mattress that would qualify it as no good.

"Better this way," he said, pointing to another pile of apparently identical mattresses at the other side of the large room. He rapped out instructions to the two employees, who obediently clambered over cupboards, chairs, settees etc., to reach the mattresses, to the accompaniment of a barrage of snapped and barked instructions. The boys finally dragged a mattress over to us for our inspection. It was covered in a blue flowered material, was about four inches thick, very firm, and encased in thick polythene.

"How much?" Queenie tried.

Another round of Malayalam from Kadhikan, the boys and the proprietor. Then the usual, "Very good, very cheap price, very good quality, long last." All in one breath.

"Yes, but how much?" Queenie repeated.

Another round of convoluted Malayalam, then silence, while we all looked at one another. One of the boys had made his way to a green painted steel ex-military style desk, and from the depths of a deep drawer he extracted a book which he duly brought over and presented to his boss. With the return of his pussycat smile, the proprietor opened the book and pointed at a picture of the very mattress, displayed within the picture of some upper class American style home. Price, five thousand, five hundred rupees!

"No," I said. "That's about three times too expensive!"

"Four thousand rupees!" He snapped.

"No!" I repeated.

"OK what you pay?"

"One thousand rupees!" It was my turn to snap.

"You want pay one thousand rupees? No, sir! No, sir! Here is one thousand rupees mattress!" And he led the way to the original neatly stacked pile of mattresses. We were, as tradition has it, back where we started. Not to worry, we were about to acquire the purchases at a price a middle class Indian would expect to pay, after all it was an Indian who would derive the benefits long term. This, along with variations of cunning, each as tiring and frustrating as the last, were thrust upon us, until, having finally acquired the items we most urgently needed, we paid up and waited for our taxi to arrive for the return journey.

Amazingly, three double mattresses, two full size plastic chairs, a low table and some pillows, all fitted into the capacious boot of the Ambassador taxi. What a wonderful machine! Deep, soft seats, wind up windows, room for four people comfortably in the rear seat with springs and a horn that could be heard more loudly outside the vehicle than inside. Luxury! After only one short stop while Kadhikan went off to purchase wet fish at a roadside market, we were home and unpacked in less than five hours. It was already dusk so, tasks completed, we walked through the coconut grove to the shore, and watched the deep orange sun slip into the sea to the accompaniment of waves crashing onto the sand and graciously rolling and rattling the pebbles to and fro.

On our return to the house, we could see flickering candle light in the windows. There was a power cut, one of many we endured in India. But as it transpired, we were to suffer far fewer cuts here in Pachalloor than in Kovalam. Valsala had indeed lit candles for us and was in the process of making tea. The kitchen was relatively bare, except for the new concrete and brick bench surfaces built on to the walls.

"Kardy," I called. "Give me a hand with this bed otherwise you will only have the floor to sleep on."

"Floor is good, Jack, always sleep floor" came the unexpected response.

"But we have double beds and mattresses, all nice and clean and comfortable!"

"Jack! No! Sir! We always sleep mat only."

"But Kardy. We don't need three beds. One is for you and Vas."

"No good sir, floor better." Kadhikan insisted. This was comfort too far.

"OK, mate we'll put two mattresses on one bed."

We dismantled the now spare bed frame and stored it in the small ante-room. I unpacked the bags while Queenie made for the shower.

"Jack, look here!" she called from the bathroom. I went to investigate, and found her standing next to the shower, with water squirting out of the sides of the ball joint on the shower head, while a single thin trickle fell, wimp like, from the centre of the rose.

"So, here we are on our first night by flickering candlelight, with a leaking toilet, leaking water pipe, and a shower that doesn't work! Some bloody plumber!" I said, exasperation clear in my voice. Queenie began to laugh, finally seeing the funny side, and as she did, so the lights came on. Good old Queenie!

I removed the shower head, allowing a strong fall of water in the one direction, downwards, gushing like a hose pipe. We showered in this way, adding the shower head to the growing list of repairs. We had discovered that lying damp under the fan after a shower was a wonderful way to remain cool for some time, and we soon fell into an exhausted sleep. Sadly, we had forgotten one important thing before retiring for the night. We had forgotten to go on a "mossie" hunt. Consequently, we were both bitten several times on all parts of our exposed anatomies. I cannot remember who woke first under the barrage of stinging and itching, but Queenie was first up and on went the light. We were still very tired. Looking about us, we saw maybe a dozen or so mosquitoes, some waiting on various parts of the wall, others zipping around us, presumably awaiting a suitable landing site on our collective mass of white flesh.

Suddenly the light bulb inside my head flashed on! I had a surge of energy! "The tent! Queenie! Let's get the tent on to one of the beds. That's if you don't mind sharing."

"Yes, yes!" She exclaimed, immediately getting my meaning. "Use the inner mosquito net! One mattress underneath it, one inside it ... if it will fit..."

"Yes!" It worked! Sweating again now, we showered once again, then zipped ourselves safely inside the mosquito net, finally falling asleep at about 2:45 am, in our new cocoon.

It was the almighty explosion somewhere close by and outside the door which woke us, followed by another bomb going off. Boom! Then the sudden sound of machine-gun fire. Rat-a-tat-tat! We clutched at each other in fear, already bolt upright in the predawn dark. Crack-crack-crack! Rat-a-tat-tat! Our hearts slowed.

"Phew! Jesus! Queenie, it's only the temple! I've heard about this! I'll go out and have a look."

"It's four o'clock. Surely temples don't start up at four o'clock in the morning?"

"I'll look." I said again. I unzipped the net, and opened the door, all in one movement, while also managing to fall over the remains of the tent, which we'd left on the floor. It was still dark outside, but I could see by the lights from the surrounding cottages that a stream of people were emerging from their compounds and were all heading in the same direction.

"Queenie, come and look at this lot. These people must be bonkers!"

Not everyone, however, had drifted off in the direction of the temple. A few moments later the familiar whirring sound of the coir spinning machine, and the soft chatter of female voices, peppered the air. The women had started work. We went wearily back to bed.

"Jack, Jack, Jack." The soft insistent voice from outside the window finally penetrated our sleep. I glanced at my watch.

"Christ! Is there no peace here?" I snapped angrily. It was still only 7:30. Up I got again, unzipped the net, and flung open the door. I immediately felt a black wave of guilt. There was Kardy, stainless steel tray in hand, with fish, curry and bread for our breakfast. "Oh, cheers, Kardy." I said, rather inadequately.

"Queenie, breakfast is served!"

"Breakfast?" She asked, surprised.

"Sure is! Come in, Kardy."

"No sir, you take!" I took.

We initiated our plastic chairs and table, with fish curry for breakfast at seven thirty, and still feeling as tired as we had the previous evening at eight. But we were very grateful for the kind considerations of Kadhikan and Valsala. We finished our filling breakfast, and returned the used dishes to Valsala. I was pleased to see that the dividing door between the kitchen and the main room proper had been bolted from her side. It made for privacy, and we were both impressed that Kadhikan and Valsala had recognised the need. Privacy is a very rare commodity here, even in places one would assume it would be essential. Valsala had made us tea, which I carried back to share with Queenie, who had crept back to bed. While we drank our tea, we discussed how we would deal with certain aspects of our stay and what the house should look like for the tourists. It should be pleasing to the eye; and appropriately rustic, but more than a room. The furniture would be simple, in accordance with the ambience of the district, comfortable and easy to keep clean. We lay on the bed, bloated with breakfast, making mental lists of items we might purchase, if we knew where to purchase them. Tables, storage cupboards, a cooker of some kind, stainless steel ware including a traditional style water carrier. Saucepans, knives, utensils, and some easy to clean attractive floor covering, probably cushion lino for the living/sleeping area. We agreed that paint brushes and other tools could be purchased as the need for them arose.

"Hello, hello." Followed by a soft tapping on the partially open door.

"Come in Kardy." I called out.

"Come in, mate!" I tried to sound more welcoming. To my surprise the round beaming face of Sabu the sadist masseur appeared around the door.

"Hello, Jack, Queenie. How are you?" He beamed.

"Fine Sabu, please come in." He stepped inside, scanning the room with interest.

"This your house?" he asked, settling himself into the nearest chair.

"No, we rent it. Like timeshare." Who knew what the effect of a detailed and true account would be!

"It is very big. Very nice bed." He added approvingly, nodding at the tent-covered bed and the one that was abandoned for the shelter of the inner mossie-proof tent. Quite a luxury locally, we assumed.

"Yes, it is quite comfortable, but very hot inside, even with the fan on." Queenie replied, from the confines of the bed.

This was the cost of being fearful of mosquitoes — the extra heat created by two bodies in a confined space.

"Is very good for you." He handed me two blue envelopes. "Invitation. Johnson wedding, two weeks. You will come?" he asked hopefully.

We were delighted to agree, but needed to know where the event was to take place, as the address, though written in English, was unfamiliar to us.

I found a map, and Sabu patiently pointed out the village where he lived, instructing us to make our way there by nine o'clock on the morning of the wedding, when we would be taken by taxi to the church for the ceremony. He wrote the address in Malayalam on the envelope, so that we could show it at the bus station. We reckoned we would need an early start on the day — we'd need to be up by five in the morning.

"Shouldn't be a problem Jack. If the temple explodes every day at four thirty, we'll be awake, all right!"

I sincerely hoped she was wrong about that.

We felt we needed a little more research on bus times and such, but assured Sabu that we would be there at nine on the day. Delighted, he thanked us profusely, then, assuming a very serious expression, he looked sternly at me and said, "This is a Christian wedding. Please Mr Jack, no shorts." This was a direct reference to my love of wearing rugby shorts and precious little else.

"OK," I agreed, "and what about Queenie?"

He hesitated.

"Queenie is lady, pretty dress please." He said finally, looking a little embarrassed.

We agreed to his sartorial suggestions, and with a sigh of relief, he left us, the popping of his scooter being slowly swallowed up by the jungle noises outside.

"Oh, God, now we've got to buy new clothes!" I wailed. "And a flippin' wedding present."

"There's always a price," put in Queenie. We agreed to dedicate a day to clothes and present buying, also to researching our travel arrangements for the day. Finally, Queenie reminded me we were here to relax and enjoy our new experiences, take things a little easier than we did at home. Queenie was right. We resolved not to work every day. Two or three days a week would be enough. Consequently, we decided that today would be a day of rest, tomorrow we would investigate the possibilities of bus travel to Trivandrum, and research the shops.

The tiredness and the heat finally got the better of us, and we dozed off again under the welcome draught of the spinning fan.

Chapter 12

It was early afternoon when we awoke. After showering, we made our way toward the main road, with the idea of somehow travelling to Kovalam, maybe suss the bus, and enjoy an evening meal at one of the beach side restaurants.

Before we left, I called into Kadhikan's half of the house, where he provided us with a key for the main door. Now we felt like real householders! Things were looking up for the first time, it seemed. We grinned at each other and set off for the main road. The blast of intense humid heat that hit us once we left the cover of the coconut palms was incredible. Of course, the sun was nearly at its highest. We paused, stunned. I looked at Queenie for inspiration.

"Come on, then let's go for it!" she said, bravely.

There was very little traffic on the long hot road, which disappeared into the heat hazed distance. Buses seemed to pick up passengers wherever people stood; there were few defined bus stops, a relaxed approach to picking up passengers irrespective of official stops, it seemed to work.

We had plenty of time so we decided to walk through the coconut grove on the opposite side of the road which would provide shade, and perhaps find another track which may lead us to the road which we felt sure ran parallel to the one on which we were now walking. Fortunately for us, our speculation paid off. We crossed. While we walked, we were interested to see how many houses, shops, temples and surgeries etc., were tucked away and barely visible within the dense coconut palm grove.

We ambled along, looking here and there around us, and responding to the occasional "Hello! What is your name?" and "School pen?" "Camera?" "One Rupee?" that came from quite elderly women, as well as children, who were either walking with baskets on their heads, or sitting in the open doorways and porches of their dilapidated but shady houses.

Each new sight was a novelty to us, while the smells of wood smoke, incense, and cooking food were intoxicating. We agreed that we were glad to be here, and in a way, regretted our dependence on the tourist area of Kovalam. Yet where else would we be understood? Where else could we change money, or order a meal, or use a satisfactory toilet? We did not know, but we agreed that we'd better find out — and soon! We had indeed a lot to learn. Finally, about one kilometre down the winding track, the anticipated parallel road did appear, the map we had looked at was correct and we had read it properly — great! A bus arrived, roaring towards us on the opposite side of the road. We would miss it! Was it even the right bus? We were unable to decipher the local scribble-like text on the front. Should we? Shouldn't we? Yes! We ran. It stopped. I looked up enquiringly at the people on the bus.

"Kovalam?"

"Kovalam." They shouted.

On I leapt, hanging on to the side bar I pulled myself upwards, leaving just enough room for Queenie to ride on the bottom step. As her foot left the ground the bus roared off.

"One could lose a shoe this way, if not one's life," I mused, hanging grimly on. I pushed upwards into the heat and press of compacted bodies. Queenie was right behind, acquiring and later perfecting the techniques of elbow power required for bus boarding.

I do not know how many of the eight kilometres to Kovalam we had travelled when the bus ground to a halt, engine off. What's happening? What now?

What was happening was that the conductor was exercising one of the many techniques required to collect the fares before arrival at the final destination. On this occasion it was a case of relying on the dexterity and not least the honesty of passengers to pass fairs from the back and middle of the bus to him as he squashed himself in an appropriate corner towards the front of the bus and took the money and where necessary, gave change on shouted instruction.

After all, collecting fares from a hundred or so passengers was no mean feat, packed as they were three wide across the aisles, plus three people sat in seats either side of the aisle plus another two people stood up in front of those sat in the seats, with another crushed in for luck every second row. It was so compact that it was physically impossible to reach down into a pocket for money.

Consequently, certain quite specific knowledge needed to be acquired by crew and passengers in order to survive any bus journey in India. The most important skill required by passengers, we discovered, was to ascertain the best bus stop to board, and at what time of day.

It did not take long to finally reach Kovalam, but because of the packed bus, and the consequential loss of vision, we were unable to discern any more landmarks than we already knew from our previous trip a year ago.

Strangely we h'd had a kind of airing on the bus, even though it was packed with hot bodies. The large open window spaces along both sides had no glass in them; the wind therefore, depending on the speed of the bus, blew in on us with a pleasant cooling effect. We alighted along with many others, and amid the barrage of rickshaw and taxi drivers, made our way to the Wilson's Money Exchange.

A phenomenon that firstly amazed me and after some weeks outright confounded me. So, picture the scene. You are seen plainly getting off the bus, you will walk the couple of hundred yards toward the beach, which is the only direction you can head, down the narrow single-track lane. The drivers and taxis are crammed along the sides, taking up most of the width and all facing towards the beach. The small cabs are parked such that it is difficult to imagine how they could turn around to drive back up the track, a mystery to me!

Each of the twenty or so drivers, spaced three to four feet apart, or just the length of the three-wheeler taxi, will repeat, "You want Tecsi? Tecsi! Very cheap price! Very cheap price!" the final taxi may be a mere four feet from the actual sandy beach, but the driver will still ask the same question, even though you are obviously at your destination, i.e. the beach.

We stepped into the cool marble office of Wilson's hotel and changed our money. Then found our way to one of the many palm-covered restaurants. We sat, relaxed, and waited for our lemon teas. As we gazed into the white/blue surf, we debated should we cool off in the sea? That is, walk into the sea fully dressed. Queenie said she's not sure, which meant "No".

I decided to go it alone and removed my shorts and shirt, down to my swimmers and went for it. I discovered the technique of missing the onslaught of these hard and heavy breakers, quite simply, either by squatting down and allow the wave to pass over me, or if one's position does not allow, owing to depth, dive underneath the mass of water which again passes over the top. It can be fun for a time, as there are no rocks in the way. It does however, after a few minutes become exhausting. One becomes so exhausted that it is not safe to carry on.

As usual the breakers diminished just a few yards into the water. Swimming and playing around in the deep is great fun, so long as you keep your eyes open for the periodic giant wave that will pick you up off your feet like a cork, and send you spinning back into the front line of breakers and on to the sand. The young locals have perfected the skill of sliding down the face of the larger waves, and are able to body surf right onto the beach.

The temperature of the water was warm, with cold streams running at ankle to knee height. The clarity of the water was such that one could see to the bottom with ease, which is an advantage for the young boys who dive down to retrieve mussels from the beds just beyond the shore.

The fishermen had finished pulling in their nets and a crowd of twenty or so people, mainly fishermen and women, stood around the large circular spider's web that was not exactly teeming with fish. Shouts and what looked and sounded like arguments ensued, the women eventually wandering off with baskets on their heads, presumably containing either their share of the catch, or a purchased amount. Crows hovered like large black clouds, chancing a snatch here and there at the small discarded fish, the crawk! of crows drowning out human chatter.

I waded into shore with breakers at my back, and spraying up over my head onto the creamy white-hot sand, and as so many times before, I ran for the cool of the shade and into the open fronted cafe. Tea has just been served, mine had cooled.

We planned to have a stroll underneath the shade of the various makeshift forecourts along the beach, to the extreme end of the bay to see what lay there.

We paid the waiter, and avoiding the usual banana, sunglasses, handbag and postcard sellers that had accumulated around our table whilst sipping tea, we walked on. The sea was certainly much calmer now, devoid of the sound of crashing waves.

"Let's go sit in that restaurant over there," Queenie pointed. "We should get a sunset view in an hour or so."

"Good idea," I agreed "You go, I'll see you there, take my shorts and things, I'm going back in the sea for a cool off."

"Should I order?"

"Yes," I shouted back, "anything. Keep it cheap though!"

The first splash into the water was a shock, it was icy in comparison to the water just a few hundred yards away. I waded to waist depth and knelt. The cool and then cold gentle waves lapped up under and over my shoulders, over my face, and down to my chest again. Instant relief! Wonderful! Again and again! It swirled, covered my head, and receded. This gave way to a slight rise of guilt. I was here in this cool blissful sea, looking into the contours of the beach line with its waving palms, and cool as a cucumber, whilst Queenie was not here to enjoy it.

I knew it would be pointless wading back onto shore and asking her to join me in the water. There would be something amiss, a shoulder, an ache in the neck or head, or even just plain disinterest due to the horribly painful and depressing fibromyalgia.

Queenie for the most part manages so well under this curse that I do sometimes forget and perhaps expect too much of her. I had to fight off the urge to rush and try to share the experience.

I waded slowly, looking around at the sights. Large pools of reflected colour drifted this way and that, to the edge of and slightly into the water. Other colours drifted between and in amongst the green of the vegetation. These pools of colour were the ladies dressed in their smart bright saris, coming down for their five o'clock promenade. Children and fathers, fully dressed in smartly pressed trousers, shirts and ties, wandered into the sea, some with trousers rolled up, some not. Slowly the ladies in yellow, purple, red, green and gold vividness, wandered deeper, into the now flat calm sea, to waist height. This informal event happened every day.

Full of laughter and obvious joy, the families came together to enjoy the cool water and to watch the sunset. "Mmmm," I thought. "Very satisfying. Observing humanity in one of its better moments. What a privilege and a relief."

I could hear a familiar voice

. "Jack, Jack, nearly ready!" Queenie had worked her magic again and ordered fried chilli beef, with mixed vegetable fried rice and a bottle of ice-cold Kingfisher beer. The condensation formed ran down the bottle, tempting me to pour out its contents.

As I reached the table, I was also dripping water on to the concrete floor.

A very smart, thirty-something year old waiter stepped over to me. I stopped in my tracks.

"Welcome sir, perhaps you would like to take this towel into the second room on the left. You could dry off if you wish." I could not believe it! What an extremely nice guy!

"Thank you!" I replied, picking up my shirt and shorts.

"Your food will be served on your return, sir."

"Thank you very much." And off I went to dry and dress myself. However, the "dressing room" brought me down to earth with a bump! Even so, I emerged from the shambles of the storeroom cum sleeping quarters of the employees feeling good and hungry.

I sat. The food appeared. Beer opened, poured, complete with a beer mat to cover the glass and deter flies.

"How was it, chuck?"

"Oh, excellent!" I replied, referring to the swim.

"Hey, and this is incredible too. What a waiter!"

"Yes, his English is perfect. He can speak about anything. Here he is! Sunjeev, this is Jack, Jack, Sunjeev."

"Thank you Sunjeev. This looks like very good food."

"Thank you sir, please enjoy your meal." And off he drifted.

"How much, Queenie?"

"Well up to now, one hundred and twenty rupees plus the beer."

"Looks like a blow-out then Queenie. Why not?"

The food was as good as it looked. The vegetables and beef had a Cantonese crispiness about them, the rice, separate and starch-less.

The pale orange sun was steadily becoming deeper and lower in a dispersed, wispy and fluffy cloud. To the high and far left, the cloud was a deep blue, running to a light blue sky. As the sun's light was picked up by the motion of the sea, it changed from light blue to red to pink. Now a new array of colour formed. Purple hazes to greens, to black to blue to flaming red.

It happens so quickly. It stops you mid meal or mid-anything.

On the beach the saris, suits and sellers, all of them stop for that moment, when the top outside rim of the sun slips between the sky and the waves, and WOW!

The final, indescribable light show, all shooting from that small central point, and slowly slipping into soft darkness.

Chapter 13

The light from the candles set in the remaining and diminishing natural light, made an atmospheric, idyllic, postcard setting.

"Thank Goodness we made it," I said, as I touched Queenie's hand, hoping that she could share the feeling.

"Yes," she said softly, or was it sadly?

"It's certainly very pretty," she replied softly. The lights came on. I hadn't realised that we had had a power cut. The rows of dainty lights, incongruously taped and tied together along the shore line, and draped as they were over bushes, plant pots, poles and pillars along the rustic promenade line, helped to pick out the other three or four restaurants nearby.

We were the only two people in the restaurant at the time. I looked over towards the business end of the restaurant. Sunjeev was already on his way, smiling.

"A beautiful night tonight," he smiled.

"Absolutely wonderful," agreed Queenie.

"You'd like a beer sir?"

"Yes, fine. Where are you from, Sunjeev?"

"I am from two places, actually. I am on border of Kerala and Karnataka. My one ration book says I am in one state, and my other ration book tells me I am in another. Who am I to argue?"

"So you get double rations?"

Ration books allow a citizen to shop at the district discount stores, which are subsidised by the government.

"Yes, of course. It works well for my wife and children whilst I am working away. I'll get your beer sir."

"I very much like English and American films. Have you seen Titanic?" he asked, as he set the bottle on the table.

"Yes we have." Queenie enjoyed that film.

"Yes, the effects were wonderful. I think it was mostly digital technology." Replied Sunjeev.

He followed this with, "The story was good, but sad, I think."

"Your English is perfect, Sunjeev. Where did you learn?"

"I don't think it is perfect, but I have learnt the difficult bits through films. English, Irish, American. I have learnt emphasis and manner this way."

"That's fantastic!" I reply.

"Also, I have spent a lot of time working in large hotels in Bombay and Bangalore, where speech and presentation are very important."

Sunjeev was definitely not like the rest. He did not wear rubber flip-flop sandals. He wore simple, leather thonged sandals and neatly pressed, light coloured trousers. His shirt was not stained nor did it hang out, the sleeves were folded neatly just below the elbow. The belt around his waist did not sport the usual ridiculous over-sized silver or gold coloured buckle. His hair was combed back, moustache trimmed into a conservatively styled but South American way. Sunjeev, was, in a word, COOL! He could fit into the Conservative club or was it the gambling casino. He was confident, and I suspect, knew more than his stuff.

"Where are you staying, sir, if you don't mind my asking?"

"Do you know Laguna guest house, near Pachalloor?"

"Oh, yes, I know Davina, the owner of Laguna. Are you staying there?"

"No, but if you were to continue on the track, past Laguna, there is a new concrete looking house, the only one with a flat roof."

"Oh, I see. Are you renting?"

I replied. "A sort of timeshare."

"I understand sir. Will you return tonight? If you go by taxi, no problem."

"I was going to go back by bus." I replied.

"In that case," he returned, looking at his watch, "you only have thirty minutes before the last bus leaves."

"Oh thanks, Sunjeev, you have saved us a taxi fare."

"No problem sir. Should I get the bill?"

We had not thought of a last bus leaving at 7:30 pm nor had we considered where to get off the bus exactly, especially in the dark, as there is, as might be expected, little street lighting, and none at all through the coconut grove. Guess who had anticipated this eventuality and had secreted about her person a small torch, designed for this very occasion?

We rushed off. We caught the bus. For once, and once only in our stay in India we were the only passengers on any form of public transport.

"Pachallor!" we said in unison. The conductor looked blank.

"Laguna." I said. "Pachalloor!" I repeated.

"School." He said understanding us at last. "Ten rupees."

We alighted at Pachalloor School, a recognised bus stop, and almost exactly where we had crossed the road earlier to get on. What luck! We heard croaking toads and the pitched throbbing of crickets, we passed cows, dim shadows in the gloom, and long-horned bulls. In the blackness we saw luminous, blue-green and hollow eyes. Then strange, soft rustling sounds. "Hello, what is your name?" greeted us occasionally from the behind hedge tops. We finally crossed the main road we had started off from earlier in the day.

We had made it down to the track into our grove. It was a moonless night, and the darkness was now absolute. All we could see and hear was a television glowing and chattering from inside one of the open doors of our neighbour's houses. This became a familiar landmark for some weeks to come. By the light of that indispensable torch, Queenie exhumed the key from the depths of her bag, light on, fan on, we're home! Yes, electricity, what a day! We decided to chase "mossies" before showering, during which I re-registered on my internal computer, "Must get some pieces of mossie net to block up the air vents."

We each fell into the shower, or waterfall, such as it was, then zipped ourselves away feeling very comfortable, and fell swiftly into an exhausted sleep.

zzzzz

Crash! Roar! Bang! What the hell! We both leapt up. I struggled out of the net first, Queenie hard on my heels, torch in hand, and headed for the shower room. Opened the door. Water was roaring out of the main water pipe that the toilet flush tank had been attached to. It was attached no more. I walked into this torrent, bent down, fumbled, located the main tap, and turned it anti-clockwise. Silence. I looked around me, dripping.

The tank, the pipes, screws, toilet seat, all were strewn around the floor. "Christ!"

I dried myself. Queenie, poor sod, I thought she was going to cry.

"Come on kid, it's not that bad. I'll sort it out tomorrow." It was two-forty-five AGAIN! We nodded off, knowing that in an hour and a half, Guy Fawkes Night would start up.

A very gentle tapping awakened us. Was I awake? Tap-tap. It doesn't sound like Kardy. But who else could it be? It was light outside. Rat-a-tat. What time is it? Seven am. Tap-tap.

"OK" I muttered, "I'm coming."

I climbed out of the cocoon, feeling weary, wondering, "Is this really happening?"

"What are you doing Jack?" came Queenie's voice from behind me.

"Someone's at the door," I replied.

"Kardy?"

"Maybe." Shorts dragged on, I opened the door, and there before me stood — half stooped, red eyed, breathing boozy fumes — our polite, conservative Mr COOL himself!

The elegant waiter of the previous evening.

"Sunjeev!" I spluttered. He didn't answer, he just leered, red eyed and sickly smiled.

This tall elegant man from yesterday was taking on the proportions of a hobgoblin.

"What's wrong?" I asked.

"My wife, my house! It's all going to end!"

"What do you mean?"

"You see sir, I need only three thousand rupees, and you can save my family."

I don't believe this, I thought, why me? I felt like a one man social security system.

"I owe money, I have been to my home last night." Which he couldn't have been so quickly. Karnataka is at least twelve hours each way travelling by train.

"The moneylender will claim my house today at one thirty if I do not pay the three thousand rupees. I can repay you at the end of this week out of my salary."

"Bullshit!" I thought. Waiters, like everyone else around here get twenty-five per day, maximum. He doesn't earn three thousand a quarter, never mind pay me back in three days.

"Can't do it." I said, as firmly but as sensitively as I could, under the circumstances.

"Please sir, I will repay on Friday."

"Sorry, Sunjeev, can't do it mate."

"Then maybe two hundred," he responded. I'll pay you back Friday."

"OK, two hundred rupees, hang on." I got the cash, he took it, and was forever and eternally grateful.

I say, "It'll come out of your tips!"

He laughs, and off he goes. As he passes the end of the building, Kardy appears, in a more than usually cowed state.

"Who he — man?" he enquired.

"A friend" I reply.

"Where he come?"

"Kovalam." I reply.

"Why he come?"

"Kardy, what's wrong, Why do you want to know, Tell me?"

"Jack, you kind sir, you must not tell in Kovalam you Kardy house stay."

"Why not?"

Silence.

"Why not?"

Sickly smile.

"Kardy, tell me, WHY NOT?"

"Jealous sir, very jealous. No tell if anyone ask. If anyone ask, say you stay Laguna."

"Kardy tell me how can you run a tourist business if no one knows about it?"

Face creases. "Is very difficult."

"Sorry, Kardy, you lie if you want to, but tell me the truth. What is the problem?"

"No sir, no sir, you forget." I did forget, but perhaps I shouldn't have, there was something here that I should have pursued, but chose not to.

It was now seven thirty. Life is fast here in the coconut grove. I had pissed Kardy off, so I expected that meant no breakfast. Wrong again! Minutes later, Kardy, with a complete change of character, re-appeared, shining smile to match the steel dishes that held the fish curry for breakfast. "Come on Queenie, brekkers."

"Here Jacky, I know you like fish."

"Sure do K, it keeps me full all day."

"You like tea madam?"

"No thanks," replied Queenie.

"Kardy, before you go, have a look at this." I showed him the contents of the bathroom. "No toilet," I poin-ted out.

"Yes sir. Toilet good, you use bucket of water from tap wash toilet."

"I could do that Kardy, but why can't we have the job done properly?"

"Later, Jack, later, later."

"When is later?"

"Tomorrow, maybe next day." He replied.

"OK, I'll do a temporary repair for today, then you get the plumber."

"I plumber, Jack." The injured tone told me I'd put my foot in it again

"OK, day after tomorrow, you fix properly."

"Yes. OK sir, no problem." He beamed.

I enjoyed the fish curry. Although it was tasty, it was getting monotonous, we did need to expand our horizons, find an alternative. Indeed we had agreed some little time ago to become independent of K's family they could not afford to feed us every morning.

"How about Pachalloor, Queenie, fancy that today? Pachalloor to Thiruvallum. What do you say?"

"It'll take all day."

"Yes," I agreed "we'll walk slowly, look at the shops, find out where things are."

"Well so long as we can get something to eat later, somewhere."

"Yes, we will research the "nosh" shops, you never know, they may be quite good." Under the waterfall we stood, swept up a little money and off we walked. It was still only eight thirty in the morning, but already warming. We retraced our steps to Pachalloor School, and then walked in the opposite direction than we had travelled on the bus to Kovalam the previous day. Looking at the map, Thiruvallum, was, I suppose, about four, maybe five kilometres, not that maps are reliable here, they give nothing more than a vague idea as to where places are.

There was lots of tree cover, so the temperature remained just on the warm side of comfortable. Let's face it, that's miles better than the cool side of freezing, as it would be in the UK in December.

We attracted lots of stares. We looked into one of the many open-fronted paint shops. We were attempting to ask the price of blue paint for the bathroom, when a local woman stuck her head down into Queenie's carrier bag, and proceeded to put her hand into it. I watched in amazement. A local man appeared, stood next to the woman, they both peered into the bag. Queenie had felt the hand and pulled the bag sharply. They both looked up and grinned, sporting red teeth and saliva, which dribbled down the side of the woman's mouth.

"Angleesh?"

"Yes," She replied.

We weren't able to get much sense regarding paint. We thought water paint or distemper probably meant emulsion paint. We were shown a small tube of blue dye. I deduced that one mixes one's own colour. We had previously agreed that today would be a "find out" day, rather than a "buy" day. We walked on, responding nervously to the demands of the many local people who either stood and glared at us, or came within eighteen inches of our faces, and looked us up and down. Those who knew any English at all would add to the usual repertoire the demand, "Where are you going?" As we walked towards Thiruvallum, the rickshaw drivers who constantly passed would slow right down, place themselves and their vehicles directly in our path, proclaiming "Tecsi?" then drive off, leaving us with the taste of burnt oil.

Kovalam, because of its familiarity with foreigners, was much easier for us to cope with. The local people there had become used to a range of visitors.

We speculated that maybe if we walked the same route, after a few days or weeks, then the people may become used to us, the novelty may wear off. Indeed, we could ignore them. Of course, there were occasions when people were very helpful, and dealt with us in a very reasonable manner. Sadly, the truth is, for the duration of our three month stay in this small pocket of India, these more considerate people were most definitely in the minority.

We reached a small, dark building, about a hundred yards from the last shop we had looked into, from which emanated a warm spicy food smell. The faded lettering above the rickety doorway proclaimed that it was a hotel. I put my head tentatively through the door, in an attempt to discern whether, and what kind of, food might be available. Indeed, to ascertain exactly what kind of hotel this was. The room was so black and dingy all I could see were the unclean dark green tables, smeared with rice, gravy and other leftovers. Two pairs of white eyes began to take on human form, as my eyes adjusted to the dark, I heard,

"Ello! What is your name?"

I looked at Queenie, who shrugged her shoulders. We stepped down into the room. The eyes and teeth took on recognisable human form as our eyes adjusted to the gloom. The voice now snapped, "What you want!"

"Food?" I enquired.

"Sit!"

A downtrodden young person came to the dirty green table, brandishing a very grubby-looking damp cloth.

A cloth which should have been discarded even as a floor cloth, long ago.

He swept the rice droppings off the table onto the seats and on to the floor.

"You want beef?" Came the voice.

"Yes, fine." Queenie replied.

Another man came in, rapped out something in the local language, and walked into the back of the cafe. We strained to see what was happening. He had a steel jug, and was pouring water from a plastic dustbin over his hand. The water ran from his hands to the earthen floor, and was soaked up. He returned, sat exactly opposite, no more than an arm's length away, and glared at us. In order to avoid the glare, more than for hygiene purposes, Queenie got up and followed suit. Then it was my turn to wash. The room at the back was the kitchen, it smelt of burning paraffin fumes and burning wood smoke. Clouds of this smoke poured out of the nearby doorway through the seating area and into the street. Piles of discarded rice and slops had been thrown into an already full dustbin, which spilt its contents onto the floor. I emerged, sat and was happy to see that the man opposite had been joined by another, they talked amongst themselves. We were no longer the objects of his attention. In came the young man, this time with no floor cloth, but two plastic trays with rice. He dropped them with a rattle on the table more or less in front of us. An older man arrived with two bowls of brown sauce with lumps implanted, these turned out to be beef. I poured the contents of the basin onto the rice, and with fingers, delved into the pile. It was a good temperature, hot enough to kill off bacteria. The food tasted wonderful! A blend of spices. The gristle gave something to chew on. Overall, we both thoroughly enjoyed our meal, and of course, so did the four people who had glared and stared at us throughout it. I looked up at the boy who had served us, and said, "Limca!"

Looking alarmed, he repeated, "Limca?"

"LIMCA" I said again. He left the premises to buy two bottles of Limca from the shop next door.

Limca is a popular Indian lemon drink, so popular, in fact, as to have its own "Book of Records." Meanwhile, we had washed our hands again while we awaited the boy's return. Later, Queenie looked up.

"Bill, please."

"Bill?"

"Please."

"Thirty five rupees" he growled. We knew the Limcas were ten rupees each, so the meals were a very reasonable seven rupees each. We paid, said our thank yous, and left the premises. We stepped out into the wet relatively smoke free heat again, feeling full and satisfied. At local prices at that!!

A few more yards along the road there was a row of shops/shacks lining each side of the road. We ambled past, stopping here and there, coping well with the inquisitive locals. By the time we had reached Thiruvallum we were exhausted.

Thiruvallum took on a small town persona, it had three banks! Situated at a junction of three roads, consequently it had a lot of buses and general traffic passing through it. We felt that the inquisitiveness of the locals had reduced quite a bit, and we risked entering a shop and bought some fruit, bread and nuts. The shopping went surprisingly well. The best or easiest technique seemed to be to point at an object and put up the requisite number of fingers, two apples, one bread, and so on. We opted to catch a bus back to Pachalloor School. It was already three o'clock, and extremely hot. It had been a long interesting walk.

We studied the buses, and where to get on. Most of them were tightly packed as usual. We hadn't far to go. We crossed the road to the stop, and there, sitting in a corner of the cafe opposite, I recognised Kardy!

In I went, smiling.

"Hi, Kardy." He smiled ,

"Hello, Jack, Madam. You like tea?"

"OK." We agreed, trying not to be unfriendly, and sat down. He ordered for us.

"No boat trips today Kardy?"

"No sir. Not good. Not many tourists. Season not start."

That surprised me.

"The season starts soon, surely, Kardy?"

"Maybe, but not good."

I couldn't help but think he was in the wrong place to catch tourists. "Kovalam is better for tourists than here, surely?" I suggested.

"Yes, this place no tourists. Only Kovalam is good."

"Then why are you not in Kovalam." I enquired, being conscious that if he had no boat trips, he had no income.

"Maybe later, later." He replied.

Tea arrived, I was getting used to it, Queenie struggled to drink hers.

"Where you go?" Kardy enquired.

"We walked from Pachalloor."

"You walk!" he repeated with raised voice, and in amazement.

"Yes, we walk quite a lot." Offered Queenie.

"You walk in your country?"

"Yes of course," we replied, "but now we get bus back to Pachalloor,"

"You get bus!"

"Yes, why not?"

"Why not you get rickshaw?"

"Too expensive," I answered.

"You want Lambi scooter?" He enquired. "Is very good bike. Engine good, needs kicking start. Mend with mechanic. You can have."

"Where is it?" I enquired.

"At father house. I show, not far. Come."

So saying, we left the cafe and crossed two main roads, entering another part of the coconut grove. A further few hundred yards or so we arrived at a clearing, with a palm leaf and wattle constructed house. The same house that I had visited a year ago as part of Kadhikan's tourist boat trip. Outside the house, there was a broken down, rusty old scooter, an Indian derivative of a Lambretta. The lights were broken, the brake cables had seized, the tyres were worn to the inner canvas, but inflated.

"Look!" he exclaimed, as he pressed the kick start with his foot.. It scraped in a disengaged kind of way on the inner ratchet.

"Ah," I exclaimed, "no good."

"You push!" I pushed, he let out the clutch. The usual pop-pop-pop, blue smoke, and off he roared, down the jungle path. He turned the machine around, and came back to us, beaming.

"Very good bike. Lambi need fix starting, good for you, you can have. You pay repair bill."

"What about insurance?"

"Insurance already anyone, no problem."

"What about brakes and lights?"

"No problem, take to mechanic, only five hundred rupees. You get on madam, I take home."

"It's got no brakes!"

"No problem. Brake no need. Short journey. Please madam, I take?"

"No. I am not going on THAT!" She appealed to me. I agreed.

"No, Kardy, it's not safe."

"Why no safe?"

"NO BRAKES!"

"OK, wait." And off he roared. Minutes later a yellow and black rickshaw arrived, with Kadhikan riding triumphantly behind.

"Here madam, now, you take rickshaw." We had no choice, the bus journey was out, we would sound ungrateful if we refused.

"Maybe you have Lambi mend at mechanics?" He enquired.

"Maybe," I said

"Later, later." Conscious of and enjoying my new-found approach and attitude.

The rickshaw popped and rattled us back to our starting point.

"I've still got to fix the toilet," I said. "I need to do something at least until he gets around to doing it." We clambered out of the rickshaw, and I ran up to the roof to a rusting tin tool box to see if could find spanners, screwdrivers or anything that would be of use to me. There were odd items, pieces of pipe, bricks, rope, four small spanners and other rubbish. The repair I made on the flush tank was not a good one, although it took one and a half hours to complete. By propping the tank up on bricks, and winding string around the pipe threads before tightening, I got it to work with a very minimal drip, drip of water.

The toilet was now usable.

Chapter 14

"So what's on today," I asked Queenie as she emerged from the bathroom, not that I really expected much of a response, early as it was. We had however managed a full night's uninterrupted sleep.

"What's on is something to eat and get away before Kardy gets here with fish curry for breakfast. If I have it again this month I'll never want to eat it ever again ever, ever."

"Hey come on Queenie it's my job to be grumpy, not yours. If we really don't want to meet him this morning lets get out of here as quick as we can, clothes on and off we go."

"OK, let's go. Should we tell him we're going?"

"Yeah, but on the way out."

We caught the bus coming the way we wanted to travel, and directly outside the coconut grove so no walking through the grove to the parallel road.

"Let's go up to the village where Johnson's salvation army wedding is going to be, to see what's involved in getting there. What do you think?"

"Great idea! After we've eaten lets grab something at one of the side stalls at Trivandrum station."

Trivandrum is the state capital of Kerela. It did make sense — after all we really did need to know how often the buses ran, and where exactly on the station the bus went from. All that would take time.

We needed directions, and information. Wrong information could easily lead us miles from where we needed to be, so we agreed we would ask three people and go with the majority decision.

As to be expected the station was absolute chaos, buses revving, choking fumes, people pushing no, fighting their way on to the buses. No special regard for the elderly, actually they were doing fine by themselves in this. An "each man for himself" culture. The secret is in the elbows. We took note.

We decided to ask the guy at the ticket office; yes, a ticket office; where the bus would leave from.

The guy wasn't sure but gave us a general idea, so we then asked a bus driver who told us, "Wait there. Don't move."

"How long before it arrives, the bus to Alaga?"

"Five minutes maybe ten." He replied.

"Thanks," we both shouted over the racket and roaring of engines. "OK that means probably an hour, so let's ask someone else, our luck can't be that good." Just as we were about to do that and having spotted a suited civil servant looking guy to ask, what looked like a runaway bus parted the crowds, and came to rest dustily some thirty feet away from us.

The passengers all but fell out of the two doors.

"Well someone's in a hurry." Queenie remarked.

"They are bloody nuts it seems to me." I replied, "Do we really want to do this? These are long distance buses it seems to me."

"Oh come on Jack, they'll know what they are doing. It looks lot worse than it is.

We don't know how far it is. Come on let's ask this driver getting out of his bus how far and how long it takes to get to Alagar." Just as Queenie stopped talking, a man in a bus company uniform, with "inspector" displayed in gold trim on his cap, walked up to us with a smile on his face, and said to both of us,

"Sir, Madam, how can I help you?"

The excitement! The response was immediate, from both of us at once and rather incomprehensibly.

"How? Where? When? To Alagar?"

"OK, OK, OK, you are in the right place, the bus is due in anytime now."

"How long will it take us to get there?" I piped up.

"One hour, and one half."

And with that we were dismissed, we thought, from his mind, as he tried to get on with the proper running of his bus station. A sudden shout from behind us interrupted our meandering thoughts.

"You bus! Here now. Run."

Our friendly inspector had not forgotten us, and but for his timely warning we may well have missed the bus. Grabbing our bags we ran into the diesel fumes and chaos of roaring, manoeuvring buses.

We claimed separate seats, enjoying what comfort we could before the bus became intolerably crowded, as it inevitably would. We were lucky, the bus was a mere one-third full. Some very long, tiring and distressing journeys are made on these vehicles, the hard plank seats, lack of glass in the windows, the heat and overcrowding, all adding to the discomfort or excitement of public transport travel here. However, for the moment, we luxuriated in the welcome space, trying to ignore the rising temperature. In the confines of the bus station, we both commented on the trickles of cooling perspiration running down inside our clothing.

With a great deal of revving and grinding of gears, our bus finally lurched into motion, still only half full. We ground our way out of the bus station and joined the chaos on the road outside, the fumes from our engine mingling with those of the rest of the early morning traffic. We made our way through the town; taking on passengers as we went, the bus becoming ever more compacted; and then finally out into the countryside, where we made enough speed to enable the fog of fumes to blow away, and for a little country air to circulate.

The passengers we had picked up as we drove through the town were gradually dropped off here and there and once again we had the bus almost to ourselves, and we could observe the passing scene at our leisure. We were travelling slowly up a gradual gradient, and before long the palm forests receded and gave way to a more varied flora. At one of the stops we counted fifteen different kinds of trees within the few square metres we could see from our window. The occasional heavy showers we had experienced since our arrival had served to extend the electric green of the landscape, originally regenerated by the earlier monsoon downpours. It is magical how very occasional showers in such heat can sustain such an amount of lush and varied countryside.

The bus conductor was also watching out for us, and had remembered where we needed to alight. "Off! Off!" He shouted above the din of the motor, turning around in his seat gesturing towards us.

"Thanks, OK." We called back, as we struggled to the back of the bus and jumped down into the dust of a village street. Within seconds of asking directions we had been bundled into the back of a rickshaw, and off we buzzed down ever-smaller lanes and tracks. The driver knew Father Salvation Army Commander's church and house, so we were able to sit back and remember and reflect on my earlier meeting with Major James, a full year before.

I had been lying on the bed in our room in the package holiday hotel, when I heard a tapping at the door. I opened it to reveal a very smart gentleman dressed in full tropical style Salvation Army uniform, and brandishing a collecting tin. In excellent English, he politely asked me for a donation for the benefit of the poor, in exchange for which he wrote out a receipt. That, I thought, was the end of it. Just another chance encounter in this land of a billion possible chance encounters. It was only later I discovered that he was the father of Sabu the Sadist Masseur, and of Johnson, the large and likeable waiter at our hotel. And now, here we were, about to see his home and almost become members of the family.

No sooner had we reflected on our first meeting than we had arrived. Before us was a small country chapel, very plain, with a neat, white painted bungalow next door. The bungalow was enveloped in brilliant pinky-red bougainvillea, some unidentifiable plants with large glossy green leaves, and the whole encircled by tall, shade-giving palms. A calm and beautiful sight, another small part of Paradise.

The bright blue door opened and Major James stepped out, looking just as smart and fit as I remembered him from the previous year. He stepped forward, smiling, arms outstretched in greeting.

"Hello, how can I help you?" He asked, obviously not recognising me. As I shook his hand, I explained who we were and our mission — to reconnoitre our journey so as not to be late for the auspicious occasion of his son's wedding. He was delighted to see us and, instructing the driver to wait for ten minutes, invited us in for lemon tea, while he finished his preparations for a trip to the nearby village. We had just caught him in time it seemed, and now we could all travel back together, at least as far as the bus stop to Trivandrum. It all seemed just too easy!

We were introduced to Mrs Major James, an equally smartly dressed person in her tropical style Sally Army uniform, consisting of a well-cut light grey sari and blouse piece with epaulettes. She didn't speak English, but greeted us warmly before disappearing to prepare tea for her unexpected guests. The house was in turmoil with preparations for the wedding, a great deal of painting and general refurbishment appeared to be going on, "Ready," we were assured, "for very special guests such as yourselves." We met a third son of the family. Spattered as he was with pink paint, not, he assured us laughing, his usual mode of dress. He was studying for a degree in Social Work, but was at home in order to help with preparations for the big day.

We asked whether the wedding was to take place in the little chapel next door. We were amazed to hear that as there would be upwards of seven hundred guests, a much larger church in a village some kilometres away would be used.

"That's a lot of people in your congregation." I remarked.

"They are not all Christians, half at least are Hindu or Muslim. We are all very happy and get along well together. We join together for many festivals and events. You must come here, to this house, on the morning of the wedding. You will travel to the church with my family as our honoured guests." He continued. "We have hired minibuses." I glanced at my watch.

"Time to go, our driver will be getting impatient."

Far from being impatient, the driver was sound asleep.

Our goodbyes and the sound of our repeated assurances to the family, that we would arrive bright and early on the day of the wedding, finally roused him, and the three of us climbed into the back of the rickshaw to make our way down to the village to pick up the return bus to Trivandrum.

An incident at the bus stop made us very aware of some of the hidden dangers of this place, and we were very grateful for the calm, commanding presence of Major James.

An old man tripped and staggered out of a nearby street-side shack, and tumbled into the shocking dazzle of bright sunlight on blinding galvanised buckets, set in neat piles outside a neighbouring shop. With a clatter they scattered into the road and into the oncoming traffic. Motorcycles, auto rickshaws, and taxis barely slowed, none stopped. Horns blared as vehicles veered crazily around the pile of metal and man. Youths standing nearby jeered and shouted, pointing and laughing as the man's lungi, an insecure garment at the best of times, rose in the wake of dust, exposing brown buttocks to the public gaze.

The two round brown mounds also aroused the interest of one of the long-horned white cows. It was passing slowly by as cows do in India. Lowering its head, it investigated the bare buttocks with its long red tongue, all to the further screams of amusement of the onlookers. The man struggled to raise his face from the dust, but only succeeded in rolling over on to his side, shouting and screaming, repeating wild exclamations. The cow walked leisurely on.

Deftly and without fuss, Major James had speedily negotiated the purchase of a lungi from the store just behind us. Crossing to the centre of the road followed by the shopkeeper and one or two other interested spectators, he bent down and placed the length of cloth over the man's exposed nether regions. Reaching out his hand for the man to take, he coolly and calmly raised him to his feet, the man clutching the cloth around his waist with his free hand. The man seemed to be calmer now, and leaning heavily on the Major and staggering a little, he was escorted into a shop on the other side of the street, disappearing from our view and into the dark interior. "Jesus raises Lazarus!" Muttered Queenie, impressed.

Major James reappeared moments later, and hurrying across to us, apologised for his countryman's behaviour.

"Poor man. He is an alcoholic, and cannot help himself." He finished, and dismissing the incident from his mind, chatted to us about the forthcoming wedding, and his hopes for his son's future, until the bus finally arrived.

We took our leave of this most humanitarian of gentlemen, assuring him once again that we would be on time on the day. Our plans had gone well so far, and as we rode back, we estimated that there would be plenty of time left to do some shopping in the state capital Trivandrum before dark.

We located a couple of shops selling electric cooking plates. The first shop assistant or owner however, entered into the usual nonsensical retailing approach, asking double the price indicated on the price tag. So we left, and tried one of the shops situated in a very Western-looking shopping precinct, where eventually we bought the kitchen crockery, utensils, in fact everything for the kitchen. An Indian habit that even after months of shopping I still had difficulty with, is that wherever you may go, from superstore to small shack, when enquiring as to the price, the shop assistants or owners, they never seem to know the price of anything in their establishment. So a meeting ensues amongst the staff of the shop, then chatter amongst the local customers then a pin drop silence. No response. I ask again "How much?" More chatter. People climb on chairs, look under counters, discover an empty box, jar or packet, and search to find the maximum retail price, and then add on something they call local taxes. I have not seen this happen to anyone other than foreigners. So it would appear that prices are set not on the basis of actual product cost but on your colour perhaps or your clothes maybe or your demeanour, expression or general look. Who knows ?

"So, how much is that cooker?" I asked, pointing to the one on the counter. Out came the ladder, young man climbed to the top shelf and extracted what he believed to be the appropriate box, brought it down, removed the cooker from the box, and replied, "Nice cooker. Very cheap."

"How many rupees?" Straining our necks to see the maximum retail price sticker displayed on the box. "Electric." He said helpfully.

"Yes." we agree. I firmly took the box out of his hands, and read "Four hundred and twenty five rupees including all taxes." I pointed to the price, and said, "Price four hundred and twenty five rupees."

He said, "Wait!" Then bobbed his way into the cashier's glass-enclosed desk space. We waited and waited. Two Indian ladies came into the shop, smiled pleasantly at us, "Hello."

"Hello." We replied. And we waited. The assistant returned. "Wait, you wait." He served one lady and then the other, two more people arrived in the shop and when the assistant began to serve them, I began to get annoyed. I made my way to the cashier's desk. Peering through the eye level hole in the glass, I pointed to the cooker on his table.

"Cooker! Four hundred and twenty five rupees! Yes?"

"No." Head wobbled alarmingly. "It is an old one. New one price five hundred rupees."

Getting a little hotter under the collar I asked, "Has it been used?"

"No, sir."

"Is it broken?"

"No sir."

"I will buy the old one, four hundred and twenty five rupees."

"Wait!" He said. Ignoring me, he took money and gave change to now a fifth customer. The original assistant returned to us.

"Cooker," I said, "do you want to sell it?

"Oh yes!" He said with a shake of the head.

"Get it!" He got it. I pointed to a label on the box, and read, slowly and clearly for his benefit, "M.R.P. four hundred and twenty five rupees. That's what I pay!" He saw it. Head wobbled. "Good?" I asked.

"Good." He agreed reluctantly.

"Now, test it." I said.

"Test?" He says with alarm.

"Test!" I repeat.

"OK, test."

Three cookers; five plugs and endless fuses later, we all agree we have a fully operational and safe cooker. We know this because we have also had to purchase a mains-tester screwdriver, the icon of electrical truth. The kettle however was not anywhere near as complicated a purchase. It required just two plug changes to render it operational. One of the plugs being mere millimetres smaller than the socket which wobbled around inside it and consequently flashed and sparked, the second had to be thumped into place.

"It all depends on the manufacture of the socket sir". It is remarkable how the simplest of transactions which should be executed quickly and easily, takes on the proportions one imagines of a major international arms contract. Buyer beware.

All in all it had been a very satisfactory day. We had achieved all we had set out to do, so, staggering under the weight of our newly purchased electrical devices, we treated ourselves to the luxury of an ambassador taxi ride back to what we were beginning after some weeks to consider as home of a kind.

Chapter 15

Extracts From Queenie's Diary 2

Jack's yelp of agony sent me dashing to the kitchen, to find him dancing and swearing as colourfully as only Jack can. He was clutching his left hand in his right, face contorted with agony.

"What's up?" I asked anxiously.

"The light switches", he gasped, "They're live. For fuck's sake don't touch them!" Stepping hastily backwards, I summoned our host, who displayed extremes of consternation and regret, as only "K" can. He promised to summon an electrician immediately.

Three days passed, by which time, not only was there no sign of the promised electrician, but we had rather rashly purchased a number of electrical items on the way back from our reconnoitre to the wedding village, and the corresponding visit to Trivandrum. Both the kettle and the single solid electric cooking plate tested as working and safe in the shop, however it turned out that the items were also both "live" when plugged into the house's electricity. As Jack later discovered to his cost.

Having now survived at least three electric shocks, his patience was running out. Having made daily, then hourly, enquiries as to the whereabouts of the promised electrician with no result, to Jack it seemed expedient to resort to threats of pulling the legs off Kadhikan. A unique phraseology, peculiar to Jack!

Kadhikan's dismissive cries of "Later, later" now assumed a hurt and dignified air, but sure enough, the very next day, after Jack's altercation we were wakened from our uneasy slumbers at the ungodly hour of 6:30 am by a discreet coughing from outside the door, followed by a rodent-like scratching. Grumbling sleepily, Jack opened up.

Kadhikan stood there, smiling ingratiatingly. Pointing to the man at his side, he proudly announced, "Electrician! He fix problem! Good man. Many papers!"

We were to understand by this that despite appearances, the man who stood before us was a fully qualified electrician, hence the papers. Bare-chested, wearing nothing but a brightly coloured lungi wrapped about his waist, and proudly bearing aloft the single symbol of his noble profession, the mains tester screwdriver, he strode, smiling confidently, into the room.

Standing barefoot on the wet concrete floor, he poked the business end of his screwdriver into the electric socket on the kitchen wall.

"Live!" he announced brightly. He demonstrated again, and leaning cautiously nearer, we did indeed observe a gentle amber glow emanating from the plastic handle of the small tool.

"Yes," we agreed faintly, "we know. As Jack can testify, it is live."

He switched off the current to the socket, and thrust the screwdriver into the hole once again. "Not live." We agreed. He prepared to leave, pleased with his assessment of the situation. Recovering our wits, as quickly as we could, which had been scattered to the four winds on observing his lethally casual wet floor behaviour, plunging screwdrivers, and uncertain electricity, we protested. "Hey hang on," cried Jack, "where are you going?" The electrician looked surprised.

We patiently explained the problem, again and in detail, with some interesting mimes and gestures for emphasis of the salient points.

"Ah, materials are problem!" He exclaimed, convinced that he now fully understood us. I must admit that neither Jack nor I understood him. He proceeded to dismantle the electric cooking ring, despite our protests that the problem had occurred before the purchase of these particular items.

We eventually retired from the fray, defeated for the moment, to watch from a safe distance as he continued to dismember the cooker ring. Finally satisfied with his work, he gestured for us to come nearer. We approached cautiously, and looked warily over his shoulder as he pointed out the bare twisted wire that was touching the metal plate.

"This problem — soon fix." he assured us.

Reassembling the ring, he plugged it in and switched on. His trusty screwdriver indicated by its gentle amber glow that the ring was still live. Not to be defeated, the electrician announced loudly, "Plug is problem — inferior product."

We were not convinced, and after more discussion, which became even more heated, he prepared to dismantle the kettle. A similar problem was found, corrected, and the kettle was still live. A similar diagnosis was made, and we were recommended to purchase "Anchor" plugs.

He prepared to leave again. We protested again, still unconvinced of his diagnosis, and explained the problem in absolute detail, with the addition of even more energetic mime and gesture to emphasise each point.

Still irritatingly cheerful, and with the electricity switched on at the mains, and still with bare feet on a wet concrete floor, he happily dismantled every socket and light switch in the building. A veritable rat's nest of wiring was revealed. The three wiring colours were carefully explained to us.

"Red — live. Black — neutral. Yellow — earth." He intoned his litany. We were still somewhat perplexed.

"What are the green, blue and brown wires as well as the black and red for?" We asked, not unreasonably, we thought.

It was his turn to appear perplexed. His suggestion that perhaps the electrician who installed the wiring had run out of wire and so had used other, randomly coloured, wires, "all good wire," did not satisfy us. Our attempts to ask how he would identify live from neutral in these circumstances were met with blank incomprehension; after all he had his mains tester screwdriver. It seemed he had suddenly and inexplicably exhausted his small store of English. Kadhikan's less than helpful attempts to translate both ways, and our mounting frustration, only served to complicate matters further, and we once again retired from the fray, momentarily defeated.

The raised and occasionally angry voices had attracted a small crowd of onlookers, who had gathered round the open door, and were watching the street theatre performance with every appearance of great enjoyment. We were often a source of entertainment and amusement to our neighbours, but their interest and chatter seemed to be voting this morning's performance as the best so far.

Jack and I decide to become a little more pro-active, so under the alert gaze of the assembled spectators, we walked around the side of the house, in order to examine the electricity meter. The electrician had by this time switched off the current at the mains, so initially our inspection was little more than a ruse to get us out of the house for a slightly more private discussion. We peered knowingly at the meter, took interest in the slowly turning wheel indicating that the electricity was in fact turned on, despite the switch lever being in the off position. This fact took a moment to register. It can't be! With the electricity switched off, the wheel was turning ever so slowly. "Impossible!" Jack exploded. We looked more closely, and at each other, and then called Kadhikan over. He peered closely too.

"Oh yes, sir. Wheel is most certainly turning." He agreed cheerfully. We gazed silently at him. Sensing a problem, his face assumed a mask of consternation. Realisation finally dawned, and he scurried off to inform the electrician of this new phenomenon. The electrician remained unperturbed, however, and continued to grapple with the live wiring. We were ever more sure that he had actually found some fault there, but, unwilling to lose face, continued to assure us that all was well. After three exhausting hours of demonstration, discussion, mime and gesture, we were no closer to a solution. The electric iron had been added to the pile of dismembered electrical goods, and the only remedy the electrician could offer us was to suggest, yet again, that we purchase "Anchor" plugs.

Apparently, those plugs are the only ones manufactured in India that would actually fit our newly installed sockets. All other plugs had pins that were too small and thus fall out. They also connected only intermittently to the earth wire, thus rendering all electrical items potentially live. The final piece of advice given to us by the electrician as he took his leave, and our one hundred rupees, was "When electricity on, do not touch any metal part of electrical equipment." We were not convinced with this advice as a solution, nor indeed grateful, which had cost us our morning, our peace of mind and one hundred rupees.

We learnt to approach all our electrical goods with extreme caution, and whenever I used the iron, I grew used to the plug leaping unexpectedly out of its socket to land with a thump on the table beside me. Even Jack's wooden match sticks forced into the sockets beside the plugs had only a temporary beneficial effect. We were also no longer surprised to note that a friend's refrigerator had layers of insulation around its metal handle, and we empathised daily with the other Europeans who lived around the area who had literally hair-raising tales to tell of electrical goods which suddenly "bit". And we never, ever, "touch metal parts when the electricity is on".

Chapter 16

The day of the wedding was getting very near. We considered this a rare chance to become involved in a close personal event, different from a usual tourist opportunity.

Queenie and I decided to buy new clothes as described earlier for the occasion, not for sentimental reasons, or that we felt obliged to Sabu, who had given us the instructions, but to show respect. We also needed to choose an appropriate wedding present.

We had to some small degree become familiar with the shopping possibilities in Trivandrum, consequently we had no difficulty in going directly to an appropriate "Clothing Emporium," as it was described in large gold letters on a green and red background. Our shopping was enthusiastically encouraged by the counter staff who did little more than confuse what, under usual circumstances, would have been a reasonably straight forward process. After the usual resignation, and as resistance was pointless, we allowed ourselves to be persuaded, then dissuaded, then persuaded, and back again. At the climax of our confusion and desperately needing someone's help we were dropped like lead weights.

Silence, no co-operation. Like an awkward old computer, they froze, stepped back, heads shook, smiles smiled. We were shocked again.

However, we left the shop with a light brown shalwar kameez for Queenie and a nice crisp white shirt for myself plus of course thirty minutes of real live impromptu theatre at no extra cost, except of course the usual fraught nerves.

The wedding present, a series of small to large "tiffin" boxes made from finely finished stainless steel, each fitting snugly inside the other and encased in a light canvas zip up container was, I thought, the perfect choice.

Queenie and I were looking forward to this wedding, although for my part I would have been even more excited had it been a Hindu or Muslim ceremony instead of a Christian one. I appreciate that's being fussy, not to say ungrateful.

It was a beautiful morning, a great day for a wedding, our earlier reconnoitre had been useful. We were finally making our way to the "auspicious occasion," and everything went like clockwork. We arrived, the bus arrived, we arrived at our destination on time, the pre-arranged taxi arrived on time, and it was still quite early in the morning at the groom's home. There must have been a dozen minibuses lining the rough track immediately alongside the Major's home. We were delighted to be met by Father who was beaming with enthusiasm, as well as sporting his expertly pressed and medal adorned Salvation Army uniform.

"Welcome, welcome you are our most honoured guests," he greeted us warmly. We were taken through the already gathered throng and into the large ante-room we had visited a few days previously. Now it looked very different, not just in colour. Glittering, multi-coloured decorations adorned the walls and ceiling. "Very Christmas like." We commented to ourselves.

Father placed us at the front of the throng. Bodies crammed into the room tighter and tighter, he held his arm aloft and spoke. You could have heard a pin drop. The throng seemed to arrange itself in to a pre-destined order; a straight line of guests; a queue in fact appeared to form facing the tall, gentle, confident figure of father. He spoke quietly in his native tongue. Johnson, his oldest son, that is the groom, appeared from an inner sanctuary, head bowed either in gratit-ude, humility or submission. He stood before his father.

Father turned and looked to me, and noticing I had my camera to hand asked in his quiet voice, "Please you to take picture." I willingly took pictures, still not a sound from the hundred or so people squeezed into the small room.

Father spoke rapidly to his son who, raising his head was clearly seen to be quite tearful; a slight hand movement made by father left a small denomination rupee note in Johnson's hand. A kiss to both sides of the face and a strong mutual hug concluded that particular aspect of the short but effective initial ceremony.

The long queue of people now facing Johnson was made up of mainly older women who passed by. Each in turn spoke quickly to Johnson and pressed their offering into the young man's hand.

Tears rolled down his face. It was soon over and father stood proudly in front of his son offering up a white linen handkerchief to dry the boy's, soon to become a man's, tears.

At this point an obviously higher-ranking and more pompous Salvation Army officer took command of the proceedings. Lessons were read, hymns were sung, all in English and as badly out of tune as any British congregation, certainly no worse. The service took about fifteen minutes whereupon father advised everyone to make their way to the waiting minibuses. Turning to Queenie and myself he thanked us once again for our presence, adding, "Please you will travel in car with family".

Father was quite right it was family. All the family. Although it would be true to say that we two extra people could easily add to the discomfort of all in such a small space, a car designed for four, it didn't however, such was the accepted discomfort anyway.

The Morris Oxford creaked and groaned its way to the main venue in the nearby town with its load of thirteen passengers. Naturally all conversations and mutterings were in the indigenous language. Consequently I cannot share them with you.

The church was cathedral-like in size and devoid of decoration. Its long backless benches in place of pews were basic but functional, while the altar was a long broad table behind which the Salvation Army officers, dignitaries and wives were seated. These of course included father and mother major, and tagged to one end two chairs that had been provided for us. Visually at least, it could have been the last supper.

On the opposite side of the table in the first row of the pew section, were the bride and family plus entourage, all looking desperately miserable. Certainly the groom's family held the power position in this relationship. We were interested to see how the groom would cope as he was placed to one side of the table, so separated from the bride and his own family as to leave him totally without support on this important and emotional occasion.

The mass of congregation was facing up towards the business end of this massive church. Father had previously voiced expectations to make up the congregation to about a thousand and I guess this was easily exceeded. The layout of the building and the long distances between congregation and main event, as well the bride's family having been seated with their backs to the congregation, served to cut off the expectant crowd from any intimate aspect of the matrimonial proceedings.

The dazzling white expanse of the building served as a perfect backdrop to the array of greens, pinks, scarlet, blues, purples, saffron, silver and gold of the saris. From the slightly elevated position and at the distances involved the colours flowed and danced to the movement of the women as they drifted with their usual elegance down the centre aisles and along the rows, contrasting, flashing, sparkling electric-like until they reached their chosen seats. There was an almost total absence of males. Those that were there were young boys and older men. Crisp, pressed and segregated.

The service was conducted in the local language so we were unable to follow the details. It took almost three long, hot hours to complete. Each member of both the parties involved, directed by one salvation army officer or another, would verbally respond when indicated and then follow on to make yet another prolonged speech. The couple to be married seemed to take a minor role in the proceedings, and totally ignored each other even at the end when signing the register. They could have been total strangers to each other, no demonstration of affection, no smile or happiness expressed.

Indeed, the groom appeared to be supremely bored, glancing at his watch from time to time, while the bride hung her head and appeared to be no less than terrified.

What was it, I asked myself, that allowed me to feel that the whole sad performance was at best for the benefit of the authority of the church and its officers, and very little to do with the congregation, or the bride and groom? Oddly I felt for some reason a perverted gratification, witnessing the sacrificial lambs to the slaughter. Maybe it pleased me, I just had my pre-judices confirmed.

The joy of the occasion came when the officers led the congregation into the adjoining great hall, where a hundred or more long tables and benches had been arranged in rows. Each table had been laid with twelve large steel plates, and jugs of water, each with the usual small stainless steel drinking receptacles. The main parties including ourselves were seated on the elevated stage in a long row facing down onto the crowd. The food was served to our number first, where father superior said grace, bent and tasted the food, and with a smile and approving nod the whole hall turned into a laughing, shouting, clanging, feeding frenzy. Needless to say the food was of the highest standard with a plethora of different flavours, all new experiences to us, and all equally delightful.

This experience was one we could have easily missed and although it made me feel at times upset, confused, even angry, I am pleased we were invited to such a personal affair and in such a personal way.

The feast completed and all thanks given, we excluded ourselves from the reception which was to take place at Father's home later in the day, though I responded to requests by members of the entourage to take photographs, and this being happily completed would be our small contribution to the day.

We left the church after saying our last goodbyes and made our way back to Kovalam to concentrate on our Christmas arrangements and of course the inevitable neighbourhood party plus whatever else may evolve, including the purchase of furniture which had been delayed owing to more interesting or unanticipated events.

Chapter 17

Extracts From Queenie's Diary 3

This was to be my first Christmas away from the UK, and I wasn't quite sure how I would react to this. As the day approached, I sank deeper and deeper into depression. Massive guilt feelings troubled me. What if this was my mum's last Christmas, and I wasn't with her? I rang her each week, and she always seemed cheerful enough. Each time I rang she told me how glad she was that I finally had the opportunity to travel, and how she envied me. I tried to hang on to this, and her reassurance that although she missed me, she didn't want to spoil my opportunity.

I tried to tell myself that I'd probably enjoy the day when it arrived, and that it could be no worse than some of the Christmases I'd had to endure in recent years. I always ended our conversations by reassuring her that I would be home in the late summer, and that we would celebrate the Millennium Christmas and New Year together.

In the meantime, Jack and I were busy with the house project, putting right the devastations of the Indian cowboy(!) builders. We had been bitterly disappointed in a number of aspects of the project, but we tried to stay determinedly cheerful, constantly reminding each other that we didn't expect it to be easy, and how glad we were to be here, in the warmth and beauty of a tropical land.

Jack announced a day or two before Christmas that he had been given a couple of tickets for a Christmas "do" in Kovalam. It seemed like a good idea to me, and solved the problem of what to do with ourselves on the day. "We both need some cheerful company," I thought to myself. I rang Mum on Christmas Eve, and as always, she sounded cheerful and pleased to hear my voice, though like me, she admitted that she was always glad when Christmas was over. I promised to ring her again in a day or two, suspecting that the phone lines would be jammed on both Christmas Day and Boxing Day, as ex-pats rang home. The rest of Christmas Eve passed off very quietly.

On Christmas Day, we made our way to Kovalam in glorious sunshine, rejoicing to think of everyone back home shivering in the winter chill of the Northern European Christmas. We hadn't bothered to buy each other gifts. Besides which, our budget was very limited. But what better way to spend Christmas than swimming in a warm, clear ocean, and then lazing away the afternoon in the shade of a beachside cafe, drinking lemon tea or ice-cold soda water? Then finally watching a famous Kerala sunset before drifting off to the party venue at the other end of the beach.

A few people had arrived at the venue before us. In no time at all, people arrived with the beer, and wishing everyone "Merry Christmas", we entered into the spirit of the occasion, opened the first bottles and settled down to an evening of eating, drinking and making merry. Sitting back with my first drink in my hand, I looked around me. The patio of the tourist home and venue had been decorated with fairy lights, and a group of tables had been pushed together to provide a large dining area under the stars. More people had arrived, and were greeting each other noisily, or sitting in small groups, chatting together and drinking. Their ages ranged from late teens to late middle age, and as I sipped my first drink, I turned my attention to a middle-aged couple across the table from me. I was just in time to hear the woman exclaim, "Gawd, I HATE Indian food!"

"Sylvie, you always say that, yet you come back here year after year!" laughed the greying man I took to be her partner,

"How do you manage?" I called across the table. "What do you eat while you are here?"

"Egg and chips, dear!" Came the laughing reply, "And they can't cook chips, either. But I do love it here!" I knew what she meant! Everyone laughed. Sylvie was obviously well known and liked.

"I've got my Christmas present." She continued.

"Oh yes, what's that then?" I asked.

"Bisto Gravy!" came the unexpected reply. "I've had a carton of Bisto Gravy sent to me from home. I'm having roast chicken, spuds and gravy for my Christmas dinner!" She announced proudly. There was a roar of approval, and Sylvie got up to supervise the final touches to her meal. While she was away, our dinner was served.

First, a large banana leaf was placed on the table in front of each guest. This was soon covered in an assortment of curry sauces, vegetable, fish and chicken, with chapattis and bananas on the side, and a huge mound of rice. Everyone tucked in with a will, pausing only to watch as Sylvie reappeared, bearing high a small jug.

"Here it is," she announced proudly, "Bisto Gravy!"

"Aaaahhhh!" we all cried in unison, amidst general laughter. Sylvie had provided herself with a plate and a knife and fork.

"I likes to eat civilised." she announced, before tucking in with evident enjoyment, to her chicken, spuds and gravy.

Jack, in the meantime, was also tucking into the food, and the beer, and was talking animatedly between mouthfuls to John and Gunda, a couple of new friends. They were listening to an older man who said he was from the North of England, and came to Kerala every year for six months, and saved his income for the other six months in order to do so.

Sylvie, another friendly lady, told us that she and her husband stayed for three months every year.

We found ourselves in good company and we felt we somehow belonged! It was nice to feel that if we were mad, there were others equally mad, and if it was madness to want to be warm, then we quite liked being mad.

I was thoroughly enjoying the food, the drinks, the company, and I decided that a tropical Christmas was no bad thing. A group of locals had been watching the proceedings from the next door veranda, smilingly joining in with the chatter and banter around the tables. The main course was finally finished, and a fruity, moist Christmas cake was passed around the table. I can't resist Christmas cake, and I'd begun to think the lack of cake might be the only downside to this Christmas, but here it was! I ate my own and several other people's portions.

The party grew noisier as beer and spirits were now being consumed in vast quantities. Someone turned up the music, and Gunda jumped over the low dividing wall to join the group of locals on their veranda. Taking hold of the hands of a woman and a child, she gyrated enthusiastically to the music, encouraging everyone to join in with vigorous movements of her shaven head. Jack and I were too full of food to dance, but most of the crowd got up and joined in. Indian and European dancing and laughing together under the stars, by the soft light of the ever present fairy lamps strung around the trees and bushes, all this was much more of a relevant reason for a festival.

The rest of the evening passed by in a blur. Finally glancing at my watch, I was amazed to see that it was close to midnight. The last bus was long gone, and I wasn't sure whether there would be a taxi driver around to take us home. I alerted Jack, who was chatting noisily and merrily with John and Gunda once again. It was good to see him so relaxed and happy after all the months of trauma and hard work we'd left behind at home, only to be confronted with more work again on arrival in Kerala. Jack agreed that he'd had enough, so we made our farewells, thanked our hosts, and tottered off into the dark, leaving the remaining few revellers to drink till dawn.

I had forgotten my torch, so we walked, weaving, giggling, and stumbling along the familiar paths under the coconut palms. Fortunately, most of the route now had electric lights along it. The rickshaw stand was almost deserted, but one hardy soul was still on duty.

"Taxi?" he enquired,

"Yes, to Pachalloor."

"One hundred fifty rupees! "

"No," we chorused, "fifty rupees in the day, one hundred at night! Taxi association rules!" We reminded him.

"OK." He agreed, grinning. Like everyone else, he could not resist trying it on. For once the road was deserted, and once the little rickshaw had struggled up the steep hill, we made good time to our destination.

We paid him off, and staggering about in the pitch darkness as I tried to dodge the taxi as he turned to make his way to the road, I completely lost my bearings.

"This way, this way." Insisted Jack.

I wasn't sure, and staggered about in a circle, further disorientating myself in the now pitch darkness. However, for lack of any other path to follow, I reluctantly followed Jack's dim shape in the darkness. I was sure we would be hopelessly lost, but secretly quite enjoying the experience. We stopped for a moment as Jack squelched into a puddle left by the previous day's short, heavy shower. His loud exclamation of disgust disturbed someone in a nearby house, and an outside light was switched on, momentarily blinding us. Shading my eyes, I saw that a man had come to the door of his house, and was looking us over. He smiled as he recognised us.

"Khadikhan house?" I enquired.

He pointed silently down the track, happily, in the direction Jack had been taking us. The next thing we needed to do was to identify the tiny, foot-wide track leading to Kadhikan's house, now that our friendly neighbour had once more extinguished his light. We knew it was somewhere on the left. Not only had I forgotten the torch, but I'd also forgotten to put on the outside light at the house. We groped about in the pitch dark, sweating, swearing and grumbling, peering at the ground, hoping to be able to make out the lighter coloured track from the surrounding vegetation.

"Here it is!" I cried joyfully. What a relief! Jack might enjoy lurching about in the jungle at night, without a light, but for me it was the sort of adventure that seemed more appealing in retrospect, or indeed, as part of someone else's adventure.

Fearing snakes, we stamped our feet on the path, which Jack, 'trepid splorer' of the world, claimed would send them scurrying away. I hoped so. I like snakes, but at a distance. Finally the dim outlines of K's house came into view.

"Home at last," we laughed. Letting ourselves in, with only a little difficulty in locating the key, and then locating the lock, and then turning the key, we groped for the light switch — very warily. I was rewarded with a flood of light, and the whirring of the fan.

"At least the electricity's on," I said thankfully, as we stumbled into our beds after the usual torrential shower from the as yet unrepaired shower head.

Looking at my watch by the dim light from my small torch, I saw that once again it was two-forty-five and the sound which had woken me this time was Jack's groans of agony.

"What's up?"

"Stomach cramps." he muttered through gritted teeth, as he tottered off in the darkness toward the bathroom. I groped for the light switch.

"Damn!" The electricity was off. Locating the candles and matches by the light of the torch, I went into the bathroom, to find Jack, pale and sweating, face creased in agony, sitting on the toilet and hanging on to the wall at each side to support himself. Now thoroughly alarmed, I hurried to fetch one of the bottles of water for him to drink. He was suddenly and violently sick on the bathroom floor. I picked up the bucket, and put it under the tap for water to flush away the mess. I was rewarded with the merest trickle, which very quickly became a drip, and then ceased altogether. Both ends of Jack were now in violent operation, and I could do no more than hold the bucket and stroke his head.

"Bloody hell!" I raged inwardly. "If it's not one thing it's another! The tank on the roof is empty, the electricity is off, and Jack is sick as a dog! BLOODY, BLOODY HELL!"

The worst of Jack's attack seemed to be over, and a little colour had come into his cheeks. Stepping gingerly over the mess on the floor, I guided him back to bed, brushing aside his apologies, and his protestations that he wanted to clear up the mess he'd made.

"You can't!" I said rather abruptly, 'There's no water in the tank!"

"Then go round and put the pump on to fill it up."

"There is also a power cut!"

"Shit!" He exploded,(not literally.)

"Precisely." I answered.

I got him to drink as much of the bottled water as I could, then blew out the candle, leaving the devastation in the bathroom until morning. It was hot and sticky without the fan, and the smell from the bathroom, despite the two doors being closed, was atrocious. As I lay down again to try and get some sleep, I knew exactly what time it was. An explosion rent the air, rocking the building to its foundations. Yes, it was four o'clock and that was the temple starting up for the day. So far, in all the time we'd spent in this house, we had hardly had one complete night's sleep. With water tanks dropping noisily off walls, early morning visitors, mosquitoes, and sweaty heat, sleep had so far eluded us. I dozed off until first light. Thankfully, with the return of the electricity, the fan came on and I was able to go round to the back of the building and switch on the pump, to send the water from the well into the tank, and from there to our bathroom.

In the early morning cool, I climbed onto the roof to oversee the filling of the tank. I could make out the other buildings around me, and in the courtyard of the next door house, the women were already hard at work spinning the coir. They spotted me on the roof, and smiled and waved, before turning their attention back to their jobs. The tank was soon filled, and I made my way down the outside stairs to our living quarters, to tackle the dreadful job of cleaning the bathroom. Jack had beaten me to it and the cleaning was well in hand when I went back in. He still looked pale and a little feverish, but had not had a repetition of last night's sickness. I was grateful that he'd cleaned up. My stomach was none too secure after the two or three bottles of beer I'd consumed. Other people's vomit almost always makes me come out in sympathy.

We spent the rest of the day very quietly, nursing our hangovers, but discussing the party. We agreed that it had been a very enjoyable evening, and somehow, we got around to discussing holding a party of our own for New Year, up on the roof. It seemed like a great idea, and we proposed to invite all the neighbours, to get to know them. We envisaged sing songs and traditional dancing perhaps. We grew excited at the prospect, and set the date for New Year's Day.

That, I think, was the sum total of the work achieved for that day, and we settled down that night, praying for an undistributed night's sleep. It was not to be.

The tiger who stalked me in my dreams, waking me with his ferocious roar as he leapt, continued to roar even as I sat bolt upright, frozen to the spot, heart pounding, eyes wide in the darkness. Finally, the roaring sound resolved itself into the now familiar noise of water gushing again from the toilet cistern and flooding the bathroom floor.

"Damn and blast all Indian workmen!" I muttered fiercely as I groped for the torch. An encounter with a coconut sized spider with extremely long legs a day or two before had left me feeling vulnerable and apprehensive about leaving the safety of the bed or mosquito net without first checking the floor and walls for any possible many legged intruders. That these might be large, hairy, and have a nasty bite, was also worthy of consideration, hence the torch, the light switch being situated at the far side of the room. The coast being clear; there were not even any cockroaches; I slipped out of bed and crept across the room to the bathroom door. I tried hard not to wake Jack, who was for once, sleeping deeply, blissfully unaware that the morning would bring him yet another problem to solve, a further repair to undertake on this seemingly blighted project. Switching on the bathroom light, I surveyed the damage. As before, the tank hung drunkenly off the wall, the temporary repair effected by Jack a few days ago having finally given way. Water gushed from the pipe leading to the roof storage tank, the toilet cistern having totally divested itself of its contents. Wearily, I turned off the supply to the pipe, switched off the light, and tottered back to bed, all the while wondering where in India one could purchase screws large enough to complete the fixing of the tank to the wall. I concluded that morning would be soon enough to alert poor Jack to this latest disaster, and settling down once again, soon fell asleep, under the comparative safety of the mosquito net. As usual, I was the first to wake, and, deciding that discretion was the better part of valour, said nothing to Jack immediately about the toilet, but prepared a cup of tea. I would then introduce the subject gently.

Jack in full spate is an awesome sight, though to be fair, it is hot air. His colourful and highly descriptive language, and his total disregard for the sensitivities of innocent bystanders, can be quite terrifying.

Imagine an amalgamation of Alf Garnett, Basil Fawlty, and Victor Meldrew, and you will have some indication of the level of performance given by Jack. In the end, however, there was no easy way to break the news. So, as he made to go to the bathroom after finishing his cup of tea, I socked it to him.

"Cistern fell off the wall again last night." I announced, casually. Jack stopped in his tracks. I hurried on.

"We'll go to Trivandrum first thing, and set ourselves the task of tracking down some large screws!" I suggested cheerfully, knowing that Jack would always rise to a challenge.

He glowered at me, blue eyes hard and cold.

I knew what he was thinking. He was thinking about the many varied, interesting and totally horrible ways one could use to induce slow death in Indian workmen.

I'd beaten him to it. After all, I'd had most of the night to invent and refine any number of dreadful tortures. Without a word, Jack turned and stalked into the bathroom, muttering blackly under his breath. Finally he returned, and forcing a sickly smile, said, "o K, let's do it! Showers, breakfast, and out — quick as possible or I'll have to strangle someone!" I knew who the unfortunate "someone" would be, so for the continuing safety of Kardy, hurriedly prepared breakfast, and set off for the bus, having showered and dressed in record time.

Much has been written about Indian buses, and most people are familiar with images of lethally overcrowded buses, passengers clinging for dear life to their tops, or hanging on to the sides using any available handhold. The actual physical real experience however, is something else entirely. We soon discovered that every bus journey undertaken in India, of whatever duration, is different to every other. Yes, the overcrowding will be the same, the lurching and grinding of gears, the smell of burning diesel, and the aching muscles from maintaining a cramped position. But the details are always different. This particular bus journey stands out in our memories due solely to the unusual, even for India, behaviour of the conductor. The main problem encountered by Indian bus conductors is the actual collection of fares, as mentioned by Jack before in this script, when movement up and down the aisle is so severely restricted due to the incredible press of humanity on the bus. This bus conductor had his own, very unique method of collecting fares on a crowded vehicle. As I will reveal without further ado!

We had noted that by boarding the bus going to Trivandrum at a particular bus stop in the village, we were generally able to procure a seat for ourselves, as quite a large number of people would get down at that point. And once again, fortune smiled on us, as if to say "Sorry about the start of your day, here's a little compensation." We were able to grab the last two available seats. After this stop, we knew the bus would fill to overcapacity in no time. Sure enough, by the time we had made three or four more stops, the conductor was reduced to clinging to the outside of the front passenger door, getting down at each stop in order to cram more humanity into every available space. We watched this performance with some trepidation, sure that each time the bus jerked into motion, the conductor would be unable to leap back onto his precarious perch, he would be left behind, and the bus would sail majestically into Trivandrum conductorless.

Our worst fears were suddenly realised. The bus pulled away from yet another stop, where more got on than off, and the conductor gave a shrill whistle which we understood was the order for the driver to continue the journey. We saw the bus pull past the conductor who was stood at the roadside, and nudged each other gleefully. Now what? We asked ourselves, assuming the worst. Jack peered out of the window, and by craning his neck, was able to see what was happening outside the bus.

He suddenly drew in his head, and looked round at me with an expression of total amazement on his face. Speechless, he jerked his head towards the rear of the bus. Craning my neck to see what had so amazed Jack, it was my turn to be incredulous. I was just in time to see the conductor's hapless body being pulled through the rear window, to be passed over the heads of the passengers in the rear of the bus. No-one else seemed at all surprised or alarmed at this turn of events, and the conductor, a youngish, fit looking cheerful chap, then proceeded to calmly collect fares from this unusual position. Struggling over and above his tightly packed passengers, determined not to miss a single fare. We couldn't help but fall into helpless laughter.

"That's one for the book." Chortled Jack.

Chapter 18

This trip to Trivandrum was one of many, fortunately none of them were anywhere near as difficult as the first. We learnt later that the municipal rubbish removal and street sweepers had returned to work after being on strike for several months, consequently the rubbish that had piled up during the monsoon months was now being removed. A stream of female workers were digging into the piles of compressed running-wet garbage, with makeshift hand implements of such design as to necessitate the women coming into constant bodily contact with the stinking mass. No mechanical digger, these poor women were not even equipped with a functional hand tool. They scattered and gathered and heaped the mess into their large steel bowls, sometimes by hand only, then lifted the bowls onto their own heads, the contents hanging and dropping and dripping down over the sides and on to their bodies. They walked and then threw their head pans up onto the side of a lorry, where another woman stood already knee deep in decaying garbage and manoeuvred the pans onto the top of the pile again with her bare hands. There was no protective clothing whatsoever. The women worked silently on, ignoring the passers-by as the passers-by ignored them. There are lots of shovels and protective clothing in India, why then, I wondered, didn't these women get any?

We walked on past rows of toiling women, enquiring as we went at the various hardware shops, about screws, rawlplugs, hand drills, bits, plastic flexible pipe, washers, moveable spanners and such. It was frustrating to say the least, that although the main hardware and tool shops might stock one of the items on our list they may not stock the other. A shop that sold a saw would not sell a hammer. A shop that sold straight plastic pipes, would not sell plastic bends to fit. A hand drill shop would not sell the bit to fit the drill, but the sweet shop had exactly the right size of washers required. Odd as it may seem, we were able to purchase nails at the tobacconists, and screws at the newsagents. Local street/shop knowledge in this respect is vital, but needs time to acquire, plus a considerable amount of patience. We punctuated our shopping, through necessity, with drinks of cold soda water or Limca.

We researched into other less dangerous cooking possibilities than we had at present, that is the electric stove. There were lots of paraffin stoves and the usual firewood option. I asked about LPG stoves, and although LPG storm lights were widely available, adapters for using the gas bottles for cooking were not. We realised that our electric ring was probably the best option after all. We were soon struggling with plumbing and fixings and various other items, though we had not been able to get any of the shopkeepers to understand "rawlplug". We opted for the only available alternative, small wooden dowels which would help to plug the already overlarge screw holes in our toilet wall that we, or I, needed to fix the cistern and toilet pan firmly in place.

Once home after the usual walk from Pachalloor School, I tackled the jobs, replaced the usual too-small screws with four more suitable ones, and then replaced the leaking flexible coupling. After securing the large black rubber washer into the back of the toilet pan with the larger screws placed properly and tightly in to the wall, and the extra support of cut to size broom handles supporting the underneath of the cistern, I was convinced all would be well. I was kind of proud of the job; it looked level, tidy and secure. I turned on the water, and although the plastic cistern distorted with the weight of water inside due to its thin and inferior manufacture, it was held and supported in every direction. It did not fall off the wall ever again. Next I dismantled the shower head, in order to ascertain why the holes in its face would not emit water. The plumber who had fixed it; Kadhikan in fact; had not removed the very large sticky backed plastic label placed on the inside of the head, thereby obstructing the passage of water. This I punctured in several places with a safety pin, screwed the head back in place and tested it. Joy! I had a working shower! It had been a busy day, but we decided to travel to Kovalam to have a meal. We may even meet John and Gunda. We were tired, and decided to take a rickshaw for a treat. After the usual silliness with the driver, we arrived at our destination, and walked towards the beach. And there in front of us was Ben.

Ben was a tailor who worked the beach, making up copies of whatever garment was requested by the tourists. He had made me two silk shirts last year. They were made with beautiful material, and were excellent value.

"Hi, Ben!" I shouted in hope that he would remember me. He turned. He was a very pleasant handsome young man, very neat and fashionable. I had found his dealings to be very honest. The technique he used for pricing was to ask you the customer to write a price for an item you had expressed interest in, on a piece of paper that you genuinely thought was fair. He would do the same, and whichever was the lowest, was the one that he would do the job for. In our case, his price was the cheapest by ten rupees. This seemed to me to be a much more sensible arrangement than starting at a ridiculously high price and having the humiliation of haggling down.

"Hello, Jack! Glad to see you again!" we sloped off to a restaurant to compare notes on the previous year. Ben was looking prosperous and dapper, and had changed his shop and rented a position towards the backside of Kovalam, away from the beach. It was not the most popular spot, but was the only one he could afford. Even so, at thirty thousand rupees for six months, it was a lot of money. He introduced us to his partner, who had a tailor's shop on one of the other beaches.

"So how is business, then, Ben?" I asked.

"It's OK, but much quieter than last year."

"Why? How come?" I asked.

"Since the package industry came, I have lost lots of the younger travellers. The new wealthier tourists go on pre-arranged tours outside the area, and buy gifts in other places."

"So, people don't stay around here, then?" I responded.

"Maybe three or four days in two weeks is all". His business partner added,

"The younger ones used to travel to here, and stay a while. There wasn't as many at any one time, but they spent more over a period, plus of course, the season was longer then."

"So package tours are a mixed blessing?"

"We only have one flight per week for the whole of Kerala, and it is not enough."

"By the way, Jack, I've got an Italian girlfriend," interrupted Ben.

"A tourist?" I enquired.

"Yes, she has been here a month already, and she will stay another month."

"Watch it, Ben, you'll be an adopted Italian before long."

"Yes, why not?" He replied, with a broad grin.

"I have to go now to see a customer at the shop. Come and meet me tomorrow. Christina will be there."

"OK," I said, "I'll see you about six and we'll have a drink together in the Coral Bar."

"Well Queenie, should we move on? Go and see Sunjeev, see what his latest horror story is?"

And there we were again. A little too cloudy for the usual sunset, a different but still interesting sky with colours and light reflecting and dancing through the various thin layers of cloud.

"Hi, Sunjeev!"

"Hello, sir, you would like a beer?"

"Yes, good idea! Two glasses please."

We avoided any conversation about our previous meeting, enjoyed our meal, and discussed the next day's plans.

"Tell me Queenie, did you notice the rough timber furniture at the side of the road in Trivandrum?"

"No I didn't notice."

"OK, I'll take you tomorrow. It's past the Gandhi statue on M.G. Road."

"OK, it may be good enough to sand down and paint up. I'll have a look, see how much it costs."

"Maybe I could paint it then stencil it." Offered Queenie.

This agreed, we travelled home in a modern private mini bus. We crammed into the only available space, which was on the luggage carrier beside the driver. The advantage was that we were dropped exactly at the top of our track, as this bus took a different route to most state buses. The disadvantage was that we would be jettisoned through the windscreen in the event of a collision. I looked into the blackness, and spotted the neighbour's television, glowing eerily under the trees, and headed for it as our beacon to home.

As Queenie let herself in, I went round the side of the house to see Kadhikan. Before I could open my mouth, "Jacky, you must give me 500 rupees, fix Lambi!"

Thinking that there was a lever here, I said,

"OK, but you must get me an electrician in the morning! The electricity is still dangerous."

"Oh yes, Jacky! Electrician. He be here morning! When you give me 500 rupees?"

Not wishing to imbue an atmosphere of mistrust, I said, "Now, Kardy, why not?" So I took him round to the front door and gave him the money saying, "Electrician! First thing! Wake me up — or else!" Needless to say, there was no sign of either Kadhikan or the electrician next morning.

I went round at about eight thirty, feeling good after a night's sleep, having been wakened only once, by the four o'clock explosion.

"Where's Kadhikan?" I asked when Valsala opened the door. She pointed towards Thiruvallum.

"He go early." The first time I had heard her use English! "Tea?" she offered.

"Thank you, yes." I answered.

Tea arrived via Deepu, her oldest son who was about ten years old. I waited for Kadhikan, thinking he may have gone in search of our little barefoot electrician, but by eleven I decided he wasn't coming. We made our way to the usual bus stop and Trivandrum, feeling let down. I'd allowed him to do it to me again. I still didn't understand why I was paying for "K"s Lambi to be fixed.

Having arrived we elected to have an early lunch, and so noticing a cafe I entered, pointed at a curry that was being enjoyed by another customer, and said, "Two." After two meals and coffees I paid the fifteen rupees and went off in search of the outdoor furniture store.

We found the furniture. Yes, it was crude, and naturally, not finished off. No screws and no glue, but nailed together with two-inch nails. All the same, it was engineered well, very sturdy and would probably look very nice once Queenie had exercised her artistic ability. They were very useful structures; free-standing shelves the size of double wardrobes, tables, six feet by four feet, benches etc. and the prices were remarkably good. Having lost five hundred rupees last night to "K" I only had enough money to purchase the kitchenware, so we resolved to tackle the furniture purchasing at a later date.

Returning to Kovalam, I changed money, and as planned, we went to meet Ben and Christina. She was plainly in love, and should have known better. A thirty-two-year-old nurse, pretty, and in all other respects, it seemed, a sensible person. She had already, however, extended her stay for another four weeks, put her job at risk, she told us, and panicked her family. She spoke of Ben leaving all that he knew, and living in Italy. I didn't know Ben all that well, but I did know that he'd told me wanted to make a business here. He had a mother and father, the usual large extended family. I wouldn't think he was going to leave them very easily for Christina somehow! I shouldn't have said anything to Queenie and kept my thoughts to myself.

"Jack! Stop it! You've got no right! He may think the world of her! You are just too cynical!"

"OK, Queenie, OK? Sorry!" I conveniently changed my approach.

"Ben, next week, if I clean the flat roof of where we live, would you come around and have a meal with us up there one evening, with Christina?"

"Yes, good idea, thanks. I'll bring beer, have a good drink." He replied.

"I thought you didn't drink, Ben!"

"Little, little, make me wobbly!" He laughed out loud.

"Jack, look!" Exclaimed Queenie, "Between the bushes. Kardy!" There he was, sliding in between the palms, glancing nervously in our direction.

"I'll get him. Kardy," I shouted "over here!" I got up and approached him. He scuttled away.

"Kardy! Come here! Where are you going?" He stopped, sideways on, not knowing what to do. A split-second later, I was standing by his side.

"Come and meet some people."

"Yes sir, very good sir," he bobbed. "I come."

"Have a seat," said Queenie, pushing a plastic chair toward him. His expression was that of a man who had been woken up from a deep and absorbing dream.

"What's wrong?" She asked innocently.

"Nothing, madam. Nothing wrong. "Where you go today?" he continued.

"Trivandrum," I replied. "Would you like a beer?" Silence. I repeated the question.

"Yes, yes sir, beer good. Yes."

I went to the bar to order, met the waiter halfway, and returned. Kadhikan had gone. "Where's Kardy?" I looked towards the entrance. He was there, pacing around in circles, drawing nervously on a thin, hand-rolled cigarette. I waited for the beer to arrive, then waved to Kadhikan who hesitantly approached again. As he reached the table, I stood up and introduced him to Ben, Christina, and as John and Gunda had just arrived, them also.

"Kardy", I whispered, in order to get his close atten-tion, "Ben is a tailor who has a busy shop with lots of tourists. Why not ask him to introduce customers to you? Maybe offer him a small commission."

"Oh, yes sir, very good."

"If you speak to him in Malayalam," I continued, "no-one else will know anything about it."

"I will, I will try. Yes sir."

I poured some beer into his glass. He could not re-lax. I created openings for him to approach Ben, but he could not take them up. I felt I was wasting my time, then all of a sudden, "Electrician" he said, "he again come tomorrow."

"OK, that's fine," I answered, not really believing him. When I had returned from the toilet he had dis-appeared again. Queenie had been asked for money, for "rice and a little fish, for children."

Why didn't he ask me, I said to myself. "Because he's a cunning little SOD." I answered myself. I was beginning to have doubts about our whole enterprise. He was not the man I thought he was. It looked like I had made a mistake, an error of judgement. It was now some weeks since I came here, and he hadn't had any boat trip customers at all in that time. If he couldn't run this simple business, how would he run a tourist home? I looked up, and there he was again. Slowly weaving his way around the empty tables. He stood at a distance, looking sheepishly in our direction. I ignored him. Surely this was not Kardy's sales technique! What on earth had happened to him? He had changed!

Discussing the situation later that evening, we both felt that last year, I had Kadhikan as a fellow traveller of sorts. I had empathised with his daily predicament of in-your-face poverty, which gave rise to the constant need to force an opportunity to make a few rupees even trying where one may not exist.

Searching the proverbial haystack for the non-existent needle for all of one's days, guarantees that awareness of a route to a bigger picture becomes unlikely. I thought that maybe this realisation could be part of his problem.

I knew from personal experience how much courage and stamina it takes to have to constantly confront strangers with a view to a sale. I have had to work commission-only sales in gas, electricity, insurance, windows, telephone lines, and various other self-employment ventures one needs to keep the wolf from the door somehow, and it is not easy.

Strangers prefer to laugh, or jeer and have fun at your expense, even insult you and your vulnerable position. Looking down from their privileged position of permanent occupation, choice, and wealth they are oblivious to the fact that you are simply trying to make a very basic living. They walk by, heads in the air, and slam their doors in your face. I have felt this pain in the UK and empathise.

I have respect for his past ability to approach people from alien cultures, and struggling with an alien language in order to get his point across.

Unlike the bigger businesses, the travel agents, money exchangers, indeed anyone with a shop front, he had no base to work from, no smart, well-educated staff to back him up.

For all that, I felt disappointed in his lack of effort in this project, his project, it was his stated belief and conviction that this modernised house would provide him with a better life.

He had seen a bigger picture. Now he had lost the drive — that extra effort needed to gain that important foothold. He appeared to be de-motivated and wretched. His ability to plan and work consistently appeared to have deserted him. I had tried to explain to him how people like himself and myself need to work longer and harder than those who have the advantages of education and other advantages.

He laughed, and by his demeanour it appeared he didn't believe me when I told him about the hours I'd had to work to enable us to be here, and that hurt deeply. I had made agreements with Kadhikan, and thought I had a common bond through hard work and struggle, but the man I saw now bore little resemblance to the man I knew last year. His distance, scowling and pacing, and furtive stalking, and avoiding issues, was worrying in the extreme. After all, he is why we are here, why we came in the first place, on his invitation, in order to improve his situation.

His attitude was now affecting my will to continue, I may have to accept my judgement and decision to support him was wrong. It would be difficult to accept this notion. I may also be wrong. I hope so,

Also, I don't give up that easily.

Chapter 19

Extracts From Queenie's Diary 4

A party on the roof for all our neighbours to celebrate the New Year had seemed a great idea, and we grew more enthusiastic the more we discussed it. Kadhikan and Valsala were most enthusiastic, however when Jack suggested that maybe the ladies might cook beef parotta, a silence ensued with a gaze towards the floor . When we asked, "Why, what's wrong?" Kadhikan informed us that the ladies could only cook fish curry. We were not convinced, although it could have been some religious mores. There are certainly contradictions somewhere. As I understand it, Hindus consider cows sacred, on the other hand beef parotta is served at most cafes we have been to. Odd!

Privately, I think the ladies would much prefer to have a break from cooking anyway, and would also welcome the chance to dress up and "eat out" for once.

This means, of course, that we will have to employ a cook. I felt confident that the five hundred rupees for the beef that Jack was asked for and had contributed to would not include the cook's wages. Right again. Kadhikan tried to hit us for wages in advance. We partially conceded, and gave him half, the rest to be given after the cooking had been successfully completed. I still had to go shopping with Valsala for the other ingredients - flour, oil, sugar, spices, etc.

On the day of our proposed shopping trip, I put all negative thoughts behind me as I waited for Valsala to be ready. I was still not sure where we were going, whether to the local market or Trivandrum. What I did know was that Valsala had a lengthy list of items, written in Malayalam by an unknown hand. Again, I didn't know what was on the list. Kadhikan had appeared at the door at about eight o'clock, to inform me that Valsala would be ready "later, later," but how much later was left to my imagination. By eight thirty I was sitting in the shade just inside the open door, watching life pass by. This house now has no garden as the little there had been is taken up by the extended building works, not even a fence around it, so we are constantly on view to people who pass by on the track, just feet from the door.

This lack of privacy was sometimes an irritation to me. This morning, however, it was a pleasant distraction and I smiled and waved at the passers-by, who were, without exception, unable to pass without peering into the open doorway. A group of children appeared suddenly, grinning widely and calling "Hello, hello", nudging each other. They knew about the party, and their bright enquiring happy faces lift my spirits. The prospect of sweets and all manner of unusual delights had made them bolder, and they giggled, pushed each other forward and jumped up and down with excitement until someone's Mum shood them away, with an apologetic glance in my direction. I indicated that I welcomed their cheerful intrusion, and she hurried away, looking pleased.

Ambili, a feisty young woman who lives opposite, appeared at the gate of her family compound. I waved and smiled calling, "Valsala?"

"Soon!" she replied, then turned away and disappeared indoors. I continued to wait patiently. Waiting is something I have always been good at, but here I have been able to fine-tune the skill, and use it as a means of observing the daily life around me, whether human or animal. Most of the comings and goings of Indian life are incomprehensible to me, but do give me much food for thought, or amusement.

I wondered why labourers, whose job is incredibly hard anyway, carry such heavy weights on their heads? I have seen wheelbarrows for sale, which would make the jobs much easier on the roads and building sites. Perhaps a wheelbarrow is too expensive, and human life apparently so cheap here, so is therefore probably considered more expendable. Why are houses built with holes in the outside wall, which are specifically designed to accommodate a protruding coconut palm which is growing on the inside of the house? Why not build the house a couple of feet to the left or right of the tree, or is the tree so precious that it cannot be felled? Mystery upon mystery.

The kettle I had put on earlier, finally boiled, and I put some of the water and a liberal helping of Dettol into a small steel bowl. I still had not been able to extract a deep splinter from my finger, and I was getting increasingly worried about it. I had nightmares about gangrene and disgusting tropical diseases. The splinter went straight down into the flesh at the first joint of my right index finger. I could see a small black dot in the hole, and had used a sterilised pin to fish around in an effort to hook it out, so far without success.

It was aching this morning, so, with gritted teeth, I plunged my finger into the almost boiling water, holding it there as long as I could. I poured on more Dettol, then dried my hand with a clean towel. Finally, I wrapped a piece of clean, freshly ironed cotton around my finger. Satisfied that I had at least for the moment staved off a germ invasion, I put away my Little Nurse kit, and returned to my position by the open door.

Valsala at last, made a sudden appearance around the side of the house, looking very nice in her beautiful red sari. I was suddenly and painfully aware of my T shirt and cotton skirt, both of which have seen better days. She looks beautiful, and as usual, quite radiant. I note that she is wearing a small amount of gold on ears, neck and wrist.

I am used to seeing her dressed in the simple house dress as worn by all the village women here. It is a most unbecoming garment, and looks no more and no less than a Western night-dress, with its frill around the shoulders and across the chest, long sleeves and skirt all in one. She smiled widely at me, I complimented her on her appearance. She acknowledged my praise with clasped hands and a bob of the head, a most beautiful gesture of thanks without one whit of servility about it. Then, gesturing for me to follow, she set off at a fair pace, barely leaving me time to lock the door before hurrying after her.

As there is only one key, I hoped that we will be back before Jack, who had taken it into his head to track down some eye ointment for me. For my part, I was not sure at that stage whether could I trust Indian medicine, so, when or if, he found some, I knew I would then have to make the decision as to whether to use it or not. I had suffered so much with this eye problem and for so long, that I felt sure it would never be cured. In fact, two of the remedies prescribed at home had actually made the situation worse. I was merely holding the condition at bay. The medication I used blurred my vision, so that I saw India through a smeary haze of ointment. I know Jack had my best interests at heart, and I really don't want to fall out with my best friend, but he does sometimes find it hard to understand how I feel about some things.

Valsala and I pause at the edge of the hot road. I knew she understood more English than the two or three words she occasionally spoke, so I asked,

"Bus-Trivandrum?"

She nodded, and hurried across the road. Once safely under the shade again, our walk became more leisurely. As we walked along everyone we passed by greeted Valsala. The words "Angleesh ledee" featured in each encounter, and I was fully aware that I was once again the centre of everyone's attention. I smiled at everyone, and greeted them, and they smiled warmly at me, nudging each other and giggling. I am still not quite sure what our final destination was to be, as the road we were on would lead us to the local market and also to the bus stop in Pachalloor village proper.

We hurried through the busy market and joined the small crowd of people at the bus stop beyond. Of course! I should have realised! This was to be Valsala's big day out in Trivandrum. After all, she WAS wearing her best sari and whatever gold was not in hock at the moneylenders. (Or was that a mere Kardy fabrication? Him saying he had sold her gold for the house.)

Since we had arrived, we had not known Vas to go further than her parent's house or to the local clinic when the youngest child had his polio vaccination. She was obviously going to make the most of the opportunity for a visit to the big city! "Good for you, Vas," I thought admiringly. No wonder everyone we had met on the road had stopped and questioned her; no wonder she looked even more pleased with life than usual today! Not only was there the prospect of a party, and visit to Trivandrum, but she also had in tow an "Angleesh ledee ."

Once on the bus, the interest in me continued, and Valsala proudly presented her new companion to all. I was not for a second going to deny this delightful lady her moment of glory, and so I performed to the best of my ability, answering the myriad monosyllabic queries of "Name?" "From?" from the women. I admired and petted all the babies. This, to the very evident gratification of everyone. The crowded bus had taken on a festive air, jammed close and shouting over each other and chatting together, as all we women were at the back, as is the norm.

I was almost sorry when we reached Trivandrum. Valsala took my hand to assist me down from the bus. She kept hold of my hand as we walked to the roadside, a look of concern on her face. She pointed at the rushing streams of traffic, and held my hand more firmly in her tiny brown one. She was taking her role as my protector very seriously, so I allowed her to guide me safely across the busy dual carriageway, the gentle pressure of her hand indicating when I was to stand or walk. Hurrying towards the Chalai bazaar, we stopped for refreshment at a chai stall. Valsala insisted on paying for this treat, just as she had insisted on paying the bus fare. It appeared to give her a great deal of pleasure to be able to play the hostess. I liked her more with every passing moment. I had been a little concerned that our lack of a common language would make this a somewhat arduous trip. This lack however, had not caused any problems at all, and we had communicated with smile, gesture and mime very easily. I hoped she was enjoying my company as much as I was enjoying hers. She is an attractive woman, totally dedicated to her family. I treasure a photograph of her, where, instead of looking at the camera, her whole attention is focussed on the child in her arms, and the toddler at her feet. She has a look of such pride and devotion in this photograph, it tells me all I need to know about the genuine character of this woman. A little of this devotion has been temporarily diverted today to her English companion, and she cares for my welfare in these strange surroundings with as much attention as she would give to her children.

I know she can neither read nor write, so she carried the shopping list like some talismanic charm, clutched in one hand throughout our journey. She presented it with due ceremony to one of the many shopkeepers whose premises line the narrow, twisting lanes around the bazaar. She was in her element. She inspected the various bags of rice, rejecting some, approving others. She looked at the various spices, sniffing and pinching between her fingers. She discussed at some length, the flour the trader offered her. Finally satisfied, her mound of purchases was packed into a large sack. The flour, ghee, spices, rice and other items almost filled it and it was much heavier than I had anticipated. I began to wonder just how many people were coming to the party. Valsala hefted the large sack onto her hip, despite my protestations and offers of help, and hurrying away, left me to pay the bill. I hurried after her, and caught her up just in time to see her order a young man help her lift the weighty sack onto her head. This accomplished, she strode along, avoiding the litter and rubbish, seemingly able, like all the ladies here in their pretty saris, to float above the mess in the streets. I could only trot along behind her tiny figure, feeling very large and useless. She seemed to be heading for the bus station, but I decided to have none of this. If we caught a bus back home, she would have a long walk at the other end, and I was convinced she would not allow me to take my share of the burden. I touched her arm and indicated a taxi parked nearby. An expression of worry crossed her face, "Please,

I pay!" I reassured her, and was rewarded with another of her brilliant smiles. Without more ado, she loaded the sack into the rickshaw, and climbed in after it. I followed her. She seemed delighted with the rare treat of a rickshaw ride, and alternately chatted to the driver or smiled happily at me. When we arrived at the track leading to the house, we were met by her eldest child, a boy. He seemed to have been instructed to wait for her, or maybe it was just luck that he was hanging around at that moment. However, he proudly took the heavy sack from his mother, knees buckling under the weight, and staggered off down the track with it, his mother offering a steadying hand from time to time. I followed more slowly, deep in thought. The whole operation had taken barely two hours. I had hoped that Valsala and I would perhaps take a walk around Trivandrum, have a cup of tea in a cafe. I had wanted to extend her treat, make it worth having gone to the trouble to dress so nicely for the occasion. I wondered vaguely whether my clothing hadn't matched her standards, and she'd been ashamed to be seen with me. I decided that this was nonsense, there had to be another reason. People here were generally very polite, and seemed to accept that Western dress could sometimes be rather eccentric in comparison to their own. Somehow, I felt, the whole thing had been taken out of my hands.

When I arrived at the house, Valsala, Deepu, and the sack were nowhere to be seen. Nor was there any sign of Jack, so I set about wrapping the gifts for the Lucky Dip. These were mostly the brightly coloured glass bracelets which seemed to be very popular, and sweets. I hoped I had bought enough little token gifts for everyone, and that our guests would understand that they were no more than that, a little token reminder of what I hoped would be a memorable occasion. It turned out to be that, but not exactly as planned.

I'd just finished wrapping the last gift and had dropped it into the basket when Kadhikan appeared. I eyed him warily. His appearances usually meant I had to dip into my purse, and like Jack, I was beginning to get a little tired of his continuous demands.

"Hi." I said, trying to sound welcoming.

"Jack, where Jack?" he asked, peering around the room as if I had Jack secreted somewhere in that large and relatively bare space.

"Back soon." I replied.

"Lights for party. Little lights!" he began, smiling in that way I knew would end up with a request for rupees. "I fix only two hundred rupees!"

Yep, I knew it! True to form as ever. I had bought lots of candles to illuminate the roof, but Kadhikan had had a bright idea too, one, which of course, involved rupees. From behind his back he produced a tatty string of fairy lights.

"I have more!" he enthused. "Put in trees." I agreed that it was a good idea, and would look very nice, very festive. Privately, I thought, "Fine, but why does every bright idea cost quite so much?"

Sighing deeply, I handed over the 200 rupees, and he disappeared.

The "lighting engineer" appeared and proceeded to wire up the lights, using my sellotape to join the pieces of wire. I stopped watching at this point, cringing mentally at the thought of imminent disaster. Somehow, by means of a rickety bamboo ladder, and lots of shouting, the lights were fixed to the trees around the roof, and it only took four attempts to get the bulbs to light. I was instructed to come onto the roof to admire the effect, which was spoilt by the fact that it was still broad daylight, and it was therefore impossible to tell just how bright these little lanterns would be after dark. Everyone else was pleased however, so I congratulated them on their expertise. As usual, a small crowd had gathered to oversee the proceedings, the same people, I was sure, that would be present at the evening's entertainment. I did note that each individual bulb appeared to be wrapped in a small piece of coloured paper, which I felt would ignite some time during the festivities, and would no doubt add to the gaiety of the proceedings.

Meanwhile, cook had arrived and so had Jack. Cook is a bright young man, with a good command of the English language. He reassured us that he is more than competent to cook for us, as he cooks at the golf club. We were suitably impressed, and felt that he at least could be left to his own devices.

Jack filled me in on his day, as we supervised the provision of a table for the cook. The main thing he had to tell me was that he had been unable to track down any Lacrilube for my sore eyes or its exact Indian equivalent. He had however, bought a few bottles of beer, which he secreted in our rooms. Feeling that we could leave everyone to it for the time being, we shut ourselves in, and cracked open a beer while it was still cool from the refrigerator at the government liquor store. He had severely restricted the number of beer bottles, we were not proposing to have a bunch of drunks rioting on the roof, falling over the edge, or worse, peeing over the parapet on to my washing below. We agreed that cook should have a bottle of beer — his was a hot and sweaty task, and he had impressed us with his cheerful manner and proclamation of expertise. The other two bottles were ours! And we finished them off in no time. Suitably lubricated internally, we set about a final run through of our party piece, a nonsense song whose first line is "There's a hole in my bucket, dear Liza."

This seemed to be an appropriate ditty under the circumstances, and I felt sure that most of the women would be able to relate to it. They spoke no English, but I hoped that the mimes and props would make the meaning clear. We proposed to make our musical debut after everyone had eaten, in order to encourage others to demonstrate their own local village songs and dances. Our imaginations ran away with us, and we decided that this party was going to be the high spot of our expedition. So in fine fettle, dressed in our best (for best read cleanest) clothes, we ventured out to check on progress.

People were hovering about, just beyond our line of full vision, in the trees, at the gates of neighbouring courtyards, and on the roof. There seemed to be a problem. We asked cook. "No chairs." he informed us. OOPS. Major oversight. We asked him to ask our neighbours if they could provide their own chairs, as we only had four. Some quick fire Malayalam ensued and dark shapes scurried off into the gathering gloom, to reappear moments later with a rich and varied assortment of chairs.

There were plastic ones, wooden ones, tubular metal ones with plastic seats, broken ones, old ones and new ones — sufficient chairs to accommodate at least half of the slowly growing assembly. I threw myself into party mode, trying desperately to be the model hostess, in the continuing absence of Kardy and Valsala. I discovered Valsala helping the cook, and she smilingly refused to join the group on the roof to mingle with her guests. Kardy's whereabouts remained a mystery, and would do so as it turned out, until the end of the evening.

The roof was now taking on a festive air. The fairy lights shed some illumination on the scene, but I am very glad I had the foresight to place candles in strategic positions, particularly at the edge of the roof where the parapet was unfinished. I had visions of some unfortunate child plunging over the edge into the darkness below. The candles also lit up the large table, which Jack had so painstakingly constructed from bricks and the base of a double bed. You never would have known. His ingenuity never ceases to amaze me. The roof was rapidly filling up, and large numbers of well-scrubbed children were looking at me expectantly. I started a conversation with the nearest one, but beyond the "What is your name?" routine, we were unable to understand each other. Each child had to go through the routine, the shy ones being propelled forward from the rear to receive the benediction from the white lady. Our conversational pieces exhausted, I resorted to handing out sweets. Sweets and children disappear with amazing rapidity. I guess they had recited their English lesson, received their reward, and then felt free to leave.

Cook now appeared, and ushered Jack and I to a small plastic table set to one side of the large table, which had two chairs set beside it. We had been watching its preparation with some trepidation, and now we were sure that the evil portent we had felt was not our imagination. Cook's next words confirmed our worst suspicions.

"Guests of Honour!" He proclaimed loudly. "Please sit."

Oh no. This wasn't on our agenda. We wanted informality, bonhomie, and jollifications with our neighbours. A chance to mix and get to know people, have a little fun and relaxation. We resisted. He insisted. We looked around, feeling hunted down and caught in our own net. It seemed that the entire village had assembled on the roof, and were waiting eagerly for the sacrifice. Jack made one last desperate plea. "Everyone, sit, eat, enjoy yourselves!" No one moved. Cook was more insistent. "Guests of Honour! You must sit and eat first!"

We looked at each other. Jack and I knew that we were constantly observed. Whenever we ate a meal in a cafe, we were subjected to the intense scrutiny of at least two pairs of eyes. We were always horribly embarrassed and struggled to ignore it as we tried to understand that for most people here, we were rather unusual, something out of their daily routine, to be talked about over a few beers or at home in the evening. But this was something else. It seemed that the entire village were going to watch us eat. Furthermore, it seemed to us, no one else would eat until we had done so.

"I feel like an exhibit in a zoo!" I wailed mournfully to Jack.

"Bloody chimp's tea party, more like!" He grinned.

"Or a King's food taster, testing for poison." I laughed bleakly, picking up the humour of the situation. Cook made one more attempt.

"I have made a special meal for you," he cajoled.

We could do no more than surrender gracefully. Cook gestured that I was to sit. Jack followed suit, and a collective sigh went up from the crowd.

"I think they thought we were going to renege, and they weren't going to get any dinner after all." Jack whispered. The situation finally hit me as being ludicrous, and comic. I started to giggle, and waving my hand to the assembled masses, I made a formal speech of welcome, struggling to contain my laughter.

"Good evening ladies and gentlemen," I intoned in my best received pronunciation, a la BBC Home Service, "welcome to our New Year's Do!" I continued. Jack was chuckling mightily.

"Regent of India and his lady, eh? Who'd have thought it?" The assembled populace looked a little more relaxed, and some of them smiled encouragingly at us. Cook had disappeared, to fetch our special dinner, we hoped. We were starving, neither of us had had time to eat all day.

We had watched cook preparing the parottas, and had been fascinated by his expertise with blobs of dough which, with a few deft turns and throws, he had transformed into wafer thin pancakes. These had then been twirled around so fast that we had been unable to follow the movements, and had suddenly appeared as small, thick, coiled cakes, which were then placed on a hot griddle to cook. He had made literally hundreds of these, and we were looking forward to a feast of beef curry and lots of parottas. We looked expectantly across the roof to the head of the stairway. "Here he comes!" I said, my mouth watering. "Just ignore the watching eyes, and tuck in," I advised Jack.

"You bet I will. I'm so hungry now I could eat a scabby horse."

"You may well be doing just that," I laughed, "we've no guarantee of the provenance of this beef."

"OOH, there's posh, provenance eh! Are you saying this could be horse?"

"It could be anything. Come to think of it, I haven't seen any horses at all yet."

"No, they have eaten them all!"

With this, Cook arrived at the table, bearing two plastic plates each with a small amount of beef curry and one small, flat, cooked piece of dough. We looked at it in amazement, surely we were going to get more than this to eat, where were the thick, fluffy parottas he'd been cooking for the last three hours?

We looked at Cook questioningly.

"Special meal for you," he said, indicating the half a tomato sliced engagingly into a pretty flower shape, with two small pieces of cucumber lying sadly beside it. I suppose it did look very nice, but what we wanted was a proper meal, something substantial, some MEAT. We had eaten vegetarian for weeks, and were desperate for a little protein in the form of MEAT. We thanked Cook, and sighing deeply, took our first bite. It was delicious. We looked up to find cook, surrounded by the entire village, looking on silently, waiting hopefully.

"It is absolutely delicious." We cried enthusiastically, in the hopes that he would replenish our plates double quick.

The two or three mouthfuls we had taken had almost emptied our plates. With a smile of satisfaction, Cook withdrew.

"Please" we shouted, "Everyone, sit down, eat."

And finally, the men sat down. Strangely the women still stood, talking quietly amongst themselves. I indicated that they should sit also. They stared back blankly, uncomprehending.

"What's up with them?" I asked Jack.

"Dunno, " he said, desperately wiping his plate with a morsel of dough, trying to extract the last fraction of flavour,

"Maybe it's always men first here." He gave up on his plate, and looked round for more. I had finished mine, too, and was staring hungrily at the mounds of food being served to our quests.

"There seems to be plenty." I ventured. "Let's ask for another plateful."

Our pleas went unnoticed, Cook's English deserted him and he seemed suddenly unable to understand the word "More." We began to regret the beer we had given him, and the beers we had drunk, which had made us even hungrier. I began to feel angry — I'm never at my best with a rumbling stomach.

"Where's that blasted Kardy?" I finally exploded. "It's bound to be his fault!"

"Oh, come on Queenie, he can't be blamed for everything!"

"Sorry. Yeah, you're right. I'm just so hungry." I moaned.

"When everyone has been served, he's sure to have some left." Jack tried to comfort me. It was now the ladies' turn to be fed, and they and the children made themselves comfortable around the huge table. They smiled happily at us, then got on with the business of eating and feeding the children. The men had vanished, so I got up and walked to the edge of the roof to look over. I could see one or two stragglers disappearing into the gloom.

"They've gone!" I called to Jack, completely taken aback. Realising that the women might also do the same, I fetched the Lucky Dip basket from the other side of the roof, and began to distribute the little parcels around the table, wishing each lady a Happy New Year. I felt no compunction about interrupting their meal, after all they had watched closely every mouthful I had taken, and I began to realise that English manners have nothing to do with Indian manners. As each woman finished her meal, and seconds and thirds, just like the men, they got up to leave. Very soon, only Jack and I were left on the roof. Valsala was last to finish her meal, as she had been helping cook, and had smilingly ignored all my earlier pleas for her to join us. She finished eating, smiled brightly at us, and left. All that was left on the roof was the memory of the ladies in their best bright saris, some guttering candles, and us. And our growling stomachs. Cook put in a final appearance.

"Gifts were gold?" he asked me.

"Gold?" I echoed, completely confused.

"Ladies want to know, were gifts gold and what is meaning of LUCKY DIP?" He repeated, indicating the now empty basket. I followed his pointing finger, and was just in time to see an elderly man with a small child, rummaging about in the bottom of the basket, to finally extract one last parcel. Without a word or even a glance, he, parcel and child disappeared down the steps and into the darkness. I had watched the same man come back several times to do exactly the same. I hoped by now he had completed his collection. I turned my attention back to the cook.

"No", I said, "the gifts weren't gold, they were just a small token to wish everyone a happy New Year. I could not possibly afford to buy gold for all those people."

He shrugged and didn't appear to believe us but continued.

"Ladies very happy. Yes, Ladies very happy. Very nice party, they ask me to tell you."

Somewhat mollified, I thanked him for passing on the message, and for all his hard work.

"Is any food left?" I enquired hopefully.

"Food all gone." He said proudly.

"Well, I'm not surprised, it was excellent food," Jack chipped in, "here take this, mate, you've worked really hard tonight." and he slipped Cook three hundred rupees.

It seemed only fair, he had done the majority of the work, and we couldn't have done it without him. But I still wanted something else to eat, all the local shops were now closed, and there was absolutely nothing to eat downstairs. Damn and blast and lots of expletives, I muttered to myself.

"Why does everything we touch turn into some kind of farce?" I asked Jack. He looked glum, and I was sorry, because I knew we would have felt better about the situation with full stomachs. He was suffering just as much as I was. Cook was very happy with his wages, thanked us profusely, and left.

We were alone with the candles, the paper "HAPPY NEW YEAR" sign I had painstakingly cut out and coloured, and the fairy lights, which were now no longer coloured red, blue, green and yellow. Due to the paper having, as I suspected, become singed, they were now all glowing a dull yellow brown. We sat at our Honoured Guest table, and regarded each other morosely.

"Shall we sing?" I suggested in a small sad voice. Jack began to chuckle, and in moments we were roaring with laughter.

"Well, at least they enjoyed it!" He gasped, finally.

A movement caught my eye at the other end of the roof. I peered into the gloom, nudging Jack to turn and look. Jack also peered into the gloom.

"Oh, guess what? It's the invisible man. I wonder where he's been lurking all evening?" he asked, cynically. Then, louder, much louder, he called across to the dim figure.

"Hey, Kardy. Where have you been? Why didn't you come to the wonderful party?"

Jack's sarcasm was lost on Kadhikan, but nevertheless he continued in the same vein.

"We missed you! You would have really livened things up! Where have you been? You missed all the fun!" Kadhikan crept forward out of the dimness at the top of the stairs. We saw that he was accompanied by two equally disreputable looking men. All of them were weaving slightly. I began to feel uneasy. They were also rather menacing. However, as they came closer and into the light, the air of menace dissolved, and they looked exactly what they were - a bunch of piss-heads.

"Good party, sir, madam? All good? Very nice?" Questioned Kardy, his voice slurred.

"It looks like the party you were at was better." Retorted Jack. Puzzled, Kardy protested.

"No party, sir. Kardy no party. Little drink, little smoke my friends." He turned suddenly, in order to include the two villainous looking characters, and almost overbalanced. Giggling, he let himself down very carefully into a chair.

"Jack, you got beer?" He asked.

"No I haven't." said Jack, rather shortly. Kardy looked disappointed, and muttered something in Malayalam to his fellow drunks. They glanced at us, and then smiled ingratiatingly.

"Little beer?" asked Kardy again, hopefully. "Not even little beer!"

The three men sat at the big table, and regarded us silently. We were just beginning to wonder how long this would go on, when a fourth man appeared out of the darkness. He was no less the worse for wear than the first three, but he did speak pretty good English, if a little blurred by alcohol and substance. He greeted us warmly, as old friends, and launched off into a potted autobiography. His quick fire, but occasional slurred delivery was sometimes hard to follow, but we understood from him that he is a very well educated man, (in his own estimation) with a BA. Or maybe it was an MA, in psychology, or same such. He now lived simply, he said, had given up riches to live the simple life. He sold ayurvedic medicines for a living. We began to lose what little interest we had at this point, feeling sure that it was just another sales pitch. Surprisingly, it wasn't, or at least, he did not pursue the matter. He went on to discuss astrology, before finally indicating the three men, who had been watching in admiration as their colleague conversed easily with us in our own language.

"These men," he informed us, drunkenly with an air of imparting some vital piece of information, "are singers!" Kadhikan interpreted this for his two companions, and they all nodded vigorously.

"In temple." Kadhikan added for further confirmation of their unique skills in the performing arts. This was marginally more interesting, and although not exactly what we had envisioned when we had practised our own party piece, we knew it was the nearest we were going to get to any form of cultural exchange. The three suddenly set up a mournful wailing, rather startling us. Fearing that they were in pain, I looked for assistance to our ayurvedic doctor. He, however, was sitting, eyes closed in ecstasy, and/or substance and following the dreadful wailing sound with great pleasure. We sat back, and listened politely.

The wailing stopped abruptly and the doctor/salesman interpreted for us. This we found was quite helpful. It was not, as we had thought, a song of lost love or other distress, but a joyous anthem to the moon. We wondered what a sad song must sound like. Our educated friend had no sooner finished his interpreting, however, than our songsters were at it again. This song, no less mournful to our ears, seemed to last an awfully long time. We were beginning to fidget long before its close, and every mosquito within a thousand yards was targeting us both, it seemed. The wailing finally wavered to a finish, and our MA (or BA) launched into an interminable and incomprehensible interpretation of its content. He stopped suddenly, sensing that he perhaps did not have our full attention. "Food?" he enquired. We were not sure whether he was offering or asking, so we suggested that he stepped downstairs to enquire.

"And bring us some if you find any." We called after his retreating back. We waited hopefully for his return. He was gone for some time. Enough time to eat at least one plate of food. He finally returned.

"Well?" We asked.

"Sorry, food all gone." He said, as he sat down. We felt sure we knew who had had the last, but we couldn't prove it. I glared balefully at him, wishing him, and Kardy and the Wailers, far enough away. I was thoroughly fed up with the whole business, particularly as Kardy and Co. had suddenly developed a nasty habit of spitting over the parapet. I knew my washing was hanging below there. I was not sure what to do. If I asked them not to spit over the parapet, would they misunderstand, and start spitting on the roof? If I went down and tried to remove my washing from the line, I would be in the direct line of fire. I decided that this was one dilemma too many for the evening, and said nothing, hoping that tomorrow would reveal not too many red betel nut stains on my best white t-shirt and Jack's underpants. Jack and I were both sick and tired of the whole business, so we wished our guests "Goodnight" and prepared to leave. They were astonished. It is only eleven forty-five! Why are we leaving so early? The night is young, let's party! We gazed at them with mounting hatred, as they tried to make us stop.

"Many more beautiful songs." said our educated man. "Please, stay and listen." We suspected that we would have to listen anyway, we can hear everything that goes on around us when we are in the house. We made our excuses and left, walking carefully down the badly lit stairs and into our room below. I felt malicious, and with a small cry of triumph, deprived them of light. Most of the candles had burnt out, and now I had unplugged the fairy lights.

"That'll teach 'em!" I said savagely.

Jack laughed at my childish attempts at sabotage.

Chapter 20

Surprisingly, despite our rumbling stomachs, we slept very well; it seemed nights ago since the four o'clock explosions had last disturbed us. We were both in good spirits, mainly because Valsala produced some fat pink bananas for breakfast. So we had banana and custard and fresh coffee.

"What's on, apart from painting the walls, Queenie?"

"Well, we could look for lino in Trivandrum, and we need more ground coffee." She replied.

"Yeah, let's go, I'm ready." I said, grabbing the eye lotion tube. Queenie beat me to the door, opened it, and there he was, the small and limp ghost-like figure of Kadhikan.

"Madam, please look, please check." He said, pushing the advertising leaflet into her hand, the very one we had suggested he might need, the one we laid out for him on an earlier occasion, about a month ago, in English of course. She took it from him, and looked through the spelling to re-discover that the already corrected mistakes from the last time she checked his or the printers work were there again. Plus a new motif had also suddenly appeared. "What's the seaplane for, Kardy?" I asked.

"Printer, he say best, make look good for customer."

"It's a lie Kardy, tell the printer you are doing boat trips, NOT aeroplane trips." she said with a half raised voice. Queenie crossed it out saying, "Take it back. Make the printer do it again properly. See you later. Let's get out of here." Off we went quickly before Kadhikan had the chance to come up with the "poor man" begging routine again.

It was a greyish overcast day, and therefore cooler. It's strange how thirty-five degrees seems twice as hot as thirty. I was thankful that it was cooler.

Trivandrum was less smoky, and the female sweepers had made a big difference, moving the stinking mass of months of rubbish.

So once past the line of beggars and taxi drivers, each tagging on behind us for fifty yards, we had a clear run to a pharmacy.

"Eye lotion." I said.

"They won't have it," Queenie replied.

"Let's ask." They didn't have it, Queenie was right and neither did the half-dozen others that we asked, but now we were near the Fort Hospital.

"Solman the tour office manager in Kovalam says there's a great place near here, modern with an eye specialist."

"A clinic?"

"A hospital."

"I don't trust them."

"You don't have to, just ask for eye lotion." Queenie looked stubborn.

"Oh, come on let's at least try." I said in near despair.

We arrived outside what looked like a Holiday Inn, with a sign saying 'FORT HOSPITAL' over a large red cross.

"Doesn't look bad." I suggested. Queenie was in her annoying and negative mood, and said,

"It'll be too expensive."

"I'll pay for it then, just let's get in."

A very smart young man wearing a deep blue suit approached, smiling.

"Good morning, madam, sir. My name is James. How can I help you?" I took out the empty tube that had contained the much-needed Lacrilube eye ointment. "We need this or an exact copy."

"Very good! Please step this way."

The reception area was like the VIP lounge at some oil-rich states' airport, with no one in it except us. He took us across the wide marble floor, past the white leather settees and tubular chrome glass-topped tables with matching ashtrays, to the mixed green onyx reception desk.

"Yes, what can I do?" asked the fashion model receptionist. Queenie took the tube off me, thank God! She was taking an interest at last! She explained the situation, and as promised I paid for a consultation with an eye specialist. A whole forty rupees.

The same young man took us up to the first floor in the silently gliding lift. Along the wide white marble corridor, to the consulting room, and there was the female eye specialist, who examined Queenie's eyes asked questions and prescribed ointment. Queenie tried it out that evening and for the next few days. It worked, the eye lesion healed, and to this day Queenie has not had a recurrence of eye pain. I claimed my forty rupees back out of the communal fund!

After leaving Fort Hospital agreeing that it hadn't been such a bad experience after all we wandered happily around the city.

As anticipated we found a shop selling PVC floor covering and negotiated a price, which was about a third of the price of the same thing in the UK. It was imitation white tile with a small blue diamond motif, cushioned and very smart. We chatted about priorities, decided to complete the painting first, and being satisfied with the location and price of the covering left its actual purchase for another day. There was a method to this apparent madness!

We had two Thali meals for twenty-five rupees each, the meals were a selection of six small and differently spiced portions of vegetables or meats served up with a huge dollop of rice. Thali meaning mixed or various.

We enjoyed this tasty selection, paid up and left saying we would return again another day. We found our way back home later in the afternoon.

Having discussed and decided to enjoy the rest of the day at a leisurely pace, we grabbed our swimming costumes, and strolled towards the sea, through the grove, and crossed the lagoon by means of a dugout canoe, this operated by a native man complete with loincloth who appeared to be about eighty years old.

His canoe I suppose served as a pension plan, based on the reality of work until you drop. What else could he do, what else was there? Not a lot, we suspected.

We kicked up the white sand as we ran quickly to the waves. Looking back at the grove across the lagoon, bright specks of red and yellow flashed here and there, people washing clothes, swimming. Palms swaying, as usual it looked like a piece of paradise.

Sea eagles swooped down to pick fish from the waves. Flocks of black crows flew down from time to time, then perched themselves on the wooden edges of the large canoe-like fishing boats waiting at anchor. The water was cool here, perhaps because of an underwater shelf leading down to the deep. A few steps into the sea and the bottom was gone. A group of small boys were throwing small circular hand nets into the sea, and pulling them back.

On this occasion, we were left alone, unhampered by the inquisitiveness of locals. We ambled along, to and fro, and I considered how on earth could this beauty, freedom and space, be part of the horror that lay just four hundred yards inland, with its chaos and recklessness. Surely, I thought, there must be somewhere in this country where a person could live, that has the beauty of this place, and where people behave in a more considered way toward each other. Or maybe not!

The predicament associated with "Kardy," the house, his laziness and the constant begging, was taking its toll on both of us and I wondered how much more of this Queenie or I would be able to take. As we wandered back to the ferry I knew it would all get a lot worse especially if I was to pressure "K" into honouring any part of his contract with us, which I felt I must complete, my part at least. I made my mind up that I must at least keep trying. I did not believe that allowing him to get away with not meeting his obligations in the way that K was trying to do, was acceptable. By a reasoned argument, maybe, but by evading, ducking and diving, no!

It sends the wrong message out to other people, that people who acquiesce and try to help are to be made fools of. His demands stood to compromise his own long term benefit, by driving us away and not completing his project, thereby ruining his chance to better his family. The completion of this project was near, and yes, it was me not "K," that was pushing to bring it to a conclusion. I could leave now, I'd arguably done enough already. It's all a damn sight better than it ever was. It was plain to see that the only real purpose we served now was to finance "K" on a daily basis.

"K" could finish his project if he needed to, but would he, I didn't think so, what he would do is use the fact that I didn't finish it to "Western standards" as an excuse to offer others for not using the house to earn a living for himself and his family.

I was also too aware that even when I did finish it there was no guarantee that he would do as he said he wanted to initially. Let's face it, his performance so far did not at all indicate that he had the will, nor the energy, to do anything else than to wander about scrounging here and there.

Yes I would keep my side of the deal, I would finish the project, I would not be happy with myself if I wasted the effort, and finance already expended. I would find it extremely difficult to walk off the job, especially so near completion. One day he may wake up and see what he has around him, and then carry on and make a success of it and himself.

My gloom at this point was happily interrupted. "Jack, Jack, look, look over there." There was a long, thick python-like snake, slithering away from us in the undergrowth. What a sight.

I had forgotten to leave a copy of a new draft agreement I had drawn up with K for his perusal. I had included a wish by me to visit his house at three months' notice at a time when there would be no expectation of paying guests, and for a length of time of up to two months in any year and to move out at a time when a paying guest was imminent. Also this arrangement was to be valid for five years. I would make a point to make sure he had a copy and discussed it with me.

"Jack, he won't agree to this! Even if he does he won't honour it, you know he won't, why bother ?"

"Yes Queenie I know! But it's up to him to argue his point of view. It's about time he made some contribution and realizes he can't have everything he wants for nothing at all, and let's face it, Queenie, I doubt if we'd even want to come back here, but he needs to know that he has to stick to at least some aspect of the original agreement, at least.

You remember Queenie, he said as part of his opening gambit that we could stay at the house anytime we wanted to. I am only asking to stay in the quiet season, and only then for a month or so at a time, like now.

We arrived back at the house. Of course, he wasn't there, so I left a note pinned on his door -"K ! Need to see you, urgently, 7 am."

Why 7 am? Truth is I just felt like being a pain.

We hurried off to Kovalam to see the gang. Now that the roof and the table had been totally completed and tested, Ben might like to visit with Christina, so we went armed with offers of evening meals for four.

We finally located Prabu, who looked awful! He was very welcoming, and delighted to see us again, but his eyes were red, his usual cheery expression was taken over by strain. I remembered he had had great losses in his life, he had not fully recovered. I talked him into having a beer, he became more animated. He and Queenie have a kind of rapport, so I left them there to their esoteric conversations, while I talked of more coarse and material subjects with John and Gunda, Ben and Christina.

Christina is what I could best describe as nutty, and on the high-pitched side, with a fair helping of confusion, a bit like a fourteen-year-old. She's in love! I could remember the feeling well.

"Jack! Would you like to visit Ashram?" asked Prabu who was by now a little inebriated, but at least he did not look quite so poorly.

"Don't really know, Prabbers. I'm not really into spiritual stuff, I am more of a materialist. Queenie is though. She'll go with you."

"Maybe we can find a remedy for your asthma. You know we have ayurvedic doctors and hospital?"

I didn't want to upset a well-meaning man ,"Yeah, all right then, why not? Maybe next week or the week after." Thinking, "Break for Queenie, also could be a wheeze."

We arrived back at the house to find Kadhikan waiting for us. He stepped out suddenly from behind a tree, and almost frightened the life out of us. "Jesus, Kardy!"

"I get note, Jack. What you want?"

"It's a bit late, Kardy, tomorrow will do."

"Yes sir, late. What is problem?"

"OK, hang on." Queenie had unlocked the door by this time and brought out the draft agreement. She put it in his hand.

"What this?" he asked.

"It's an agreement, Kardy. Can you read it?"

"Oh, yes, read OK. Wife illiterate." (He spoke the word very carefully, with a certain pride). "I read three languages."

"Oh, brilliant! Then read it, make any changes you want to it, and bring it back to me tomorrow."

"Why this agreement?"

"Because, Kardy," I explained carefully, just like the last time and the time before that. "You broke the last agreement we made last year. You did not spend the money on the agreed items. You spent it all on the roof and concrete structure so that means that I have to spend a lot more money and time, doing the things YOU should have done with the original money I sent you.

"So, this time, I need to have a legally binding agreement, with a lawyer to confirm that you agree to it, and that if you or I break the agreement, we will go to the court. I don't mind too much what it says, but I do need guarantees that you will allow us to stay here, in return for the money and effort that we have put into the house."

"Oh no Jack! I make rich you! Not agreement!"

"I don't understand, Kardy!" I turned to Queenie, "What's he saying?"

"Listen Jack, now I am poor man, but tourist come. You write your friends in Europe, tell them come Kardy house. Then I give you money, make you rich."

"No, Kardy! Definitely not! If I wanted to do that, I would buy my own house and do it. That is NOT what I wanted to do. I have built this place for you to run as a business, as you wanted. YOU, Kardy, NOT me! So I want you to look at this agreement and tell me how long we can stay, and when. Do you understand?"

"OK, I look tomorrow. I take to lawyer, he see."

"Great. Good idea. So how long will this take?"

"How long you stay here Jack?" Was his reply.

"I will go, Kardy, when I have finished the job that I came to do, and when you have made an agreement with me in front of a lawyer, and not before. So, when will you bring the agreement back to me?"

"I will come day after tomorrow, after see lawyer."

"OK, that's very good. It's late, we are tired, and are going to bed." And with that, I went in and closed the door. I told Queenie I was angry because I believed he knew exactly what was needed but he was a clever little toad.

"He is not getting away with it!" I muttered, trying to convince myself.

It was late; we were enjoying our hot chocolate before climbing in to our beds. A voice broke the silence outside.

"Mr Jack Mr Jack hello MR JACK!" The voice grew louder, who was that? It didn't sound like "K".

"HELLO MR JACK." It was getting louder, we looked at each other, then I finally gave in and went to the door. It was Sadanand, our Pink Flowers landlord from a few weeks ago in Kovalam. What was wrong, had something happened to our friends John and Gunda? Perhaps they had run off without paying the rent, or worse had an accident.

"Sorry Mr Jack you go to the bed?"

"Yes," I said "what's the problem?"

"Volleyball championship you must sponsor, big final for all the district many people see, you sponsor yes!"

"I don't know, don't know anything at all about volleyball."

"You guest of honour! Only one hundred rupees big event of the year Jack, one hundred rupees only! You will enjoy very much bring wife. She also she very much enjoy." There was no way out of it.

"Can you hear this?" I called to Queenie, "apparently you're my wife!"

"Give him the money and go to bed!"

He pushed the receipt book into my hand in such a way that had I not taken it, it would have dropped to the ground.

"OK, you win, when is it?" I asked.

"You sign here now, and here, and again." He ripped off the top original receipt and passed it over.

"You must come to the temple, you know Shastramaawi Temple, over other side of road, turn right. I meet you five thirty tomorrow, you must come. You must promise me you will come Mr Jack." He faded into the night.

"OK!" I shouted after him as he disappeared, one hundred rupees better off. I returned to my interrupted cocoa and bed.

Tomorrow arrived, neither of us knew what to expect at the volleyball championships, that in itself was exciting. Thankfully, it had become much cooler , the wind was gusting in from the sea, as it did before a downpour. "It's going to piss down." I said.

"Great stuff! Let's hope so," Queenie replied with a grin, "it'll add to the chaos." The trees were offering the occasional roar and rattle from on high. I quite liked Queenie's notion of an aquatic volleyball game,

sounded like fun. After all sports people do take themselves a bit too seriously, I thought.

(Unlike myself of course)

Up the track, down the road just a few yards, turn
left, no right, there it was. The temple. We approached
the entrance to the outside area, there were already a
couple of hundred people standing around the dusty
pitch. Queenie was the only female in attendance. We
were spotted, Sadanand came over to us beaming and
obviously pleased to see us.

"Good very good Mr Jack please come sit." He led us
to a long, narrow wooden table behind which six
smart crisp important looking people (males of
course) were sitting, sipping water with lemon out of
long clear glasses. By the time we reached them they
had left their seats and were standing to attention. We
were introduced to each person in turn; after shaking
our hands they resumed their seats.

This surely was indeed the Full Monty! I mused, as
two soft chairs were placed in line at the end of the
row of dignitaries. Sadanand reappeared with lemon
sodas and smiled sweetly.

"We are all very proud you have come sir, very
proud." I now realised I had been endowed with some
responsibility and I'd better start appreciating the
fact, cut out the flippancy even if it was mere self-chat.
My thoughts were blown away as an explosion shook
the earth, and fire-crackers exploded around us. The
gentleman seated next to Queenie leant over and explained that the old people believe that the explosions
chase away illness and bad spirits. I didn't laugh just

remarked, "How interesting." At which point I felt a hand under my arm pushing gently upwards, it was Sadanand urging me to my feet.

"Please you meet players". It was all happening quickly now, I needed to pay attention, think on my feet, I was being directed towards the players lined up and to attention each side of the net, twelve each side waiting in anticipation, for what!! OH YES! The Prince Maharajah routine! By now the whole crowd were into the slow hand clap. Clap, clap, clap, clap! I shook every player's hand firmly and sincerely. I voiced instantly dreamed up positive statements, smiling, "Have a good game, may the best team win, do your best, nice day for it". Clap, clap, clap! Until finally I completed the whole performance, turned and walked slowly back to my seat, at which HEP HOORAY sounded three times. I sat, considering that I had already had my hundred rupees worth.

I asked the gentleman who was seated next to me about the championship. He explained that this was the result of a year's eliminations and these two teams were the crème de la crème of teams, the best in Kerala. Probably the whole of India! "WOW", I hadn't appreciated this fact fully. A pistol shot rang out. The games began.

For those of us who have rarely taken an interest in, or even heard of volleyball, unlike the 84 million who play, and of course their supporters, a simple explanation of events may be useful. Those in the know please forgive any misrepresentations that may occur.

The game is played on a court not too dissimilar to a tennis court but there the similarity ends. A net is suspended ten feet above the ground and stretched across the centre of the court. There are twelve players per side, half of which are reserves, very confusing for an ignorant observer. It has no pre-determined overall time in play, the winners are decided on a best of five game basis with a two game lead to win a set, there are a plethora of rules that have developed, but I don't intend to go into them here.

The main object of the game is to score points by hitting the football-sized ball over this extremely high net in such a manner as to hit the ground on your opponent's side. This demands stealth, cunning, and force delivered all at the same time, or in various combinations. As you may have already imagined getting the ball over such a net and not having it returned with the same intent as it was delivered is no mean feat.

The skills by which the object of the game is achieved are remarkable, this has to be one of the most involving games devised or witnessed by man, or woman, not that there were as mentioned earlier, many women present at this particular rendezvous. The players, like ballerinas, fly through the air. The ball is tapped, patted, bounced, danced into position. Way above the net the most dynamic surge of energy from a team player crashes the ball downward into the opposing side. At this point three, four, or five players are airborne, the head and shoulders of the player who delivered the smash is far and away above the top of this ten-feet-high net, his nearest comrades seem suspended, awaiting the retaliation. Instantly, like lightning the ball is returned from the upwards thrust of an opponent's inside forearm smash, his team-mate anticipating this leaps up, overtaking the ball at its maximum height, crashes it in to the opposing sides' court, back where it started. A forward horizontal dive is executed three feet from the ground, clenched fists deflect the ball high into the air. This player having achieved his goal, drops into a forward roll, and into position for his next move. The ball meanwhile is immediately patted vertically downward into the other side, misses the net, hits the ground. A point scored.

This is a game of acrobatics, beauty, gymnastic elegance, trapeze with no wire, stamina and sheer power. All of this and more were exhibited at the Shastramaawi Temple. The green and gold tall guys against the green and pink short guys, the pirouettes against the gravity-defying bullets. What a contest. It lasted about an hour and a half, as a tie was not acceptable, this being a final in a championship. There were no signs of poverty in these men, lithe but not scrawny, big but not muscle-bound, weighty but not fat.

The game over, we waited for the speeches from the committee, the captain, the main sponsors — not me thank God! — the presentations and the photographs.

Caught up in the excitement of the game, I had been snapping away merrily with my little camera. I was sure I had some excellent action shots, and had saved a few frames for the presentation. The cup was presented by the owner of the Rockholme Hotel, the most swanky and most expensive accommodation in Kovalam. In fact the very place where our newly-wed friend, Johnson was head waiter. Strangers shook hands, asked the usual polite questions. Sadanand came over, beaming with pride.

"You give me pictures, yes?"

"Yes, sure, tomorrow. I'll get them developed."

"Thank you, Thank you. You can come to my house. You can see."

"Excellent idea." I replied. And having got a fairly good idea of where his house was, a mere five hundred yards from Kadhikan's, along certain explained tracks, I said goodbye. Queenie and I left, still bursting with enthusiasm.

"What a superb performance." We enthused, as we wandered the few yards back through the palms to Kadhikan's where we enjoyed a rare good reception of the BBC's World Service, showered, and went to sleep.

Early rise, short walk to the bus stop and away into Kovalam. I crossed the beach to the instant photograph developer, which in reality meant that a young man took the films to Trivandrum on his motorbike, waited an hour, and brought them back. A round journey of about three hours, whilst I paddled, drank lemon soda, enquired after Ben, whose trade had further declined. He told me, "Tourist plane land on Monday, so maybe Wednesday, tourists will come here. Today, Sunday, is not good." I sympathised, had tea with him. He was concerned, very worried in fact, that Christina was expecting too much of him.

"She is very nice, but she must go home soon." He complained.

"Absolutely!" I agreed. I gave him an order for three pairs of shorts, which cheered him up a bit. "I'll see you soon, maybe day after tomorrow." I said, as I left to pick up the pictures.

They were back. Brilliant! I had taken three rolls, so I knew I would have at least a dozen really good shots to take to Sadanand this afternoon. The pictures were good, brilliant dives, smashes and passing shots and of course, the presentation. I put the best twenty pictures with the negatives, into a pocket-sized album, ready to give to him. I made my way to see Queenie who was painting a deep blue seagull on a light blue sky that formed part of the house's interior decor.

"Should we nip over to take these 'pickies' and see Sadanand's house?"

"Yes, OK, as long as he doesn't want us to buy it off him." She only half joked.

The track he described was as he had said it would be, and it led us into a part of the palm forest we had not been in before. I suppose because the palms and the many other kinds of trees — we counted thirty-three kinds in all — are not planted in rows, and nature has evolved the area according to its own plan, all parts of the forest look different. It is therefore surprisingly easy to find one's way about. There were various clearings and houses on the way, but none had the half round tile on the roof which he had described to us earlier. Half round tiles sounded Mediterranean to me. Anything is possible in these parts. There are many remnants of past times, incursions and civilisations, why not Mediterranean.

There it was, the high, circular, palm leaf woven fence just as previously described. We walked around it, we couldn't see inside. We could see, and taste, smoke. The haze sat over the compound. It was, as you can probably imagine, quite dark on the ground, with shafts of blinding light penetrating the canopy here or there. A large, deep, loud bark, another and another invaded the silence. The guard dogs inside the compound had heard us.

"Hallo, hallo, hallo." We shouted, time and again, competing with the racket from the pack.

"I'm not going in there with those bloody things." I said to Queenie.

"Me neither." She agreed.

Just then, Sadanand appeared from around the outer curve of the fence.

"Mr Jack! Mrs Jack! How are you?"

We have the pictures." Queenie replied, and offered them to him.

"Oh please, you must come in. See my house."

"What about the dogs?" I asked. They had gone quiet by now.

"My son, he take them away. Come." He retraced his steps, pushed at a panel of the palm fence, it swung open, and was the entrance to the inner compound. This was mostly clear of vegetation, picked over by the chickens that roamed the ground. Three goats stood, perched statue-like on boulders, their horizontal, slit-like green pupils looked demonic, emphasised as they were by their short horns.

"Wait!" He half snapped.

We stood, while he bent to enter into the low doorway of this very large, single storey house.

The smoke emanating through the part thatched roof was thick and drifted in swathes around us. There was no wind. Smoke dusted the ground. It was almost silent again, apart from a small voice from inside the cottage, the occasional cluck, and the clack of bone on bone as two of the goats sparred. The strong smell of wood smoke penetrated my nostrils, then a rustle from above, and a soft breeze wafted the smoke to another part of the compound.

"Have a seat. Please sit." He was back, breaking the moment. He placed two battered bentwood straight backed chairs onto the earth.

"You like tea? Kerala tea? Very good, you like?"

"Yes fine, thank you. Very nice."

He left us again.

The house had a covered veranda. I could see a young woman moving into the house, and out again to the covered space, looking shyly from time to time in our direction, partly hiding in the shadows, offering a distant half smile. The house was once white, but algae had taken over leaving only grey-white patches amongst the green. The small ferns seemed to thrive on the surface of the house walls, and small pink flowers, clover-like growths, flourished alongside. A huge crack had evolved from the eaves to the ground, a few feet from the corner. The side elevation leaned outward. The half round tiles, which were covering this section of the roof, had become dislodged, and had slipped onto the ground and smashed.

Blue plastic sheeting covered some parts of the roof, and thatch the rest. This house, despite its size and large compound, was a mess. Worse than Kadhikan's had ever been. Like a dilapidated stately home it had, I felt sure, seen far grander times. Sadanand was not a poor man. He owned a very nice, well-built, clean property in Kovalam, from which he earned a living. He'd been a sergeant in the Indian Army for twenty or so years, and had, he told me, a good pension. Why, I could not help thinking, was he allowing his house to fall apart around him? He returned with a tray on which were two china cups of tea.

"Please you take." We took.

Queenie handed over the photographs.

"Very good pictures," He said, beaming. He was obviously happy with them, that was all I cared about. He was particularly impressed with the presentation pictures, smiling faces, shiny gold cup, and all that. The action pictures, the expressions on the player's faces, were merely given a glance, but the presentation pictures he liked very much and said so.

"Yes, they were very professional!"

"Is the young lady your wife?" Queenie enquired.

"No, Madam, daughter. She look after me. Mother, she die long ago. I have two sons also. One, you have met at Pink Flowers, other is here, he just go now for fish."

"How old is your house?" I asked.

"One hundred fifty years. Very old. I need new house. Is very broken. Also, monsoon, many mosquitoes. One day I make new house." We discussed the volleyball match. It is very interesting that someone like myself who knows so little about it, can appreciate the game. It is a positive reflection on the players. Sadanand agreed, and was pleased at my compliment.

I felt I was turning into an Indian, learning the arts of flattery and compliment. He didn't introduce us to his daughter, although we glimpsed her at a distance. We waved goodbye to her, she waved back. It was a strange encounter, one of many. We strolled back, finding our way to the backwater. We followed the shore up to Kadhikan's house.

Chapter 21

This had to be a painting day. It made sense that I should do the bathroom first, so after carrying in the chair and table, and balancing the one on top of the other, I attempted to, and later succeeded, in opening the first tin of paint after only ninety-five minutes. It was a moulded plastic, sealed, gallon size paint container, with no visible access point. The lid at the top — or was it the bottom? - was moulded over the sides and heat-sealed. A very strange affair. I gained access by rendering one of the newly purchased kitchen knives as hot as I could by placing it on the electric cooker plate. It took ages to heat up sufficiently to penetrate the flat surface of the lid. The plan I had in mind was thwarted by the discovery that to pour the paint through a hole pierced in the top, and then into a bucket, was impossible. The block of thick white sludge within was secreted not only in its rigid plastic outer, but also in a strong polythene bag inside the outer container. Consequently, the heating and cutting process took longer as the whole top had to be removed in order to extract the inner bag. This finally completed, the contents of the bag were not poured but shaken into the bucket. It was not quite solid, and certainly not liquid, nor consistent in texture. I looked at the instructions, of which there were a whole list printed in various languages. Plus, in English, "Add water to thin." The problem was not the shortage of instructions in English, but that they had been smudged into a blur. Nonetheless, "Add water" was good enough advice and after another 15 minutes trying cold and then warm water, I had a fairly good texture of emulsion paint. I added a smidgen of blue dye. And like magic, the dye had slipped through the molecules of white, and produced a glorious, strong, bright blue. With the able assistance of Queenie, I clambered up onto the chair. Bucket in one hand, brush in the other. It took two gallons of paint, i.e. six very thick coats to cover the ceiling, plus three days to apply to the small bathroom. No sooner had one thick coat been applied, than it was sucked through the cement. The first 3 coats virtually disappeared and only through a painstaking build up did the job look any good at all. And it did. More; it looked beautiful. Expensive, time-consuming, frustrating, but worth it. Learning from this experience, I decided that the next paint we bought would be different. Indeed different paint, different source. A day's search in Trivandrum brought to light eight gallons of conventional Crown plastic emulsion, known locally as distemper!! It worked! It was already coloured. Sunshine Yellow! on the tin. It certainly was. Plus a conventional means of getting at the paint, through a lid in the top. What more could we want? Sadly, however, the walls were not finished with the usual cement sheen, or some such application, which I learnt later acts as a sealer, it took another four days to complete the tiny kitchen — more than enough time to paint a whole house in the UK.

During this time Kadhikan had arrived with yet another proof of the leaflet, with some interesting new spelling mistakes, which Queenie corrected. No aeroplane motif. As we expected, no sign of an agreement, modified or otherwise. He did admire our persistence with the paintwork and said it was most beautiful, better than temple. A compliment indeed.

Queenie then set to work and turned the simple crude wooden structures into something resembling Habitat styled attractive furniture. She had made beige cotton curtains for the windows, which I hung from string. The whole place was looking a treat. Much, much better than the average tourist home or hotel. People would most certainly want to stay here. All Kadhikan had to do was to get people to come and look at it. Once seen, we felt sure it would sell itself, and would give Kadhikan every opportunity to have a lucrative little business.

A great deal of time had passed since we first started this project, and yes we had our days and half days and evenings off, nonetheless I decided I was going to take us both into the mountains for a long weekend. We had been advised by both Ben and Prabu about a hill resort where it was cool, green and restful, and inexpensive. It was accessible by bus from Trivandrum, at 8:30 every morning. However before we left, I felt I needed to tidy up the ever-annoying loose ends with

Kadhikan. The leaflets, why can we not get them correct? They really should be printed and ready for distribution, this should be the simplest of jobs. What about the agreement? It took me a day or two to catch up with him. I left messages in all the usual places. Of course this was having the reverse effect, he ducked and dodged even more. We eventually did discover him walking along the road to Thiruvallum at about nine o'clock one evening. We noticed a figure wobbling in the distance, and slowly coming nearer.

We were walking from Thiruvallum where we had been watching the "Great Elephant March". There had been something sad and eerie about those gigantic looming figures, walking slowly in the dim moonlight, the only sound the rhythmic clanking of their restricting chains at each slow step. They were carrying large amounts of vegetation trapped between their trunks and tusks, which we had watched them eat as they had been taken down to the backwater to rest and drink.

Now the small figure was getting closer with every moment. It resembled the slight hunched figure of Kadhikan. Yes it was!

"Hi, Kardy, how are you? We've been looking for you."

"Oh sorry, sir, madam. Kardy son of a dog!"

"What are you talking about?"

"I am taking a little something, sir. Maybe I am not good."

"Come on, Kardy. Everyone gets a little drunk from time to time! Stop worrying. Where are you going?"

"Maybe see friends. Have a little smoke. Maybe sleep until tomorrow."

"OK. Kardy, will you promise to come and see me tomorrow morning?"

"What for?" he replied.

"Leaflets, Kardy." I reminded him.

"Oh yes! Tomorrow I get."

"Yeah, see you tomorrow. Careful, don't get run over." As I suspected, Kadhikan was into dope and booze, that would go a long way to explain his behaviour. I hoped he'd turn up tomorrow, we could get the agreement and such sorted out.

We had only to buy the already located floor covering and fit it, and the job would be complete. So as soon as the agreement was settled we could leave here and travel further into India, and maybe visit Prabu's Ashram on the way. Also, I really did want to take Queenie away the next weekend. The next time I saw "K" was two days later at about ten in the morning. I was due to go away the following day with Queenie, to Ponmudi, the tea plantation/resort in the hills.

We had not bought the floor covering, that would likely be our next mission as the hard work sourcing it was done. Queenie had painted a series of beautiful wave motifs in blue all around the walls of the main room, it looked very professional. The room was now two-tone, light blue/grey for the top and ceiling, and a deeper, brighter blue painted in attractive wave like curves half-way up the walls. Kardy walked in after his usual "Jack, sir madam" routine. He beamed, I had not seen him look so pleased about anything. "It is very beautiful." He said.

"I'm glad you like it, Kardy. You'll earn a good living with this."

"Yes, oh yes, sir, very good."

"What about the leaflets?" I asked.

"Yes sir, leaflets. I see, very good." He handed me a pile of glossy yellow, good quality leaflets.

"Very professional." I approved.

"Madam very good artist." I couldn't be bothered to ask about receipts or bills, he wouldn't have them anyway.

"So, how much do I owe you?" I asked.

"Fifteen hundred, I say before Jack." He whined at me. I handed over fifteen one hundred rupee notes.

"We are going away in the morning, for a few days. Have you got the agreement?"

"No,sir! Not good agreement. Cannot sign agreement."

"So what's wrong with it?" I enquired.

He complained in the tone of voice which did seriously irritate me.

"You say five years I say too long, three years only then we see after.

I have to say I did deliberately say in the revised agreement that I could visit the house, when it wasn't being used, for a further five years. As I explained to Queenie at the time, It is up to him to read it, and negotiate. In short have some real input.

Consequently if I asked for five years and he had agreed I would not know that he had read it. As it appeared he had read it. "Excellent" I thought.

"OK, I'll alter it. How's that? Then we go to the lawyer, yes?"

"Yes, I go today, make appointment."

"Next Tuesday. Is that alright?"

"Yes, is good. But first, you write new agreement." He demanded.

"Yes, I'll do it today, get it typed and copied, and have it ready tonight for you." I agreed.

"Is good!" And off he went, with the leaflets under his arm.

"Things are moving, Queenie — at last!"

I rewrote the agreement there and then. From our point of view, it did not make any sense at all, but at least it would now be easy for him to agree to. I got this typed up and copied at an agency in Thiruvallum.

I handed one to Kadhikan that evening.

"I need you to get an appointment for Tuesday, Kardy." I insisted.

"Yes, no problem sir. I have already made."

Happy with this we packed ready for our trip in the morning, which would be an early start.

On arriving at Trivandrum bus station at seven am , one and a half hours early, I have to concede that, had Queenie not insisted on what, until that point, seemed an outrageous time in the morning to set out, we may well have been in trouble. The bus station that the Ponmudi bus left from was two kilometres away from the local one where we had arrived. Burdened only with our small, fairly light rucksacks, we walked on to find the correct bus station opposite the large main railway depot.

We asked an inspector looking fellow, who told us where exactly to catch the bus, and that it would usually arrive at eight thirty. But today, it would be nine thirty. We applied our system of asking three people the same question, to verify information. If they did, we agreed it would probably be correct. Any other permutation would mean that we would have to seek another three people. So we searched and found another inspector, and a booking clerk, and all three confirmed nine thirty as the time of departure.

It was now eight thirty, so we looked around for somewhere more relaxing to wait. About a hundred yards away we spied the craziest looking coffee house. It was a fifty feet high, round brick chimney, with the words "COFFEE HOUSE" emblazoned on the outside. How could we resist?

We entered, to discover that the inner concrete floor at ground level spiralled upwards, helter-skelter like. The tables and benches were placed level step-like on the outside edge of the spiral. Consequently, as one sat looking downwards one's feet were level with the next person's head. Looking upwards, one was able to look up the trouser leg or lungi of the person behind. The waiters ran up and down the spiral, carrying coffees, puris, masala dosa or whatever to the customers who may be at the top, halfway down or at the bottom of the spiral. The food was retrieved from openings centrally placed on the inner column, via dumb waiters, as in the hub of a wheel. The whole crazy arrangement was just that, with waiters running up, down and around the spiral.

A novel structure, but in the usual environs that seems to be the norm here, it was very dark, grubby and lit by forty-watt light bulbs. Dust, grime and fumes whistled through unglazed openings and around the structure. It was like having coffee in a wind tunnel. It was fun and a good talking point for us, a good start to our short break. At nine o'clock we decided to head for the bus stop. We arrived. No one was there. Panic! Had it gone? Queenie rushed over to a driver.

"Ponmudi?" she asked.

"Fifteen minutes." Was the welcome reply.

Thank goodness. We were in time. While we waited we studied the chaos in the bus station. Each bus blocked the path of another and all fifty or so were revving their engines and belching black diesel fumes. Each bus with its driver's hand glued to the horn. Sheer madness! Some buses were in grave danger of reversing into and hitting passers-by, and each other. Others would drive into the space left by a reversing bus, not allowing any forward motion so no bus could move at all. Slowly, the jam untangled itself, only to retangle itself, and so on. At the times of untangling the station resembled a bumper car track at a fair ground in the UK, with no two vehicles going in the same direction. The driver, who Queenie had asked about the bus a few minutes earlier, came over, to us.

"You, Ponmudi, there," he indicated a bus struggling to get near the stand. Moving slowly, with twenty or so people following, fighting each other off, running to try to board through the narrow opening at the rear of the bus.

We also ran with it, until it stopped. We fell up the steps, and were bulldozed up the bus by the press of people, to two waiting seats. Brilliant! In fact, as on our trip to the wedding village only half the seats were filled before we left the bus station, this being a service bus. However, at one point along the journey it must have contained at least two hundred people. The slow upwards progress of the bus and the windowless window seat afforded us a view of this enormous city, its centre, and its parks, colleges and suburbs. The bus started to empty once again near to the outskirts of the city.

We were impressed at the cleanliness of the small country towns and the greenness of the countryside. We passed small houses with front yards full of red chillies laid out to dry. The bus drove around the sacks that were laid on the surface of the road; each and all covered in the same red chillies. Washed clothes also adorned the covers on the tarmac road, drying in the burning heat.

We drove from town to town, each looking much like the last, until we reached the rubber plantations. Very ordinary looking trees they are, very un-exotic, I thought. Each one had a dish tied to its trunk, with a tell-tale leakage of sap into it. The cups were quite small, maybe holding a litre, not much more. I guessed the latex must be very slow running.

We advanced slowly into areas where houses, shacks and business premises were piled high with light brown, circular pancakes the size of hearth rugs. This I deduced was part of the rubber making process. Hardened latex probably awaiting transport to a rubber factory.

The road opened out, and ran alongside a wide and winding river, through forests and gently up into a high mountain range. The incline grew steeper, and the bus slower, the road narrower. The old bus crunched into first gear as it negotiated the first of eighty-three hairpin bends, now taking up the whole width of the road. The scenery seemed to grow more beautiful every few yards, each new bend revealing mountain ranges or vast green plateaux. We had driven through apple and mango orchards, sugar cane, banana plantations and bamboo the thickness of telegraph poles, glistening yellow in the bright sun as we ascended.

The bus stopped periodically to allow one or two people on or off. Some carried items concealed in large cotton sheets, each patterned and brightly coloured. As we reached the full height of one ridge, another appeared, miles away. The air was clean and cool. Around the next bend it was hot as the sun reappeared.

At the seventy-first bend, the bus pulled in to the side of the road next to a small wooden shack. The bus emptied, and the conductor shouted, "Chai!"

We spent fifteen minutes stretching our legs, ate a small cake, and drank the over-sweetened chai. And off again, refreshed, and delighted with this beautiful journey. We were passing through miles and miles of mountainous forest. We looked ahead, and to the left, and almost perpendicular, several hundred feet up, on a ledge there appeared a settlement cut in to the mountaintop. Three rows of modern western style eccentrically shaped dwellings, each with its own private patio. The same type of structure you can see from Australia to Spain designed for tourist occupation. Each self-contained, and offering a view over the mountaintops and the forest below.

Fifteen minutes later we pulled past the "Welcome to the Government of Kerala Tourist Development Corporation Ponmudi Mountain Resort" sign. I felt a little apprehensive. The place looked a fair bit more up-market than I had anticipated.

"How much money did we bring, Queenie?" I had the horrible notion that we may be asked Hilton prices.

"What will we do if we can't afford to stay here?" I asked.

"Go back down Jack, what else? We've got about five thousand rupees, we'll be OK. In any case it will have been a nice day out, even if we can't afford to stay.

"What a great idea of mine to get away for the weekend." I had thought to myself earlier as I collapsed into my seat on the bus, just what we both needed - a complete change of scene and pace. We had been working at something almost since the day we arrived, and although we both enjoy a challenge, and being busy, things had been getting out of hand. I smiled happily at Queenie as we settled back to enjoy the journey, the three hours passed surprisingly quickly.

Our first glimpse of the tourist complex, far away across the valley, raised our spirits to new heights. "It looks lovely." I breathed. "What a backdrop it's got. I bet the view from there is something else." I continued to enthuse.

Queenie was looking more relaxed and cheerful than she had for some weeks past. We could hardly wait for the bus to pull up. We were the only passengers left on board, so we climbed down easily, taking our first look around as we walked away from the bus in search of the reception office. It was hot here, with the sun high overhead, it being noon, but we had been assured by all that the nights would be wonderfully cool. "Just taste that air, Queenie!" I exclaimed. "I am, I am," she laughed, breathing deeply of the fresh scented air. "No fumes!" she crowed joyfully.

We paused, looking about us. The place seemed to be deserted. "I hope it's not closed, a day here would be lovely, but a night or two would be even better, funds permitting", I thought to myself. A young man appeared from one of the nearby buildings, and walked over to us, smiling. "Reception?" We enquired. "Come," he said, indicating for us to follow. We climbed a long flight of steps, pausing halfway to take in the view and get our breath. The sun was getting hotter. We finally reached the top, where the young man was waiting for us. "Key?" he enquired. "Key?" we asked, puzzled. "Room key." He confirmed, holding out his hand. "No key yet, we need reception office." Explained Queenie.

Understanding dawned and the young man indicated that we should follow him, this time down the steps. "Just a little language difficulty," we agreed, laughing, determined that nothing was going to spoil this day,

The young man pointed us to a door marked Restaurant, and made us understand that this is where we were to go. Maybe someone in here will be able to help, we reassured each other, and in we went. It was much cooler inside, and surprisingly clean and light. A man stood behind a tiny desk in the corner behind the door. He smiled at us.

"Yes sir, madam?"

"Do you have any rooms, " I asked, "and if so, how much per night?"

"Yes, sir, many rooms. Many cottages. Cottages 80 rupees, rooms 45 rupees." We stared at him in open-mouthed amazement.

"Is that each person?" I asked faintly.

"No, no. Each room, each night." He smiled broadly.

I gathered my wits, and asked, "May we see a room, please?"

"Certainly," and a key was produced, and another young man appeared as if by magic — where do they all hide? I wondered - and led us to inspect a room.

"It can't be much of a room for that." Queenie muttered.

"Well, no harm looking, as you often say." I replied.

We were led down a cool broad corridor to an end room. The young man flung open the door with a flourish, and once more we were open-mouthed with amazement. The room was huge, high ceilinged and airy. The bathroom was palatial, and was reached via a small dressing room. The sheets were clean, there was a blanket — "so it must be true, the nights are cool," I thought to myself. There were two large and comfortable armchairs. I was reminded that I hadn't actually sat in a comfortable chair for months. But the best was yet to come. Flinging wide the enormous drapes, our guide slid back patio doors that formed the whole of the back wall, and swept his hand in a magnificent gesture indicating the view. And what a view. Tiny in the distance, we could see the thin line of the road that had brought us here. We stepped out onto the vast patio.

I was for once, devoid of speech. Finally, Queenie managed a weak, "Yes, that's very nice, we'll take it."

We hurried back to the reception, hardly daring to believe our luck. We signed in for three nights, booked breakfast, then hurried back to make a full inspection of our room. It was magnificent, and the view glorious. The water in the shower was cold! But clear, not brown, and very soft, so that the soap lathered wonderfully. We giggled and splashed in the enormous bathroom, feeling like a couple of kids, its size dwarfed us so.

Refreshed, we decided to take a walk around the station, and set off in fine high spirits. We discovered a post office, a small shop, a police station, all closed for the afternoon, but due to reopen at about four. Twenty minutes to go. While we waited we wandered up the steps where the young man had taken us, to search out the other restaurant and coffee shop. Only the coffee shop was open, so we had coffee. A sullen young man, who looked as if he would rather be anywhere other than Ponmudi, served it to us in grimy cups. We sat on the small terrace, and admired the view.

"I think we may have the place all to ourselves" I gloated.

"Yeah," said Queenie "I really need a day or two to unwind. I think you can get some great photos up here. I'm glad you packed your big camera."

We sipped the dreadful coffee, content to simply admire the view, and finally relax. The past few weeks were receding fast and we were determined to enjoy our few days holiday.

We could see the shop a little further down the hill from where we were sitting, and finally the door opened. We strolled down to buy peanuts and water. A policeman was standing outside the now open door of the tiny police station. We wondered if he ever had anything to do in a quiet place like this. We decided to make him earn his money, so we approached to ask him about bus times from Ponmudi to Trivandrum. This took some time, but we finally understood one another. It seemed that buses left at seven, twelve noon, and five pm. We decided that when we were ready to leave, we'd take the early bus, to take advantage of the coolest part of the day, and so that we could enjoy once again, the magnificent scenery on the way down. On our way to the restaurant we had a few beers, then a meal and, thoroughly tired, but very happy, rolled back to our room for our first cool night's sleep in months. And it was blissfully cool. We opened the huge patio doors, and looked out over the moonlit mountains. We could trace the tiny lights of cars and other vehicles far away across the valley, but the silence was complete, the noise of their engines lost, swallowed up by the forest, and only as they entered the hill station proper, could they be heard. We finally fell into our beds, uncaring now about their hardness, and slept like the dead until morning.

I woke at first light, and ventured out onto the cool patio. Looking to my left, I could see the sun about to rise over a distant mountain, turning the sky a soft pink, heralding another glorious day. I crept about, unwilling to wake Queenie, who so seldom gets a full night's sleep because of her chronic pain. It was still and quiet, so I sat in one of the armchairs we had dragged out last night, and watched the sun rise, occasionally glancing at the "India Today" magazine that I had brought with me. Queenie awoke about half an hour later, and joined me on the terrace, stretching and yawning. "Isn't it great!" she enthused.

"Yes, yes, yes, yes." I agreed. "What's on the agenda today?" I continued.

"How about finding that waterfall the guide was talking about yesterday?"

The young man, who had offered his services as a guide, had approached us the day before. His English was good, and we had toyed with the idea of taking him up on his offer, even though three hundred rupees had seemed a little steep. He had told us about a waterfall, a deer park, and other delights which would involve about two hours walking. In the end, we had decided against using his services, preferring to go exploring by ourselves. So, agreeing that a waterfall and deer park hunt would be the order of the day, we set off in search of breakfast.

In the restaurant, we still seemed to be the only visitors around, as the only other people eating were the resort staff. We were served in a kind of off-hand way with sweet tea and large flat steamed dough cakes, which seemed to be very light in texture. However, on the way down to the stomach, they would suddenly take on a leaden quality, and would land solidly with a distinct internal thud. There was the usual fiery vegetable curry accompaniment. We munched our way stolidly through as many of the pancakes as we could manage then, rising with some difficulty, left to spend the rest of the day in our explorations.

It was clear and sunny, the air fresh and sweet. We set off up the road, and higher up the mountain. It was slow walking, the rising temperature and the stunning views combining to stop us in our tracks every few paces, not to mention the leaden feeling in our stomachs. The road wound around the mountain, and very few vehicles seemed to penetrate this far. We had noted a road block further down, at the junction, and as we had rounded the bend, the reason for the block became clear. Several trucks and a steamroller blocked the road ahead. They looked abandoned, scattered over the road. We were told later that the vehicles had been left there over the weekend until the workers returned to carry on with the road repairs. We edged around the steamroller, which was effectively blocking the road for both foot and vehicle traffic, and continued on our way.

Butterflies danced in the early morning sunlight and birds called to each other from the dense tree cover across the mountains. We stopped to inspect the remains of a dead chicken, which had been neatly cut to pieces, the gory bits scattered around a large stone. The head, feet, and tail feathers were all complete, the head lying precisely on the stone, while the feet were scattered to right and left. Bright brownish red feathers were scattered about, and the entrails lay in a pool of congealed blood next to the head. We were puzzled. This did not look like the work of an animal, yet neither did it look like the work of a hungry human. We tried to scare each other with tales of bloody sacrifice and evil curses, and feeling just a little disturbed, walked on.

Around the next bend we came to the deer park. The large gates were closed. We walked up to them and peered through. In the distance, a bunch of bored looking red deer stood about aimlessly, not even bothering to make use of the shade of a nearby tree. There was no sign or notice on the gate to inform visitors of opening hours, feeding times or anything else, except to say it was a deer park. We gazed through the bars of the high metal gates for a few minutes, and the deer gazed back. "Very nice." I said.

"Lovely." Said Queenie, and we went on our way. Strange how we expect animals to perform, or how disappointed you can feel if they don't. It was getting hotter, with no sign of the road coming to an end, nor of the promised waterfall. We passed a children's play area, the equipment having a lost and abandoned look, as do such areas all around the world, I suspect, when there are no children playing and laughing in them. I wound a scarf around my head, to keep off the sun, and we stopped to sip some water. We'd been walking for about an hour, though the distance we'd covered could probably have been achieved in a quarter of that. We both like to stop and stare, it is something we have not always had time to do. We tried to mentally work out how long it would actually take us to travel around India at this snail's pace.

The road ended suddenly. A flat area, with the marks of the tyres of numerous vehicles on it, this gave us the clue that this might be lookout point for the waterfall, where cars would park and their occupants could gaze in wonder at the mighty spectacle. We trudged to the edge of the flat area, and looked around. The view certainly was magnificent, an almost sheer drop beneath our feet. The view took our eyes way, way, down and away across to the other side of the steep sided valley, and up to the distant hazy blue heights. We looked in all possible directions but we couldn't see a waterfall. "Maybe it's the wrong spot." Said Queenie. "Mmmmm." I sort of agreed, but I had my suspicions.

Taking the binoculars from Queenie, I focussed them on a distant flash of white, far across the valley. Even with the aid of binoculars, it was difficult to make out, but I began to feel ever more certain that the distant white speck was the elusive waterfall. I handed the glasses to Queenie.

"You have a look." I urged. She spent some moments gazing through the binoculars, trying to focus on the distant white flash.

"It can't be that. Let's walk on. There's a path over there, I'm sure I can hear water."

We set off along the rough stony path, scrambling occasionally on the steep bits. I was getting hot and longing for some shade and a swig out of the water bottle.

"Down there!" Called Queenie as I was scrambling down a particularly steep and slippery slope. "I'm sure I can hear water."

I stopped to listen. Yes, I could hear it too, and mercifully, it appeared to emanate from the area of a stand of tall bamboo and other vegetation, offering the welcome prospect of shade. I followed Queenie into the sudden darkness under the trees. It was much cooler here, and I paused to take a few deep breaths, and to enjoy the sensation of sweat cooling on my skin.

"Where is it?" I called to Queenie, who had disappeared a little deeper into the undergrowth. She reappeared suddenly, looking baffled.

"Don't know! I can still hear water, though."

We both listened intently. Water was definitely falling somewhere. But not anywhere we could get to, it seemed. We thrashed around a little longer, admiring the lizards, beetles and other wildlife we disturbed, and then finally agreeing to give up the search, we climbed back up the steep slope and to the car park area once more.

While we had been away, several motorbikes had been manoeuvred around the road block, and were now parked in the car park. A group of young men, dressed in their best holiday clothes, stood or sat around the viewing area, gazing in the direction of what we suspected to be the waterfall. They smiled and waved when they saw us, and as we approached, we asked, "Waterfall?" We were correct, the waterfall was so far away it was impossible to see with the naked eye.

"Yes, very nice." They replied. We left them to their sightseeing feeling just a little cheated, but not as cheated as we would have felt if we'd paid a guide three hundred rupees to escort us to view the distant white speck on the mountainside. It didn't actually matter, the surroundings were so beautiful and peaceful and that was what we'd come for. A little thing like a distant misnamed trickle of water was not going to dampen our spirits. So, in good humour we began to retrace our steps, stopping off at the children's playground to rest in the shade, and play on some of the equipment, agreeing that it was really great that there were no adults around to spoil our fun.

The leaden breakfast now seemed hours ago, so we headed in the direction of the restaurant, the downward journey not much faster than the upward one, as each bend of the road brought a new vista to our attention. We spent the rest of the afternoon in the restaurant, and, several cold beers and large helpings of curry later, headed back to our room for a shower, as darkness began to fall.

There were now a few more visitors about, a few Europeans on a day trip, but many more Indians, families and larger groups of young men. The car park was full, the grounds in front of the main block of buildings was full of picnicking families, as was the outside flat roof of our room, which had a glorious view over the mountains. It seemed a very different place to the one we had arrived at only the day before. It had burst into life, and we enjoyed watching the children and families playing and relaxing in this spectacular setting.

"It gets better and better." said Queenie. I could hardly disagree! We also agreed that the only jarring note was the hideous sculpture, a reclining concrete figure on the lawn in front of the reception building, and even it was mightily improved, we felt, by the presence of the small children climbing on and around it.

There was a fall moon that night, and I spent an hour or so setting up my camera to get a good shot of it. It was eerily beautiful, bigger and brighter than the moon we were used to seeing at home. With no street lights to compete with, the moon's radiance filled the valley, illuminating the mountains in a pale silvery light. Queenie was content to watch, and let the peace seep through. We had neighbours next door, and although they too were out on their patio, they sat like us, without lights, and in virtual silence, speaking only occasionally to each other in quiet voices. They too, were transfixed by the magical beauty of the moonlight over the mountains.

With no need for the fan to be on at night, we could sleep without listening to its eternal clattering, the height and temperature meant that we were undisturbed by mosquitoes. We slept soundly once more, waking again at first light to catch the sunrise over the distant peaks.

Today we were determined to go down the hillside, to explore the tea plantation settlement we could see in the distance. Once again it was bright and sunny and hot, the air fresh and clean. As we walked down the road, we speculated on where the people who lived in the pretty bungalows, set in delightful gardens, could possibly do their shopping. As far as we remembered, the nearest shops were some miles down the mountain, the only businesses we had seen nearby were two small cafes, set next to each other on one of the bends in the road. Our question was answered as we walked on the track leading to the small settlement. We heard the familiar sound of a motorcycle, coming ever closer, and stepping to one side, allowed him to pass. On reaching the settlement, he rang a hand bell, which he produced from the basket on the back of his bike. Several women appeared in the doorways of the cottages, and made their way towards him. From the large basket strapped to the back of his bike, he was doling out items of food. The women paid him, and business completed, he turned around and came back up the track. "Only one way in and one out." said Queenie, adding "Just look at the backdrop to those bungalows". They were set against a backdrop of steep hills, which were covered with tea plants. We stopped on the track, unwilling to go nearer to the houses. We were never sure whether we were intruding into people's lives, and I was always conscious about where I pointed my camera, never feeling that I had the right to photograph someone without their knowledge and consent.

Lower down the hillside, the factory for the tea plantation looked more than merely deserted, it looked derelict. Appearances can be very deceptive here, we had been told that it was a working factory, so we assumed that this being Sunday, the place was closed. It didn't seem to have much to recommend it aesthetically so we made our way back up to the little roadside cafe, in search of food. We enjoyed surprisingly good coffee, ate a simple meal along with a group of workmen, and then made our way back to the resort. The fresh mountain air had made us sleepy, and we did little more than drink beer, watch the tourists at play, and stroll about the immediate area of the resort, watching and speculating about the people around us. We were by now deeply into this relaxation thing, and spent another quiet evening watching the play of moonlight over the mountains, and reading the books and magazines we had brought with us.

Our final day dawned, and this day, we promised ourselves, we would find the source of the sound of water that we could hear from our room. We followed some unfinished concrete steps down to an open area, deep in the trees. A small bridge appeared and led over a stream, which disappeared down the hillside. We followed it under the trees, scrambling over the rocks, enjoying the feel of the cool water on our feet. The stream led to an almost vertical drop, and disappeared over the edge. Was this the elusive waterfall, we wondered? Once again, the views were breath-taking. We sat on a huge flat rock, overlooking the steep valley, watching the birds sailing high overhead, and trying to capture just a little of the beauty around us on film. The day passed pleasantly enough, and we were feeling refreshed, restored ready for the fray once again. We slept well on our final night, and we felt we had finally caught up on all the lost sleep of the previous weeks.

We happily paid up the bill for our stay, which was the equivalent of about £6.50 for meals and accommodation, and set out in the early morning light to catch the first bus of the day back to Trivandrum. As promised, it was waiting for us, and we along with a couple of other passengers, started on the long trek back down the mountain.

We were sorry to leave Ponmudi hill station, it had given us a much-needed breathing space, and we promised ourselves that we may one day return, or perhaps, when the need arose, we'd set off for another hill station somewhere to rest and recuperate. We now fully understood why the British had constructed and made good use of such places. We felt we had seen another side of India, one that was very different to the one we had experienced down on the coast or in the city. We settled down to enjoy our journey home, the three hours to Trivandrum passing swiftly. This had been a well-earned relief from the tensions and frustrations of this extremely demanding project.

Chapter 22

It was a nice afternoon in Trivandrum. There was no rush to get home to "K"'s.

We were calm, relaxed, so it seemed a good opportunity to wander up the well-known M.G. Road, i.e. Mahatma Gandhi Road, without the pressure of having to complete any particular task. It was an opportunity, we agreed, to enjoy the chaos, instead of needing to fight it!

The four lanes of traffic raced in opposite directions, with a centre lane reserved for police boxes and mainly rubbish.

A worn out auto rickshaw, a lorry, a bicycle, tipped on to their sides, twisted wheel rims that had long ago kicked off their threadbare tyres, all presented a barrier across the central reservation we were not prepared to negotiate. Ahead in the far distance we saw one of those skeletal iron footbridges, the same as you can see in any city, it clearly was the sensible way to cross the road. Our choice made, we set off to walk the half-mile or so to safety.

We passed the statue of the Mahatma, the cycle shop, the big, new but already strangely rust-stained and crumbling insurance offices next to the two banks offering loans to purchase houses displaying the usual over-optimistic messages.

The lovely hot bread smells permeated the diesel fumes, we wandered past the garish wild colours displayed in shop after shop that eventually led us to the foot of the steel steps where we were to cross.

Queenie's ability to walk these distances was slowly diminishing so we stopped and stood for a while for Q to rest. Eager to see the sights from the top of the bridge I ran up the steps and passed a young man who rather oddly I thought, was wearing a hooded parka jacket in this heat? I waited for Queenie who was now cheerfully making her way upwards towards me.

"Come on Queenie you old bugger," I laughed. I waited until she had climbed to the top before proceeding. We looked over and through the wire mesh and into the blue haze of fumes. Queenie spoke up. "I won't miss this, Jack. It makes London seem like a walk in the park. Let's get back home. I hate cities at the best of times."

We ambled past the young man with the heavy looking parka jacket. He didn't appear to be doing much, just peering into the oncoming traffic below.

I don't hang onto Queenie even when she is struggling; I've tried that before to try to help, it doesn't work. I get an earful for my efforts. She only suffers these events periodically but it is difficult to have to watch her suffer and hobble in pain, it is also difficult for me to constantly break pace, stop and wait, to be unable to walk at a pace that has been normal to me for all my life.

Difficult for both of us at the best of times, much more so in the brain-boiling heat and fumes.

We reached the other side together and started off down the stairway. At this point I ran down the stairs ahead of her, shouting as I went, "Not long now kid — a nice cool shower.

Then — a SCREAM, a shout, **"JACK"**. I spun around to see Queenie's teeth sink into the bare brown flesh of the young man's out-stretched wrist. I ran upwards to help, to grab him. He took flight up a couple of steps and across the banging, clanking metal bridge.

Queenie held out her purse as I passed, "He tried to snatch my purse, but I've got it back."

" OK." I shouted, and took little further notice of her for the next minute or two. I was determined to not let him get away. WHY? I am not sure even now.

I raced up the stairway two steps at a time. The young man was more than half the length of the bridge away already. I'd never catch him! He was fading into the distance, by the time I'd reached the top of the stairs at the other side of the bridge he was three steps from the bottom. I had all but lost him! My last resort was to try to elicit help, I shouted, screamed down to the shop and stall owners at the foot of the bridge. "STOP HIM! STOP HIM! CATCH THE THIEF!" I yelled, pointing to the running figure.

Then I paused, confused. Was this instinct? Or some perverted attempt at retribution? What could I, what would I do if I caught this man? I didn't know, I only knew that something was gathering momentum. Almost on command, with a mechanical precision, faces turned and looked up. Then voices in native tongue rang out, like the slow build-up of a storm, the surge, then a wave of bodies poured from every available opening.

Out of shop doorways, the people sitting and lying on the sidewalk rose, customers from tea shops, all ran after the man I had pointed out. What had I done? Perhaps more to the point what would happen next? I had a short time to think as Queenie, having caught up, appeared at the top of the steps. I descended to meet the crowd who had now caught the thief.

He was screaming in terror, tears rolling down his face, wriggling and squirming as he tried to avoid the slaps across the head and punches in the back. An older man who had so promptly responded to my earlier demand to "STOP HIM!" stepped forward.

"Is this the man?" He enquired. I looked up towards Queenie. She confirmed what I knew already.

"Yes," I shouted above the racket, "it is."

"What would you wish to do with him?" he asked. Detecting my momentary pause, and I guess trying to be helpful, he gave me a choice. "Either we deal with him here or take him to the police station." Not wanting to be responsible for unknown consequences, and possibly the life of what might easily become the victim, I unhesitatingly opted for the police station. The young man was now a matter of inches away with tears streaming from his eyes and falling from his chin, still hysterically protesting his innocence. This attempt at shameless deception, inviting me to distrust the evidence of my own eyes, removed any pity I had for this man. An apology to Queenie would have worked in his favour, and likely have freed him.

"The police station over the road." The old man said, pointing to the large building we had passed a few minutes ago.

"OK." I turned, making my way to retrace my steps back up the stairs.

"This way." Shouted the man, as without warning he pushed the young man in to the oncoming traffic. Cars screeched, swerved, and wove around us, four people held the young man out before them with his arms twisted upwards behind him. An excited crowd of twenty or so men followed us into the traffic. The rest of the crowd not prepared to take the risk of crossing, dispersed, or stood their ground at the side of the road. We were now thankfully in the centre reservation, safely hiding behind an over-turned truck. Then out again in to the blaze of shrieking horns, fumes, dust and drivers.

The young man stumbled and fell at the kerb side, and was dragged from there up the knee-high concrete barrier at the other edge of the road. He was safely across. Our number had now reduced by at least half. Queenie was also doing well, spurred on I expect by the adrenaline and the occasion. The young man was pushed up the steep steps in front of the police station feet first and at a backwards angle, supported by outstretched hands.

Two khaki clad police officers were waiting, having emerged from the darkness of half-open twelve feet high arched doors. In response to the locals exclamations and protestations, the waist to ankle length inch and a half thick batons were unclipped from their waist belts and held shoulder high. A final push from the men holding our charge sent him sprawling through the half-open door. A black shiny boot reflecting from the outside light connected with the victim's chest. The unclipped batons were pounding him on the back amid screams and yelps. I rushed up the few remaining steps shouting,

"Hang on!"

The door space cleared as the young man was dragged into the blackness, he was pulled to his feet, tears rolling. Queenie was cringing at the sight. A voice at my shoulder spoke firmly but kindly in my ear.

"It is the only way" It was the old man. Another voice rapped out, and the beating, now concentrating on the back of the legs, finally ceased.

"Please you come," Queenie and I were escorted down the dark but cool corridor, officers in military-style regalia fore and aft with our friendly old man leading the way.

Once into the large office the inspector in charge greeted us with a big smile. Orders snapped, we were alone in the office with him and the old man. The prisoner was outside the office we could still hear his crying, and the occasional yelp of anguish.

"Tell me," the officer asked, with his educated British middle-class accent, "exactly what took place with this boy." I looked at Queenie. She told the story, occasionally interrupted by the splatter of local language between the officer and our after-the-event witness, the old man. The smart good-looking officer, sporting rows of pips, stars, epaulettes, and two bronze medals, stood to his full six feet six inch height. He shouted to someone outside, the door opened wide and the young man was brought forward, still sobbing, held up under the arms by two officers. The inspector opened his desk slowly and produced a small packet of tissues, which he handed to one of the officers. He opened the pack and proceeded to gently wipe the tears and stains from the prisoner's face.

"Is this the boy?"

"Yes." We both agreed.

"Very good."

The inspector withdrew his shorter baton while the third officer, a sergeant, held out the prisoner's arm, tucking it under his own and leaving the hand and wrist exposed. The boy roared and screamed in anticipation, but there was no escape. Queenie looked away; I looked on, crack, crack, six times across both hands.

Twelve of the best. This was some kind of lesson to me as well.

"Sign here please." Queenie shakily signed the large account-like book. The boy was removed. The inspector beamed at us, pleased it seemed, at a job well done.

I cannot say I liked what had happened, knowing that poverty was the main and perhaps only culprit here. I also realised that I did not want Queenie to be robbed. In comparison languishing in a prison cell, or hostel, to be released months after an offence is committed, is not much of a solution to street crime or poverty either.

Neither of course is allowing attempted street theft to take place un-answered.

We left the police station feeling thoroughly confused, we were angry at ourselves and I was personally embarrassed for what I had started, instead of leaving well alone. I could have let him go.

Chapter 23

Queenie was making tea, I hadn't seen Kadhikan on our return, it was possible that he was distributing his leaflets and actually out working. I needed to see him about our lawyer meeting date.

Their door was closed but there were still embers glowing within the concrete block square that served as an outside cooker. "They can't be far away," I thought, and tapped at the door. A female "Hallo?" sounded from the next door house, and turning I saw Valsala at the window. She came to the door, smiling as always.

"Hi," I said, "where's Kardy?"

Her shrug of the shoulders I interpreted to mean "Don't know".

The weather seemed to reflect our mood. A wind began to rise soon after nightfall, followed by torrential rain. The weather worsened as the night wore on, and I gave up all hope of trying to sleep. Instead, I opened the window to watch what had become a violent tropical storm. Queenie joined me, and we watched fascinated and awestruck, a welcome distraction. Thunder rolled continually around the heavens, and lightning flashed like strobe lighting amongst the trees, lighting them suddenly in stark black and white.

We watched, entranced and stunned, at the trees bending, some cracking, falling, water lashing in sheets, chairs flying — the ferocity of nature.

The lights failed, and with them the fan, so we spent most of the night sitting by the window, occasionally exclaiming in amazement at the spectacle before us. The rain looked like silver curtains against a black backdrop, while the wind drove the cool spray through the open windows. Faces wet with rain, it was difficult for me to tell whether Queenie was crying or not. I do know I felt like crying myself.

I, at least, slept lightly after the storm finally abated sometime during the early hours of the morning. I heard the temple explosions, I got up hoping to make tea. Bottled soda was all I could offer, the electricity was still off.

We lay talking for a couple of hours remembering the events in the police station, Queenie worrying about whether we had done the right thing, until the morning light emerged.

The first thing I needed to do was to investigate the extent of the damage caused by the storm. I felt sure that not all the cracks and crashes and booming sounds I had heard had been thunder. Sure enough, when I looked out of the door, and then walked a little way down the track, I could see that several large palm trees had indeed fallen during the night. One was the culprit for our lack of electricity, as it had fallen on the electric wiring and had pulled down both post and wiring, and was leaning crazily over a neighbour's fence and into his courtyard.

It looked like there wasn't going to be any electricity for some time. I walked along the edge of the backwaters, and was amazed when I found that the sea had actually breached the high sandbank between the inland waterway and the ocean, creating a completely new vista of extended seascape.

I hoped the fisher people who lived next to the shore had survived the storm's violence. Everything dripped with moisture, the rising temperature was creating an incredible amount of humidity and steam.

I felt I had seen all I needed to see for the present, so returned to the house, with news of my discoveries.

Queenie's mood had also lightened a great deal, even at home she was fond of a good storm, and the previous night's had certainly been one to remember.

I then decided to go to relocate, and purchase, the final touch to our project — the PVC cushion flooring, which I had admired previously. But first I needed to find Kadhikan who had told me before we went to Ponmudi he had arranged an appointment with the lawyer for this morning at nine o'clock. It was now eight thirty, had Kadhikan already gone? I tried not to get annoyed. Maybe he had gone up to the lawyer's and expected me to be there. I had thirty minutes to get myself up there just in case. "You never can tell, it could all run smoothly".

I had been optimistic; in fact there was no lawyer's office anywhere near where he said there was. I enquired, re-enquired, and enquired again but no lawyer

"K" had fooled me again. To keep our chins up, I prepared to spend vast amounts of rupees on the lino. I announced my intentions to Queenie, to the effect that I would, after changing money at the Wall Street Finance Company in Trivandrum, locate the aforementioned lino, get it cut to size, pay for it, then use the rest of the day to amuse ourselves in Trivandrum. That would give us both more positive things to think about than Kardy's indiscretions.

Trivandrum has an enormously high, intricately carved column. Built several hundred years ago, close inspection of our travel guide reveals that it is the Shri Padamanabhasamy Temple, dedicated to Vishnu and for the sole use of the many ex-Maharajahs of Travancore. That being the name by which this state was previously known.

That was before the last Maharaja had given it up to the elected political party of the time which was, and still is at the time of writing, the communist party. This temple, along with the associated palace residence, is now a tourist attraction. The problem is, no tourists are allowed in the temple. There is however, a saffron lungied, bare-chested person who calls himself a priest, hanging about outside.

After having recited the contents of the tourist handout, he demanded two hundred rupees, while at the same time warning us to be careful as all Indians are villainous robbers, who would extort money and belongings from their grandmothers.

Taking due note of this useful piece of information, I gave him twenty rupees, instead of the two hundred he had demanded, on the grounds that the higher rate would constitute two days pay for a mere mortal, which he surely was.

The palace was, however, open to tourists, so I paid another twenty rupees to go in, another ten rupees to an elderly lady whose purpose in life it was to collect and guard visitor's shoes. This of course, being another of the many job creation projects. I collected our tickets from one man, and gave them to another, who tore them in half, and put one half in the bin provided, and kept the other half. He then motioned for us to follow him, and proceeded slightly ahead of us, describing the various items inside this small but perfectly formed wooden palace. There were indeed some remarkable sights. A huge crystal throne totally obscured by dust, the glass dull and yellow from lack of care. There were rusty cannons; muskets; bayonets; and lots and lots of dim 'n' dowdy paintings of "auspicious" occasions, most of which prominently featured one Maharaja of Travancore or another. More recent paintings were of British, Dutch, or Portuguese Viceroys and the like. Many of the paintings are a few hundred years old, and executed in, to be kind, a very unsophisticated manner. "Primitive art?" The guide was very impressed with these, so I thought they must be OK too.

The wooden structure of the palace itself was impressive. The whole thing was carved from end to end with gods, demi-gods and all manner of intricate hand-cut wood work. It had the feel of a semi-derelict haunted house, and I bet someone, somewhere, has used it as a film set. If they haven't, perhaps they should, as I'm sure the Government of Kerala could use the money.

From the palace we wandered down into the centre of town and dined in an "American" bar, complete with plastic vacuum formed Marilyn Monroe, James Dean and Humphrey Bogart all fastened to the walls, and to complete the scene, a pink heart-shaped bar.

The paint work was dirty and pale. The black PVC-topped chromium seat cushions were ripped, revealing the sponge inner. A dark brown Elvis Presley, complete with gold neck chain, served us fish curry, and quite good espresso coffee.

From there, we wandered the side streets, noting that they were lined with a plethora of private computer schools. Good for them!

We entered the gateway of an enormous church-like building. A large sign announced grandly that it was "The Official Government Kashmiri and Tribal Craft Emporium". How could we resist?

Displayed within were life-size, carved dark wooden elephants, elephant feet umbrella stands, punkas with wooden wallahs and many other, less interesting things.

The problem is, almost ALL the shops in India look like second hand antique shops. Dusty and gloomy with items which although new, look as though they are from ages past.

Time was getting on, and having taken a couple of wrong turnings, we did eventually arrive at the sack shop that I knew also happened to sell the PVC flooring we had previously reconnoitred, and priced and ordered.

It was all ready for us. Queenie on one end, me on the other, we hoisted the twelve-foot length onto our shoulders and wound our way round the back lanes and streets towards the bus stand. Queenie stopped suddenly, pulling me up with a jerk.

"Jack, stop! Let's get a rickshaw!"

"How are we going to get this in a rickshaw?" I called back.

"Leave it to the driver." Was the educated reply.

"OK. Let's try it!"

She was quite right, the driver was enthusiastic in his efforts to squeeze our particular quart into his pint pot. We drove the fifteen kilometres with the roll of linoleum standing perpendicular, poking out of the top of the rickshaw, bending in the breeze slightly, which meant I had to stand up all the way in an effort to support it. It worked though! We got back to Kadhikan's house with much less fuss and to-do than a bus ride, and all for fifty rupees. (The rickshaw that is). That really did surprise me!

"I won't lay it today, Queenie, I'm too tired." I said, as we placed the roll on the floor.

"Hey, there's Kardy! Kardy! What about that appointment?"

"Not today, sir, tomorrow."

"You said, before I went away, 'today'."

"No sir, no sir, not today."

"I know what I heard Kadhikan, you told me the time of the meeting and where to go. What are you playing at?" I could feel my temper rising again. Kadhikan recognised the signs, too.

"I go now. This minute. Get for tomorrow, sir."

"OK, GO!" I snapped.

"Plastic very nice for house sir. How much you pay?"

"Never mind that, Kardy, go and get the appointment. Also, before you go - where is the Lambi?"

"Lambi no good sir, it break."

"So that's a thousand or is it fifteen-hundred rupees wasted!"

"Sorry sir, I go now." He scurried away.

I was determined that he was going to get a lawyer. It seemed that he was equally determined that he was not. We would see.

That night, I did sleep, and made up for the previous night. When I awoke, Queenie worked her breakfast magic once again — banana and custard! Added this to her repertoire of omelette and pineapple and more recently, porridge. Yes, porridge! In the tropics! What a title for a book! After breakfast, I systematically carried each piece of furniture outside, much to the amusement of the ever-gazing neighbours. I swept and washed the floor, then laid the first piece of PVC.

"Oh dear!" Was the most printable exclamation I made that day.

The room where the lino was to be laid was not square, or was it? I laid the next piece and then the next, and for some inexplicable reason, I could match the pattern at one end, but it would not match at the other. I could not leave it like that, so with Queenie's help, I juggled the pieces around. I had lots of spare length on all the three pieces, the only way I could get a near enough match was to place each on a longitudinal angle, and cut the PVC according to the pattern. The pattern of squares and triangles had in fact been printed on the skew, so what could I expect? It may or may not also be the room. I measured it diagonally corner to corner, the measurements were a foot or so out. I'd never get it straight.

With much wrestling and crawling about with water pouring from our collective brow, we did it. Next the ex-ante room, now a smart yellow kitchen with a blue and white floor. It looked superb. I replaced the furniture piece by piece.

It was truly a palace in the backwaters. Who could resist it, I thought.

It was four thirty already, and no Kardy.

"Where is he? Do you know, Queenie, I wouldn't feel so bad about this guy, if he would just say what his problem is."

"He is not aware he has a problem, Jack."

"I suspect I am his problem."

"His bloody nightmare I expect."

Both Queenie and I had the uneasy feeling that we were no longer welcome here, so would be glad to leave Kadhikan's house. We were weary of the ups and downs, and even Kadhikan's presence annoyed us both. We had originally decided to stay a week longer to enjoy the environment we had created, but now could no longer ignore the occasional indications from Kadhikan that he wished we would leave. Almost before the last brush stroke of paint had dried I had been confronted by his whining presence.

"I am poor man, son of dog, I have not much room, you have big house."

It was plain we had to leave, though I didn't want to believe we weren't welcome. I expect that not only did he want us to work on a daily basis, but as Queenie suggested, to pay for the privilege as well, which we were not prepared to do.

India, I discovered, is plastered with mission statements, agreements, rules, directions, etc. to which no actual commitment, in actual deed, is exercised.

India is becoming more like the UK every day. However, attempts to extract commitment from "K", had taken months of discussion, arguments, rows, and now it seemed, missed solicitor's appointments.

The only conclusion I can draw from his behaviour is that he is an incredibly short-sighted person. If he had been more straightforward, our wish to help him could have continued. He had effectively killed the goose that laid the golden egg.

I had wanted to help Kadhikan because of our similar positions within our respective societies. This should have given us I thought, a kind of affinity. In a way we could both cock a snook to society by saying, "if you won't assist the likes of us, then we'll assist each other."

It must however be a strange feeling for Kadhikan; exciting on one hand, and humbling on the other; to observe and have contact with people who can afford to spend ridiculous amounts of money on items of everyday living. His inability to discriminate between tourists as individuals to any extent puts all tourists fair and square into the same category. The urge to shake the proverbial mango tree for all it's worth to the extent of breaking all the branches is too much of a temptation for him.

High income, high spend meets low income, low spend. It's all relative!

When I first met Kadhikan he appeared to us to be using all his available resources with imagination. He planned his days, he worked carefully, nurturing his prospects, was enthusiastic, and spared no effort to provide a valuable and worthwhile service for tourists. They all agreed they'd had good value for money. He also had plans for the future, to extend his sphere of influence in the tourist market. If his performance to that date was any indication, he would be very good and successful.

Now I question whether any of this was actually true. Had we, in our enthusiasm, filled in and coloured the picture according to our tastes, seen what we wanted to believe?

I do not know, really, how Kadhikan thinks or feels about anything, but I do know that the Kadhikan we met on our second visit was a different person than on the first.

He seemed very nervous, churlish, had mood swings, happy one minute, very cautious the next. "I am son of a dog!" he would say to me.

Perhaps in trying to help him, we had destroyed the only really valuable possession he had — his dreams. A fantasy of ownership and wealth, to be like his European neighbour he observed through the trees half a mile away. "Laguna, on the backwater" earning thousands of rupees per day.

It was a respectable fantasy. It lent itself, given the circumstances, to "I could if only... Maybe one day..." indeed, so far away was the "one day," that there was no point, consequently the fantasy remained healthily intact.

It is not a comfortable feeling, realising that I may have colluded with him in destroying his own fantasy, transforming it into the reality of constant hard work.

While the tourist home was in its dream stage, it had the benefits, without the harsh reality. Maybe the toil of arranging the work to be done had been too much for him, maybe even guilt, knowing that he was breaking his agreement with us.

The concern perhaps of not knowing what our reaction would be.

Maybe he toyed with the idea or hoped that we would not return at all.

Maybe the domestic demands of relations, in-laws in particular, for him to ease their financial burdens in precarious times were too much for him. We can only speculate.

One thing is certain, he had hardly made a single positive contribution to the project while we were there. Attempts on our part to get him to do anything was met with the same response. "Later, later" which in fact translated into, "never, never."

With annoyance, I have to accept that because of my keenness to assist and improve this man's lot, I have reconfirmed what he and millions of others in this country know already, and that is — that we tourists and foreigners are fools. Sent by gods to be like carrion to the crows. At least that's how it feels to me, such is my limited perception at this time.

Chapter 24

Where should we dine tonight? Not a great deal of menu choice, lots of restaurants/cafes, the food is good, freshly caught fish mainly. Queenie and I decided to visit a different restaurant, probably one behind the beach, near Ben's shop. In actual fact you don't get much Indian food in Kovalam, not in the same way you would in the towns, or cities, or for that matter in the UK. I reckon the most interesting places to eat for variation, freshness, and sheer speed of delivery, are the bus stations. Dirty, smelly, busy, chaotic they may be. The quality and the freshness of the food however make it all worthwhile.

I caught up with Ben, who had just finished making four pairs of shorts for me. We sat and chatted. He was a little worried about Christina, who by now had made him an offer she hoped he wouldn't refuse.

"You come to Milano, I work, pay all expenses." She had told him. He did not want to go. His life savings of forty thousand rupees would not last a month in Milan. He had to make his decision very quickly; she had to leave in a couple of days' time. Soon after our arrival she joined us, sat down, and looked nervous, jumpy. I don't expect she could understand why he would turn down her offer to go with her to Europe, leave this glorified cess pool and live on the continent of plenty. I felt her pain, well part of it, sort of. She had a motive, and she loved him. I guess this offer was a good one, could be the offer of a lifetime for him.

His reluctance was difficult for her to understand. This place, however difficult, was his home.

John and Gunda arrived. They were leaving the next day, for the UK, together. This looked like it could have a happy ending, a nice feeling for us. Gunda handed over her tea maker as a parting gift. A brilliant device, a pocket immersion heater complete with cup, packed up in a plastic container.

I resisted any more than two beers, as I was conscious of the need to keep my wits about me. I was aware that I had to be more on the ball, even more so as Queenie was not having things too good at all. I must admit it's all a bit of an added mental and physical strain and was not having a good effect on me either.

We got home at about eleven thirty. I went around to Kadhikan, who it transpired was asleep by then. Not knowing this I knocked on the door. Kadhikan had disturbed my sleep on many an occasion. So the consequences were guilt free, I was past caring.

"Kardy, you there?"

"Yes Jack, wait." He came to the door, and I walked away, so as not to disturb Valsala and the children. He followed.

"Why didn't you come to see me today?" I asked quietly, in his ear. "Did you see the lawyer?"

"Tomorrow, Jack, tomorrow!" he said in muffled tones.

"What time tomorrow?" I replied.

"Afternoon, Jack, I come here tomorrow to get you."

"Kardy, Why don't I believe you! Where is the lawyer's office?"

"Thiruvallum. I go tomorrow!"

"WHERE EXACTLY IS THE LAWYER'S OFFICE, KADHIKAN?" I raised my voice in order to project seriousness into these proceedings, and forgetting for the moment his sleeping wife and children, but remembering all to clearly Kardy's previous wild goose chases I had been subjected to.

"Opposite the printer's, next to the bank, Lawyer office there." He gabbled, obviously nervous.

"What time?"

"Four pm sir, four pm, I come here."

"No, Kardy, I don't want to hang around here if I don't have to, I will go straight to the lawyer's and you meet me there at four." Knowing that the village was so small it would be impossible for us to miss each other but suspecting, if not knowing, that he wouldn't turn up, not at four, not at all.

"You go?" He seemed surprised, though I often found it hard to assess his body language or expression from his intonation. He could simply have been checking that he had heard correctly.

"Yes, why not? You must bring your copy of the agreement." I replied.

"OK, I bring sir. Please tell me, when you leave here, when you leave my house?" He asked with a wimpish and pathetic-looking cowed expression

I thought a moment, "About three I suppose, I don't know really, I may go somewhere else but I will be at the lawyer's office for four o'clock as you say. I will be there, don't worry."

"No. NO when you leave my house forever, Jack forever."

"I will leave here when you sign the agreement and not before." I snapped, plainly annoyed.

My thoughts at that moment were that he was an ungrateful, mean little toad. I walked off quite upset.

Queenie had made tea. I told her what he had said.

"He won't be there." She replied.

We then had to try to reassure ourselves yet again that we, or I, had and were doing the right thing. Yes, we agreed, I had and was.

I was aware that I really had had enough of Kadhikan as he had with me, and was I developing a bullying demeanour? I really could do very well by planning an exit sometime very soon, what was stopping me was the idea that he was making a fool of me, having taken everything on offer but continuing to make further financial demands that I could not afford. I was not to be responsible for the daily financing of him or his family, and that refusal by me did not go well with him.

An hour or so before the pre-arranged time of four o'clock, I thought I might make a move towards the village of Thiruvallum. John and Gunda arrived to say their final goodbyes, so we walked together as far as the crossroads. We wished them well, and thanked them for their friendship; it really had been a privilege to know these young people. We watched their rickshaw until it vanished into the dust and fumes of the late afternoon.

Finally turning away and walking up the road slowly and in thought towards the printer's shop that "K" had described. There was no bank opposite. No lawyer's. After checking both sides of the road, and the single small bank in the village, the only lawyer's office we could find was about a mile away from Thiruvallum towards Trivandrum, the state capital. There was no printer's or lawyer's near any bank either. I should have known, I did, but had hoped, Queenie certainly did.

"The lying little sod! Let's go to Kovalam and find him! I'll wring his neck!"

"No! Wait!" Queenie said. "Wait until four at least, we'll stand outside the printer's. He may turn up." We walked back, to and fro, we waited. No Kardy. Now my blood was boiling. This snivelling little SOD had taken the piss all along! Made a fool of me yet again! Something needs to happen here, I thought to myself, he needs to feel some consequence, to share the burden of humiliation with us. He must believe we are total fools.

"He's a con man, preying on our good nature", Queenie said.

"I'll show him some good bloody nature!"

Walking the three or four miles home in silence, all good sense and reason were worn out. We waited and waited. Kadhikan did not return home at all that evening.

The following day we took the bus to Kovalam to find a room where we could stay comfortably for a week or two, having deciding to leave Kadhikan's house on the following Monday or Tuesday, irrespective of any agreement the tasks in the house had been completed. I had kept my end of the deal.

I didn't like this feeling of defeat. I must try again, I thought. Kadhikan should not be allowed to get away with this. Queenie and I had put ourselves out a great deal, both here and at home in order to meet our commitments to him, he must be forced to meet his mutually agreed obligations. This left only two days to find, meet, and try for a final attempt to get "K" to do the right thing. After that I'd write the whole thing off, I would never return to "K's" again.

A good and early start in the morning meant we were in Kovalam early. We easily discovered a large, almost airy and lovely room at the edge of a paddy field, surrounded by palms, tropical plants and bananas. A quiet place away from the crowded beach area. The lady who looked after it seemed pleasant enough.

"So that's it," I said, "Move in here, why not?" Queenie agreed. It was now Sunday. "On Tuesday, definitely then?" Queenie nodded. I left a deposit, and we got the bus back to Kadhikans.

Once again, probably for the last time we walked from the school past all the houses and people we had come to recognise so well over the past few weeks. Although we had got used to them, the people we met still asked the same questions as they always had asked and we replied with the same answers every time we had passed from the first day we had arrived.

I turned my thoughts to Kadhikan as I walked, Queenie strolling along by my side, lost in her own thoughts. "Well, that's it," I mused, "he's got away with it. Taken all and for nothing." By the time we reached the path leading to the house, my reflections had not done me any good at all. I had become very upset indeed. I did not want to see him ever again.

There he stood.

He was in the gateway of his neighbour's courtyard. I gritted my teeth and passed him, saying nothing, and walked in to the house. He looked like he hadn't noticed me. I closed the door, and turned to Queenie.

"This is it, Queenie."

"What?" She exclaimed, startled by my tone.

"I am going to have the little SOD." I muttered angrily.

"No! Jack! You'll kill him!"

"Stay out of this, Queenie. You needn't be involved." I pleaded. She turned and walked into the kitchen.

I stormed out of the house knowing very well that this was to be forced compliance, not at all what I had originally expected it to come to. It was now to be payback time. He would discover exactly what a soft touch we really are. The calculating part of me knew that if I lost my temper totally and hit him, I would be in trouble, I must protect myself, and there must be no witnesses. I must get him away from his neighbours, and into my part of the house. I would give him one chance.

A SON OF A DOG'S CHANCE.

He saw me. I adopted what I hoped appeared to be a pleasant smile. I dared not get too close. He and his neighbours might detect my true feelings, my upset.

"Kardy! Hiya mate! Come, see! I've got a surprise for you."

If I appealed to his greed, he would hang himself so to speak, very appropriate I thought.

"For me, Jack?" His sheepish smile opened wide to one of enthusiasm, of anticipation, his eyes opened wider.

"Present, Kardy. Yes. Come on." I waved in the direction of the house. I casually turned my back on him, and walked back inside. Moments later, he followed. Head thrown back, laughing, sure of yet another undeserved prize. He stepped over the threshold. I stepped out from behind the door.

"Oh no." I saw that Queenie was slowly advancing toward me from the other side of the room, mouth open in silent protest. She knew! I had to be quick.

I grabbed him with one hand by his shirt collar, pulled him around to the inside of the door, and out of sight of the neighbours. His eyes bulged as I threw him back hard against the wall, his mouth wide in sudden terror. I lifted him to the full extent of my arm, his scrawny neck encased in his shirt collar, and that in my hand.

"NONONO!" He gurgled in fear.

Queenie had now leapt on my back, desperately trying to pull me away.

"Stop, stop, you'll kill him!" She gasped.

I tried to push my other arm backward to get her away. She was screaming, he was crying pitifully "No, no, not kill! Please, please."

I shouted as loud and as hard as I could, right into his face.

"You will take me to a lawyer now, or Valsala will be a widow. Do you hear?" Emphasising each word with a violent shake of his limp body. He was choking, and could not speak. I held on, and let him choke a little more, I needed to emphasise that this was it for him, his nonsense had gone on for far too long.

His neck was taking his full weight; his feet were off the floor. It occurred to me that I could easily hurt him. I slowly lowered this flapping, disgusting creature to the ground as it also occurred to me that if I did hit or hurt him even accidentally, it would be the end for all of us and not least Queenie. I could see quite vividly the possibilities of me on the inside of an Indian jail.

"Do you fucking hear me?" I bellowed.

"Yes," he coughed, "yes. Now, I take." He made a move to the door.

"If you fucking run away, Kardy, I'll catch you and pull your fucking head off."

I was calming down now. Relaxing my grip, I thrust him back against the door, where he cowered, too terrified to move. I was ashamed of myself. I had blown it, lost control. Queenie was shocked, speechless and staring. This was unanticipated collateral damage. It had not occurred to me the harm my actions may have.

"Queenie, Queenie, come on, it's all over." I said gently. She lowered herself carefully onto one of the plastic chairs. He scrambled around the door.

"WAIT!" I commanded. "Wait for me!" He stopped.

"Yes, Jack, yes, I wait." And he stood trembling by the door.

"Queenie, I'm sorry you were here and in the room," I apologised, "but I am near the conclusion now, please try to understand."

"I do Jack, I do. I know how you must feel. It's just very frightening."

"OK, now, I'll go to a lawyer. Will you come?"

"Yes, I will. Otherwise I'll just sit here and worry."

"Right OK. We'll go by rickshaw with him to a lawyer. I will explain to the lawyer just what I want," and turning to Kardy, I concluded, "is that OK?"

"Yes sir, yes sir."

Walking over to him, I said, "We'll go now. Go and get your copy of the agreement and bring it back here."

He scurried away, to return moments later with the agreement in his hand.

"Open it." I commanded. "Can you read it?"

"Yes sir" and he commenced to read it to me very competently.

"Which bit of that do you NOT like?" I asked.

"Is all good, sir. No problem."

"If you have a problem, you can change it." I persisted.

"No sir. Good. Agreement good."

"OK, then, let's go."

It was getting dark, but I knew that local businesses would be opening up again as they always did after the midday heat, about now. I flagged down a rickshaw, and we travelled without speaking. There did not seem much left to say. Only the popping of the rickshaw's little engine disturbed the silence. Kadhikan finally indicated for the driver to pull up, and I paid him off. This office was neither near a bank nor a printer's. In fact, there was no indication that this building was a lawyer's place of work or residence at all. I followed Kadhikan up the narrow garden path, wondering if he was about to have the last laugh after all, and that this lawyer was no lawyer at all.

Kadhikan rang the bell hanging by the door of the large conservatory, fronting an impressive-looking bungalow. A smartly dressed, very large, youngish man appeared, wearing European style clothing.

"Well, what can I do for you?" He asked me in perfect English, ignoring Kadhikan. I explained that I needed a lawyer to witness the signing of a contract and I needed the contract verbally explained to Kadhikan in Malayalam. I needed to know whether Kadhikan agreed with the contract, and to modify it if needed. Finally, if the lawyer was convinced that Kadhikan fully understood and agreed to the contract, I needed us both to sign in the lawyers' presence. Then all parties would keep a copy.

"Let me see." He snapped. I handed him a copy, he disappeared into the house with it, leaving us alone on the doorstep. A pleasant-faced middle aged lady appeared, and invited us in, indicating for us to be seated in the conservatory. We were no sooner seated, than a heavy-set, elderly man appeared, introducing himself as an attorney.

"You want to make contract?" He asked us all. I nodded, not looking at Kadhikan.

"Fine, no problem."

He read out the agreement in English, then again, for Kadhikan's benefit, in Malayalam. The pleasant lady reappeared, bearing tea and cakes. We all munched and drank gratefully then signed the agreement. I paid the five hundred-rupee fees, and we left. Job done.

Why had this simple task taken so long, and at such emotional cost? Somehow somewhere I have, I hope, learnt a lesson, what is that lesson?

K had reverted to his usual laid back manner much as if it all was water off a duck's back. "Jack I think you going kill me."

"I was!" I replied. He laughed out loud and left, saying he was to pick up the Lambi from his father's house, he waved bye bye.

Queenie and I walked towards home in the pitch blackness, down the long main road that we had crossed over and walked down so many times before, myself apologising for the previous upset. Queenie insisting she was OK. We passed a double sized shack on our left-hand side, and looked down in to that dip that ran alongside the length of the raised road. The sign on the shack declared, in English "Government Toddy Shop."

Assorted males were falling and stumbling about outside it. One man, who for some reason probably least known to himself, had removed his lungi, or maybe it had simply dropped down. Now he struggled with it, entangling it around his head. All these guys were in a drunken bad way. I left Queenie standing on the side of the road, while I scrambled down the embankment and into the almost unlit toddy shop. Everyone inside stared wide-eyed, entranced, each man with his particular lean, gait, stance or wobble, all caught in the glare of my invisible but blinding flash light, melted, staggered, lurched, wanted, needed, to shake my hand. Like small demons congratulating me on my questionable success.

"One bottle." I shouted.

"Twenty rupees," the barman snapped. I took the bottle and got out quick.

Toddy is supposed to be fresh coconut liquor, strictly controlled by the government. This being a government toddy shop, I assumed that what I had in my hand was good stuff. I had tasted toddy; most tourists don't seem to have much access to it for some reason. Maybe it was too cheap to trust. Maybe tourists don't know it exists, why should they? Package tourists don't usually get involved with local activity at this level and are actively discouraged from doing so, and now of course I understand why. We continued our walk home in the darkness. We were almost there, when up rode Kadhikan on his newly reclaimed Lambi.

"Hello, madam, sir. You walk home?"

"Yes." I replied. Kadhikan spotted the bottle of toddy.

"What this, toddy?" He asked, sounding shocked.

"Yes, from government shop."

"No, no, no, sir. Not good. Will do great harm." I laughed.

"It's only booze. Is it so strong?"

"Yes sir. Not toddy. Is chemical spirit and Diaza-morph, like use in hospital make very ill. OK for me, we used to it, no good for European."

"Diazamorph sounds dangerous," I thought. It sounded like a Diazepam and Morphine cocktail.

"You must not drink. Make crazy." He was genu-inely concerned. I threw the bottle into the canal at the side of the road. Poor SOD probably thought I would set about him again if I went crazy on chemicals. Maybe I had accidentally discovered a reason for K's behaviour. DIAZAMORPH??

In an ideal world, there would have been someone or somewhere to go to, to debrief, talk to, unpack all those dangerous feelings. I wish there had been, it might have prevented the explosion of my compoun-ded confusion, anger and frustration. I felt like I had been stretched on some mental rack, and it was still stretching. There was no satisfaction in extracting compliance through duress. A natural extension of events, a natural willingness should have culminated in Kadhikan being enthusiastic about the prospect of our return. I was very aware that forcing the contract was not in the spirit that we had when we had begun the project. Kadhikan and I were poor examples of our respective cultures. I had resorted to physical violence. I felt that he had reneged and cheated.

It was my mistake for not realizing that a wide cultural gap would exist. Maybe unknown to me jealousy had emerged in the village, with him having what appeared to be a new-found wealth, how was he, their poor friend entitled to all this and not them? It could be that somehow the construction of his house had been influenced by people out of his control, the builders perhaps, his neighbours maybe.

Maybe his and their expectations were due to their ignorance. I had explained to him in many ways that I, and all working people like him, need to work to live. I, Jack am in my country a poor man, the same as he is in his, and I am treated with contempt, not that much different than a Dalit in India. That is why, I explained, we needed to help each other. We could share our skills and efforts for the good of all of us.

There was a feeling of immediacy to leave the house, get away from this place; to run away, to get Kadhikan and my dilemmas out of our heads. We both shared this urgency.

People would like it here. It could work. It just needed "K" to do his thing, to get the customers from the airport, to make contacts. It was now theoretically possible for K to improve his life and that of his wife and children, and to set an example to his needy peers.

It was going to be a hot day for everyone. It was about eight thirty. A power cut. No fan. We were wet with sweat when we awoke, wet and already exhausted. Today was leaving day. We had to get to Kovalam. It took an hour to pack. The fan came on. We stripped off again, and ran for the shower, to stand cool and dripping under the swirling heat. We had to move! Packs in position, we walked round to say goodbye to Valsala., whose beautiful oval face creased and her big brown eyes filled with tears. She at least was sorry to see us go. She and Queenie hugged. I said goodbye. If her husband had been half of what she had been to us, we all would have benefited much more than we had.

Extracts From Queenie's Diary 5

To be able to write this short piece offers a degree of catharsis for me, and hopefully an explanation to you the reader of my feelings about these matters. It is a relief to finally leave Kadhikan's house. I had enjoyed completing the project, and the experience of living in a small South Indian village. However, I was deeply disturbed by Jack's outburst of anger towards Kadhikan, even though I felt Jack had some justification for it.

Kadhikan had not only expected us to provide for him, and stubbornly tried to evade making an agreement with us as he had said he would, but had avoided carrying out one single hour of work alongside either of us. Not a nail did he knock nor paint brush did he lift or broom did he push.

I felt strangely embarrassed, and could barely look Kadhikan in the face. He had annoyed and disappointed me enormously, but I felt, as I knew Jack felt, that Jack's apparent lack of control was at best inappropriate, and at worst, extremely dangerous.

Deep down I had the uncomfortable feeling that we might have misjudged the man, because we had been unable to overcome our language and cultural differences. At the same time, I was sorry to leave Valsala, she had never altered in her attitude to us, she was as warm and pleasant towards us as at our first meeting. I hoped I would see her again, and in pleasanter circumstances. As I hugged her for the last time, and saw the tears in her eyes, I consoled myself with the thought that whatever else happened to her, she now had a fine house to pass on to her daughter. In the meantime, she could hold up her head amongst her neighbours, now that she also had a house which was at least as good as theirs, if not better.

I knew Jack was sad because he had not felt able to develop the project further for the family's benefit. I know that had Kadhikan been more positive and actively involved himself and been less demanding Jack would have contributed much more than he had already. He had mentioned the possibility of building a further storey on top of the flat roof. Kadhikan however had thoroughly demotivated him and consequently had lost out a great deal. So it was with very mixed emotions that I walked away from the little house where I'd had such a variety of experiences.

Now I understand why it is that people who like to help others in need or want, usually do so through the aegis of an arm's-length charitable organisation, and perhaps also why it costs so much to deliver that charity to the actual people who need it.

There must be much money and resources wasted, how can it not be? It is difficult to imagine anything but complications when dealing conscientiously with other people's needs and contributions.

Chapter 25

We were quieter than usual as we rode in the rickshaw to Kovalam, each absorbed with our own thoughts. All our possessions were with us, which meant four heavy packs. Initially, I had been worried I would not be able to carry all these rucksacks as we moved around India, but I had discovered there was a knack to it, and certainly over short distances was able to carry quite heavy weights. Even so, we were both glad to dump our bags on the bed in our new room, and collapse in a heap beside them. "Let's have another holiday now." smiled Queenie.

In an effort to clear our minds of the accumulated bad feelings of the past few weeks we leapt immediately into action, and decided to spend the rest of the day in Trivandrum. We conceded to the calls of the rickshaw drivers and found ourselves rattling along avoiding the usual selection of obstructions human, bovine and otherwise. The driver finally dropped us off at the spot where hell was conceived amidst the roaring buses and manic crush. It was too much and we decided to opt out for a while, and went to the pictures as surely that would be the distraction we needed.

After the glare outside, the foyer of the picture house was so dark it took our eyes time to re-adjust, and then to make out the people lurking in the even darker corners, white flashing eyes here and teeth there. The people shouted excitedly at each other across the twenty feet or so of space between the small groupings.

The wall spaces above their heads were plastered with large exotic posters, each with its own dramatic perspective. The clash of the once alarmingly bright colours had their over-stated tales to tell. The script was illegible to us but served as added decoration. Black frills across the centre, top, bottom. It added to the strangeness of the occasion.

We had been told, by Surjeen I think, about this place and the way he described it to us had left sufficient impression to put the prospect of visiting in our collective memory and here we were, quite aware, expectant even, that anything could happen, and most likely would. The wooden kiosk seemed out of place in this great hall. It somehow looked as if it had not been constructed in situ, didn't belong. It looked a bit like wooden home-made shed, and would in fact have been more suited to a building site, or perhaps a British allotment garden. We waited for a few minutes for the designated time, then the single forty watt light bulb above the shed flickered on and off and on again. At which the people who had previously stood around looking bored, ran to the kiosk pushing each other aside like school children at break time. Ha ha, we had beaten them to it, as we were already in place having considered which queue started where. Most people went for the cheap seats, we on the other hand decided on first class at twenty-five rupees each, for which we had to wait until the mass of cheap tickets had been distributed.

For some reason it seemed to take forever to issue the tickets. By the time one ticket had been issued, the previous person had disappeared, walked the length of the theatre, upstairs through the doors and into the auditorium. We discovered why it took such a long time as our turn came — each ticket was issued with a hand-written receipt.

We paid our twenty-five rupees each and peered up the semi-circular stairway. By now our eyes had adjusted and we could see a little further into the gloom. Three young men in their haste and excitement rushed by and all but knocked us off our feet, before we were able to place our first steps on to the marble stairway, however and unlike most Indian people we had contact with, the boys stopped and apologised profusely and by way of penance walked slowly behind us up the winding stairway.

I opened the door into the large dark space. We stepped forward into the unknown and met with the most amazingly life-enhancing breeze. Goose pimples stood erect, a delicious shiver crept down our backs. This was a different world, tiers and row after row of spacious, luxurious leather armchairs. Chairs to curl up in, to really relax in, to cool right down to a temperature so previously unknown it could make you cry. This promised heaven. The blissful moment haunted only by the distant possibility of being driven back into the sweltering heat after the show was over.

Jackie Chan, super hero and gyro-dynamic master of martial arts and detective work, was upstaged only by the all-round digital three, or even maybe four or five dimensional sound system. From theatre shaking thunderbolt, to a pin bouncing from chair to carpet, to the tinkle of cut glass on cut glass. This surely was the new beginning. WOW.

The pre-film advertisements had a more down to earth quality, as if designed by the local primary school. Even this wonderful sound system could not improve the high-pitched screeches pouring out from the screen. As the belly dancers sang, the roars, jeers and laughter of the mainly indigenous audience rose. It was infectious. Tears poured down our faces as this highly interactive audience revelled in the inadequacies of the very amateurish and plainly silly sales clips. The exotic dancers were decked not in the fine jewels of the orient but in cooking oil bottles, six-inch nails and paraffin lamps. As English-speaking people and readers of English subtitles we had an advantage of a sort, as we did not need to decipher the Hindi and Malayalam voice-overs. We felt fairly confident that these rapid and completely unsynchronised high-pitched languages were, if not the cause of such hysterical merriment, must certainly be adding to it.

Just as the film reached its peak of excitement, the screen went dark. What now? We wondered. The screen flickered, and then burst into life once more. A single word spread across the screen, the writing blurred and jagged as if that particular piece of celluloid had seen better days. "INTERMISSION" it announced boldly, in faded gold on a red background. The lights went up, and all around us people left their seats and rushed back down the stairs, to return in short order with ice-creams, drinks and other delicacies. Another sudden plunge into darkness and off we went again, rollicking around America with Jackie Chan and co, accompanied by the vocal delights of the audience.

Ninety minutes later we stepped into the blinding light and forced our way into the hot, fume ridden air. In order to hang on to our enlightened spirits we opted for a proper taxi home. We drove straight to Kovalam in a virtual straight line with auto-rickshaws swerving and parting to the blast of the taxi's horn. Black smoke parted as our taxi overtook buses and gaily painted trucks. As usual the cyclists, like the cattle, didn't seem to care, and neither did we. An unfamiliar emotion for both of us. We were tourists.

Back in Kovalam, we wandered slowly into the breeze. The sea air was having a cooling effect so we decided to spend the rest of the day sitting in the shade and in between pouring ice-cold beer down our throats, discussed what we might do with the spare time we were making for ourselves. For a day or two, we headed for the warm clear sea, the beach cafes and some good company. The days slid by peacefully. We did the usual tourist type things for a couple of days around the immediate area of Kovalam, and then both agreed we would really like to do something special, go somewhere, **"do something"** had become the motto for both of us.

Having heard about Hampi from a small group of young tourists at the Christmas party we were convinced there must have been more to this historic city than it just being "cool" as described by the girls. Also everyone we had met sang the praises of Goa — so we agreed to try and combine them both if that were possible. We knew very well we were tourists now, what with no work to do. We thought we could get used to taking photographs, swimming, and generally lazing around. As it happened, a couple of days lazing about on the beach and in the beachside shack restaurants was about all we could take! For us, "holiday" does not read "relaxation"! We like to be busy, to have a goal.

A reconnaissance of the train station seemed a good way to spend a day, so off we set, bright and early, to discover for ourselves the means of getting to Goa as quickly and cheaply as possible. We'd passed the station numerous times, so locating it was no problem. Traffic, beggars and street sellers, however, presented their usual barriers to progress, and I was at times, sorely tempted to lay about them with my trusty umbrella as a means of creating a passage through the crowd.

Hot, dusty and tired, we finally negotiated the turmoil on the street, and burst with relief into the comparative cool and shade of the train station. It was as if someone had pressed the "pause" button on the video player. Everything was at a standstill, it seemed. People stood, lay or squatted about, patiently waiting for their trains, or queuing stolidly for tickets. We skittered to a halt, blinking in the sudden dimness after the glare in the street outside. Taking a second or two to get our bearings, we spotted the sign which read confidently in large red letters, "Information." Good start. We approached the dusty glass box and waited our turn. Now in confidence having taken the precaution of writing down the name of our destination, we had found that most people here could read English considerably better than they could understand our spoken words. Surely the information clerk would be able to read our destination? No doubt our strong Northern accents were a puzzle to them.

We struggled to understand the logic of the gentleman ensconced in the glass "Information" box. He was not, it seemed, in possession of any useful information whatsoever, or that's what we thought he said! "No information sir" but he did very kindly direct us to an upstairs office, which was where, he assured us, we would find all the information we required. We threaded our way through the press of humanity, up the stairs, along the corridor, and joined the line patiently waiting outside the office. When our turn came, the clerk was impeccably polite, but felt sure that the information we required was held in the "Information" desk, which was situated down the stairs, turn right, and along the platform, just outside the station manager's office. We were equally sure that the information we required was not held there, having just been told so, some twenty or so minutes ago and had been directed here to him, from the afore-mentioned information box clerk.

This clerk's face assumed such an accumulated ex-pression of hurt, surprise and dismay, that we felt un-able to pursue the matter further in view of the threat to his sensibilities and continued good health. So con-ceding defeat for the moment, we returned to the glass "Information" box. Where we joined the queue again. When our turn came, a sense of deja vu hovered about us. Sure enough, we were directed to the up-stairs office again. "We're being given the run-around!" I exclaimed, as we headed wearily for a tem-porarily unoccupied bench situated charmingly just outside the "Gents", with all its accompanying acrid perfume.

"Seems like it." Queenie agreed, in rather choked tones, we had been at this now for two hours!

"I'm going to try the station manager's office." Queenie followed, glad to be away from the strong aromatic area where we'd been sitting, yet expecting another queue, and another futile waste of time.

Wrong again, the manager's office was bare, apart from a large desk, a couple of chairs, some filing cab-inets, the manager, and someone we took to be his as-sistant, who lounged against the filing cabinets throughout the interview. The manager was impec-cable in his uniform, spoke perfect English, and couldn't have been more helpful. A full list of train times, fares, destinations to all parts of India, and a cup of tea later, we left the office, feeling satisfied that we'd accomplished at least that part of our mission. But wondering, why? Why two information offices without information but with long queues, and one man with all the information at his fingertips, but no queue? We could only mutter once again the mantra. "This is India — go with the flow."

It now seemed expedient to examine the trains that would take us to our destination, or at least a similar vehicle. I feel confident now that you the reader can share the assumption that you cannot assume anything here, so best check everything first. There was only one train to Goa, which left on a Friday evening, so we had plenty of time to book a seat, pack our bags, and spend another day or two lazing about.

As we left the manager's office, a train pulled into the station on the platform where we stood. This seemed to be an ideal time to take a closer look inside one of these enormous beasts. As people poured off the train, we peered as best we could through the high, grimy windows. There was little to be seen of the gloomy interior in this way, so as soon as practicable, we climbed aboard to take a look at the accommodation on offer. We had seen, stencilled in faded lettering on the rusty exterior of the coach, the words "Sleeper Car". We were not expecting luxury, which was a good thing really, for even though the words "Sleeper Car" were followed by "First Class", luxury was not the first word that came to mind as we gazed in amazement at the sleeping arrangements. I would not have thought it possible that six people could fit into a six-foot cube, but I was wrong. They can. The third tier of bunks looked pretty challenging to me, as there was no ladder, and hanging suspended from a pair of rusty chains on a two feet wide plank was not going to induce restful sleep on my part. "I think we should just assume that we won't be sleeping, and make the best of it. We'll just book seats. It'll be cheaper that way." I ventured. "Yeah," I assured myself, "it'll be a wheeze".

"We'll see quite a lot of the country as we pass through." said the voice behind me.

I didn't want to remind Queenie that we'd be travelling through the night, and we would be lucky to see anything at all.

In somewhat subdued mood, I clambered down from the train after Queenie, trying to convince myself that yes of course it would be a "wheeze."

"Well, this is as good as it gets, let's book the tickets." Suggested Queenie, looking at me for approval.

"OK, come on."

Ninety-five minutes later we had spent three hundred and seventy-eight rupees on two tickets to ride second class, which meant there were wooden bench-like seats to sit on, and we were to travel three hundred miles or more, through the state we are in, namely Kerala, across another state, Karnataka, and half-way into the third, Goa. A journey that was at best twenty-four hours, and at worst, a shrug of the shoulders, a smile, literally days. Anyone's guess!

Not to worry too much, we had the tickets and in three days we would be going on our way. Another advantage being that we wouldn't have to wait to get on the train as we were told it was parked up here all ready and waiting for Friday. "Excellent!" We wouldn't have to wait for the train, we both agreed and drifted back to the digs to pass the time until we left for Goa.

When we finally arrived back we couldn't help noticing the three young Indian boys hanging around the door of the apartment next to ours. We nodded and smiled. They looked nervous. The door of the apartment outside which they were hanging around suddenly opened, and out ran another young Indian boy, brandishing a small radio. He held it out to the boys who immediately became excited, with big smiles and loud chatter.

I stopped to open our door as a middle-aged, bald-headed European followed the boy out saying, "You come" in accented English. He noticed Queenie and then myself but exclaimed quite distinctly to the boys, "Go, go, go." Each "GO" louder than the last.

By this time we had unlocked our door and let ourselves in, now interested in next door's affairs. Seemed strange, "Come in." then on seeing us, reverse the command to "Go, go, go!" I returned to the doorway and shouted to the boys, "Are you OK?" They looked, giggled like schoolgirls, and made gestures with fingers to their heads implying that the man, who had now gone into his own apartment and closed the door, was "screwy". Attention went back to the squeaky little radio as they continued to hang around. I stood a moment longer, and not knowing what to make of this event, decided to take the tea Queenie had offered, and lie down on my bed for a while, before going down to the beach bar huts for a beer. I woke about eight thirty that evening to the noise of shouting and laughter outside. I opened my door, and there were now half a dozen young boys outside next door. Now with the addition of an irate landlady, who was half shouting, half shooing the boys away.

On seeing me, she approached, saying, "Bad man, bad man, he take boys in. Dirty man. He Go. You tell him, go."

It appeared that our next door neighbour, who had arrived a couple of days earlier, was giving away small gifts to the boys. The landlady believed he was doing so in exchange for some sexual favour or other. Well the guy had certainly behaved strangely when I had seen him. Perhaps she was right. I was in a strange position here myself in so far as I couldn't prove any of this. How could I, should I, ask him to leave on her behalf?

She was now banging on his door, saying, "I bring police, get out!" There was no light in the room, so was he hiding in there? The situation was getting out of hand here. I decided I would tell her that I would ask him to leave if she went back to her living quarters on the roof. Whether or not he was up to no good, he definitely wasn't going to reveal himself if he thought he was going to be assaulted by the irate landlady and jeered at by the boys. I pointed this out to her. She told the boys in their own language, they drifted off, and she came into our room, and told us again that she knew he was playing with the boys, and attracting them with gifts.

So I said, "OK, it doesn't look good, therefore I will tap on his door and ask him to go on your behalf."

She replied, "He German, can speak English sometime."

"OK," I replied, "let's wait a while, give him time to think, then I'll ask him to go." She agreed, and said she would go to the roof where she lives. Three quarters of an hour later, I decided to go next door. The light was on. Tap tap.

He opened the door. "What you want?" he said, grumpily.

"You'll have to go." I said.

"Why?"

"Because landlady upstairs is upset, she says you have to go now."

"OK." He said, went inside, and closed the door.

I decided to go to the bar, and off I went. I'd done as I was asked, so if he goes, he goes, and if not, I guess the police will move him. Perhaps they should anyway. I got to the bar and told Ben, who has not gone to Milan. Ben said he knows about the man, everybody knows. People like him come here all the time.

"I'll ring the police if you like, Jack."

"OK, why not? He may be wanted, they may know him." So Ben rang. The police say they know of the man, what can they do? No proof. We all agree to change the subject. We have no proof either. However, as we walk home, in almost blackness, going up towards the main road picked out by passing moonlight, we see the neighbour with a case in each hand. So that's it, he's gone.

We let ourselves into our apartment, turn on the fan and drop to sleep after another eventful day.

The couple of days we had left to wait before we caught the train to Goa were very relaxing, dipping in the sea, chatting to passers-by, taking a few pictures, finding new tracks into the forest areas to the back of the beach area, scrambling up hillsides, spotting the odd snake — at a distance of course — and before we knew it we were ready for the off and down we went by usual means to the Trivandrum main railway station.

The train had that old-fashioned, pleasant rhythm da da da da clunk! The same sound and rhythm we used to experience in the U.K. before longer railway lines were introduced, how reminiscent, romantic even.

We weren't crowded, the seats didn't feel too bad either, after all we were sitting on wooden slats that bent a little. The couple sat opposite were facing us about ten feet away, well outside any normal hearing range, they were all tidy and sparkling, looking eager. It turned out the man had passed his civil service exams and was off to take up a new post in Mumbai which probably cost him a small Indian fortune in baksheesh. Civil service, the best job to have in India, apparently. He looked a little bit like Gandhi, a suit, small head, small round glasses, pleasant expression. They all seemed very happy, and enjoyed telling us of their expectations.

We decided that the train would probably stop quite often at the stations on the way, and therefore we needn't carry food or refreshment. We were right, but the refreshment came via the vendors who were either on the train or hanging off it, or indeed, waiting on the platforms. We were certainly spoilt for choice! Various meat dishes, thalis, vegetables, fruits, dished up on newspapers but very satisfying. Our friends opposite had brought a complete picnic with baskets and posh looking stainless steel tiffin boxes and munched their way throughout the journey. The smell of food stripped away the usual nasty smells of excreta and urine that permeate the air on approach to any station or town. The liberal use of jasmine and rose oils by most people also helped to keep the bad smells under control.

The jugglers and dancers, made up with various masks and paint, entertained us for a few rupees, as did a dancing musical troupe with flutes drums, rattles, simple trumpets and the occasional performing monkey thrown in. In fact the whole trip was nothing less than a rich, exotic, cultural event that changed at every one of the forty or so stops the train made. It certainly was a much richer and less frustrating journey than we had imagined. I'd say we thoroughly enjoyed it. Yes, it's true we didn't sleep much, and our bums were definitely numb, and as the hours rolled by the cramps came and went, as did the scenery. With the beautiful Western Ghats on our right-hand side, and flat coastal plains on the left, I sat musing in one of the rare lulls of the evening. I pondered the colours, and how the bright strong reds, yellows and greens of the paintwork and signs on the buildings outside, the saris indeed most fabrics brightened up the dark and dinginess of the evening carriage. On the one hand they complemented the natural deep colours of the flora and on the other, the bright sun of the daytime with the white bleached hills and concrete structures that one sees so much of. It could all have been planned that way.

We awoke sharply with the screams of metal on metal, and the crashes and clunks of the rail coaches buffeting each other. We had arrived at our destination. Goa, the land of Portuguese conquest and terminating hippy trail. We allowed the Indian folks off our carriage first. Where did they get the energy after such a journey and so early in the morning? The sun was coming up already, the air was damp and the coolest it was likely to get. Thankfully we didn't have all the packs with us, our grateful landlady of the Kovalam apartments had stored them for us on her roof, so we strode out easily into this not-quite-fresh air, into a new place completely. The capital of Goa. Panjim.

Our trusty Lonely Planet travel guide, which was getting more dog-eared by the day, informed us that we needed to make our way to the town of Mapusa, and from there to Calangute where we would find plenty of choice in cheap, clean accommodation. The guide also told us that there were plenty of buses throughout the day. We were soon to discover the truth of this statement. The guide also mentioned that these buses were often very crowded. We discovered that this was also true, what else would we expect? Yet somehow the written word never really conveys the absolute truth or reality of a situation. We had thought that buses in Kerala were pretty crowded, and were sure we would cope admirably with anything a tiny state like Goa could throw at us.

Goa was a different world from the one we had left such a short time before. This was immediately apparent. No one took the slightest notice of us. We were not hassled in any way. Our question, "Where is the bus for Mapusa, please?" was answered swiftly and courteously, then we were left alone to find our way. The streets were cleaner, the people although Indian were rounder somehow, less bony, less dainty I suppose; mostly in European dress, almost a sari and lungi free area.

The whole place had a Mediterranean rather than an Indian feel. We began to relax a little as we made our way to the bus stand. We were too tired to take in everything, but our first view of Goa certainly lifted our spirits.

"This is gonna be good!" We chorused, as we trudged along real pavements, unmolested by beggars or touts.

We soon found the right bus, and were even able to find a seat. In fact, the bus was almost empty, so we felt it was perfectly reasonable to spread our bulky packs and ourselves over a couple of seats. We settled down in the developing heat to wait for the bus to move off. No one seemed to be in any hurry, except that the driver constantly revved his engine, while a frantic young man we took to be the conductor, shouted himself hoarse as he tried to tempt more passengers onto the vehicle. Slowly, very slowly, the bus began to fill. First with exhaust fumes, then with more and more passengers. Soon we had to move our bags, and we both disappeared under our large packs, which we balanced on our knees. It grew hotter. Through the narrow gap between my own pack and Queenie's, and several heads, I could see a notice painted roughly on the rusty metal of the bus, just behind the driver's seat. "9 Person standing" it read. Some wag had added a couple of noughts after the 9.

By way of much neck stretching and peering around packs, we were able to make out a little of the country we were travelling through. We careered along, rocking and scraping past ancient houses on narrow streets, until we were out into open country. The bus lurched to a halt from time to time, and more passengers somehow squeezed themselves on, or struggled and scrambled off. What we could see of the country looked interesting, and very different from Kerala. There were more open fields, red, dusty and empty of vegetation, the houses were generally a lot larger, some defiantly mansion like, and of enduring construction. There were no ramshackle huts and tea stalls at the side of the road, and no women breaking rocks. It all looked very promising, and much more affluent than we had become used to.

At Mapusa, we sat and waited for the bus to empty, refusing to join the mad scramble to get off. After all, we reasoned, the bus wasn't about to go anywhere in a hurry, judging by the amount of time we'd waited for it to move off after we'd got on. To while away the time, we counted the people as they disembarked. We counted one hundred and fifty. Taking into account that some had got down at the various stops en route, an awful lot of people had squeezed onto this one small bus. I was grateful that there were no double-decker buses operating in the area. There were more than sufficient opportunities for disaster operating in these parts of India as it was.

We finally staggered down off the bus, and made our way through the chaos of Mapusa bus station to the stand indicated by our driver. Sure enough, a bus to Calangute stood waiting to leave. No one was on it, except the driver, and the conductor, who shouted encouragement to all and sundry, pleading with them to board his bus. We felt we had seen it all before. We sat wearily down, and waited for the bus to start. It only took one and three-quarter hours this time. We had learnt to be grateful for small mercies. We were too tired by this time to take much note of the passing scenery, and were eternally grateful to be deposited, shaken and not a little stirred, outside one of the finer hotels in Calangute.

To Hell with the expense! We were too tired to search for cheaper rooms, so we opted for one night of luxury — and at five hundred rupees for two bedrooms, washroom, balcony and bathroom, all clean and a fridge with a selection of drinks. It was all too much. I sank wearily on the bed, and prepared to sleep, dusty and hungry as I was. Queenie, however, had different ideas. "Come on, let's get showered and take a look around. I'm starving!" Grumbling and muttering, I followed her into the shower. Ten minutes later, I had to admit I felt almost human, and though not exactly ready to paint the town red, I was at least ready to eat and perhaps undertake a gentle stroll around our immediate environs.

We opted to eat at the hotel, and were pleasantly surprised. The food was quite good, though not as 'Indian' as we liked, the chips weren't that bad. There was also live entertainment to enjoy as we ate. This consisted of a small group of singers and musicians, whose repertoire included such gems as "Viva Espana" and "The Birdie Song." Delightful. We hoped this wasn't a portent of what was to come. It was exactly like being in Gran Canaria, the year we'd made the mistake of going there. It was all somehow refreshingly normal, if a little silly and perhaps we needed that. After dinner, we strolled down towards the beach area, along a road lined with stalls selling overpriced tourist tat. It seemed to me to be just like any Mediterranean package tour destination.

When we reached the sea, we were able to put some of the 'WOW' factor into the day. The beach was busy, as everyone strolled about taking advantage of the strong cooling breeze that blew steadily from the west. There was a huge moon, and the stars shone fiercely in the inky sky. The sound of the waves, the cool breeze, the chatter and laughter of people from all around the world, gathered here on this beach to simply enjoy being there, made a perfect end to a couple of days hard travelling. We strolled slowly back to our hotel, and fell thankfully into our beds, luxuriating in thick soft mattresses and the cool air from the air conditioning. We slept soundly, the sleep of exhaustion, and woke early next morning, refreshed and once more ready for anything.

After breakfast in the hotel, our first priority was to find cheaper accommodation for the night. We found a pretty looking guest home only a few minutes walk from the hotel.

It was an old house, with only three or four rooms to let. It was owned by a man who fitted the description "gentleman" to a "T", and an older lady we took to be his mother. The office was in what appeared to be their sitting room, a large, high-ceilinged space with a tiled floor, and some quite exquisite pieces of furniture. A conversation with the owner revealed or claimed that the current M.P. for Leicester, Mr Keith Vass, had been born in the house. I remember meeting Mr Vass at a Labour party do! This smiley rotund politician, with a handshake that somehow sends out the message "GO away!" With a slight push! Why bother? O yes, he is a politician.

Strange methinks, how these vague contacts or references with the UK, however tenuous, cheer me up. After all, I would be going home, I was not in exile.

I wonder if many travellers feel that.

The mattresses were biscuit-like, thin and hard, the toilet Indian style, a hole in the ground with a bucket for water, and the room gloomy, with small piles of dust and debris littering the corners.

The house had a certain charm however, being situated off the busy main road, and set in a pretty garden. Having moved our gear in, I sat for an hour by the open door, drinking in the minutiae of the garden while Queenie snoozed on the bed after yet another shower. I watched the butterflies and insects busy about the flowers, listened to the muted sounds from the other rooms, watched as lizards came and went on the tree trunks, smelt the overpowering scent of jasmine while I too drowsed in the all-enveloping heat. It was suddenly all very foreign again, like a stage set made just for me, and I felt a million miles from home.

When Queenie finally awoke and announced that she was ready for her assault on the town, I was right behind her! Daylight confirmed our discoveries of the night before. Except for the humidity, we could have been anywhere in the Mediterranean. However, food and alcohol were surprisingly cheap, the people friendly, the beach a blistering white expanse. We were suddenly on holiday again — this was becoming a habit. However one night was enough on the rock-hard beds. The sound of the water tank overflowing every hour or so through the night, the water rattling down onto the galvanised tank below, coupled with the savage snapping and howling of a pack of dogs somewhere very near, convinced us that a move to quieter surroundings was a must. We paid our bill and left, carrying our bags. Not ten minutes walk away, and overlooking the sea, Acanoa Guest House beckoned.

Chapter 26

Number thirty-three, Acanoa, a room with a view, in a large ex-colonial, three storey dilapidated hotel. It could be a forties film set, outside looked like several bombs had dropped, consequently most people were probably dead or had moved on. This was a place for the oddballs with a few quid. A sort of Colonel Blimp place I suppose. That's what it felt and looked like. A remnant of an old bygone world, interesting, but dying on its feet.

In reality the lights, shower, toilet, and most importantly the fan, all worked well.

Costing the equivalent of two pounds twenty per night for two people, and seventy-five pence for breakfast, it seemed like a bargain for a short stay.

The bright blue Arabian Sea is washing up calmer today, the light foaming surf breaking gently into the white sand and rippling between the minute shells. Between the beach and number thirty-three, a circle of low, mushroom like buildings, with red tiled roofs, their eight serving hatches which once seduced the tourists with every commodity from travel packages to cakes, now closed, shuttered. Business is plainly bad.

Three mid blue uniformed women carrying very large baskets balanced on their dark hair and heads walked slowly past the relic of a motor cycle, which over time, probably years, had slid slowly down the wall leaving scratches and old paint scuffs on one side of one of the buildings. It had, I guessed, been adorning the ground for some time. Positioned like a huge, rusty, sleeping dog, its very broken-tyred rear wheel exposed to the sun, its head, and corroded bars like broken legs, clinging desperately to the last remnants of shade. No one would ever ride this bike again. A large advertisement hung above it, declaring in faded red letters "City Link Travel Services." Oh dear!

The blue clad women returned, their wicker baskets full of collected rubbish. The blue saris, and red baseball caps in place, uniform of the local panchayat (council) given to the once backward classes, whatever that means, (now called scheduled classes) are better, I supposed, than no clothes at all. I expect the women were grateful. They look well fed. One was even sporting a gold bracelet and nose pin.

The blue plastic bags, water bottles and paper they had collected were thrown in a heap on the ground directly in front of number thirty-three.

One woman collected the dried and part-burned remnants of a defunct fire, and rearranged them in order to burn the newly collected rubbish, yes outside the hotel entrance, well at least it was outside.

To the right, a dozen women were laying a new road on top of the old one. The initial layer of hot tar had been laid down earlier in the morning. It was now nearly one o'clock, and extremely hot. I expected the women to knock off soon, to return when the heat subsided sometime after three o'clock in the afternoon.

These women also carried rocks previously broken by hand in another place. These small pieces of rock, no more than one to one and a half inches in size, were carried on their heads in large steel bowls, piled high to overflowing. So heavy were they, that it took two women to lift each one on to the head of a third. A thick pad of cloth held in place by a scarf tied at the back of the neck cushioned the bearer's head from the hard steel bottom of the dish.

The weight of all the roads in India is carried on the heads of women such as these.

In blazing heat or drowning mud, the rock is blasted, broken down from the quarry sides, carried away, and broken into useable sizes, and laid, by these women.

There were no vibrant, buoyant, confident women here, just lined tired faces, resigned women, working the production line from hell. Lift, under, walk, bend, tip. Lift, under, walk, bend, tip. Endlessly for the rest of their miserable lives. The job finishes. The money runs out. What there was of it, for what? Maybe the equivalent of a pound a day.

The diesel road roller rumbled heavily into action. The women were gone. The roller stopped. The operator climbed down from his shady cab. He combed his neat black hair and strolled away, his still clean white shirt gleaming in the gathering dusk. All was well at number thirty-three, no fires yet. We slipped off for tea.

We were both more than a little relieved by the arrival of the occasional monsoon shower. A relief from the moist heat that not only induces suffocation, but forces its way into your insides, through eyes and pores.

The buildings, the floors, the tracks, the roads, even the water, radiate heat. Arms, muscles, leg joints ache. Energy is sucked from the body, leaving it lifeless. To lift a cup is an effort. Sleep would be the only escape, except that the brain will not concede. The light rain shower, then heavy downpour, and gusting warm wind, blowing now through cooler, colder water, emptying down. Then falling back to lighter, smaller droplets, and to beautiful fresh air was a delightful reprieve.

Out we went and played in the rain, we enjoyed the walk to one of the cafes that commanded a view over the ocean, the multi shaded sky enveloping the sea.

Being conscious of time passing, and wanting to experience more before we finally had to leave, we resolved to explore further along the beach. The next village, Anjuna, hidden from view by a large headland, had a reputation of being one of the "hippy" colonies of the late sixties. It has been written up in numerous tourist guides as a small and interesting village, with an exciting Wednesday flea market, which attracts buyers and sellers from all over this state, country and indeed, the world. It was also, we were informed, by another, this time an Indian tourist book, where the discriminating traveller could find peace and quiet at very affordable rates during the season.

We decided to walk the six or so kilometres over the headland to the market, and to explore new vistas. We set off early, before the heat became too intense later. With a little cash carried in a money belt, and wielding newly purchased umbrellas with which to ward off the sun, we set off up the long white beach, feeling for the entire world like a pair of pioneering explorers. In the far distance the headland jutted out to sea. Our map showed a village just over the other side, and as we trudged heroically along, we discussed how we might tackle the steep slopes of the promontory. Direct as ever, I was for climbing straight over the top. Queenie, the cautious one, was for going around the base. As mentioned we were a good few kilometres away, which would give us plenty of time to make a decision before we reached its foot.

The hot sand burnt our unprotected feet as we walked. We changed course slightly to walk along the water's edge, where the outgoing tide had left the sand cool and damp.

We must have been a couple of hundred yards from where we started out, when the enthusiastic young Indian boy beamed at us as he stopped us.

Instead of trying to sell us hats, scarves or sarongs, or conduct us to overpriced accommodation, he had something we were not averse to purchasing. He was offering a quick and easy route to the next village via fishing boat, for only fifty rupees each.

We agreed to the price and wading into the surf, pulled ourselves over the side and into the boat to join the other half dozen or so passengers. We were launched on an outgoing wave, and with a roar from its outboard motors, the boat leapt into the rolling swell. We were soon drenched in spray as the boat bounced into and through the water. The spray was oddly warm, yet cooling on the skin as the boat raced out to sea and around the picturesque headland, red rocky coves contrasting brightly with the green of grass and palms, until, finally rounding the point, we had our first glimpse of the next beach and the famous market stalls.

We were set down immediately below the famous flea market, after receiving another welcome soaking in the process of disembarkation. Lemming-like, we followed the gathering crowd moving along the beach in the direction of the market. Our anticipation soon dissipated when we saw that the famous flea market was nothing more than another extremely overpriced and tatty craft fair. Not to be put off by this minor disappointment, we set off at a tangent across the beach, heading for where we could see a row of beach side shacks.

I have always had a yearning to stay in accommodation that was as close to the beach and sea as possible, so long of course, as it did not cost more than our budgeted one hundred and fifty rupees per day. I had already discounted a previous option in an idyllic location, owing to the costs of accommodation and food on offer.

We asked the rotund Mexican-looking proprietor of one of the beach side cafes where we might find a less expensive room on or near the beach.

"My name eet eez Pedro." He informed us, and putting aside our question for the moment, he regaled us with a more immediate concern of his own.

We were amused to hear that five minutes before our own arrival, and shortly before his, his staff had had a visit from a group of government officials. They had summarily confiscated the few dozen large bottles of San Miguel beer from his refrigerator, for which he had no official licence to sell.

He was more amused than angry. "More stock under sand!" he grinned, "refrigerator stock for stupid officials. No more problem now until end of season." Then he roared with laughter, his staff grinning and nudging each other behind him. Abruptly changing the subject, he pointed to a house a little behind and to the right of his café.

"Here is house. Man Tulseedas".

"OK thanks."

"No problem" We took this to be an answer to our earlier question and set off in search of "Man Tulseedas."

The room available appeared to be a partly converted cow shed, clean, in need of painting. Its main attraction was its proximity to the beach and café. The room itself was a good twenty-five feet square, with one corner partitioned off. This area served as the bathroom, and consisted of a squat-type toilet raised on a concrete plinth, a shower, and in the corner inside the entrance to this long narrow cubicle was a plastic water butt. I should at this point in the proceedings have taken more interest in this item.

"Why water butt?" I should have asked. But I didn't and was pleased to agree four days rental of the cow cum human shed for one hundred rupees a day.

Feeling satisfied with our explorations we returned the same way as we arrived, by fishing boat. Talking our usual nonsense, we agreed that the next day we would walk the whole distance like the intrepid explorers we really were, and with full kit on our backs. We would enjoy the benefit of a minor but real exploration and trek, and then rest in our newly acquired cow shed.

We set off to our new-found destination and cow shed early the following morning after enjoying our boiled egg breakfast, with barely browned toast. So into the bright and early sunrise, fully loaded fore and aft with our two heavy bags, our trusty umbrellas raised against the sun, and a bottle of mineral water we took to the elements.

Somehow the clarity of the air, or our complete misjudgement of the distance involved, made everything seem nearer and lower. However two hours later and we had only just reached the base of the headland. The raging sixty feet wide water torrent at its base was a surprise. We knew not how this torrent was to be negotiated. We now had not only the headland to negotiate, and the long stretch of beach on the other side, but somehow had to get ourselves, and our packs, safely across the tide-swollen river. A river we had not noticed on our previous day's boat trip. All that was lacking to complete this tropical exploration, we felt, were piranha, a crocodile or two, and maybe a few vultures thrown in for good measure.

We headed for the nearest beach shack cafe. Our consternation on seeing the river in full spate had not gone unnoticed.

"Ha, ha, ha, ha! Oh, dearie me!" Exclaimed the waiter with a shake of the head. "The river, it will not go down soon. Maybe four o'clock." He continued. "You sit, wait, have beer?" He offered, in greedy anticipation. "No," I snapped, feeling totally disgruntled, "soda water."

"Soda water?" he questioned, apparently never having sold such an innocuous liquid to a white man before.

"Yes." I insisted.

He disappeared to fill our order, and no doubt, to chortle malignantly about our predicament with his cronies round the back of the cafe.

We dumped our packs onto the hot sand, and faced each other across the grimy plastic table.

"How are we going to get across?" Asked Queenie, indicating the torrent roaring a few feet behind her.

"I'll try wading across without a pack, to see if it's at all possible." I naively volunteered.

Queenie's expression was not encouraging, she was unconvinced. She had no plan of her own to offer, so three bottles of soda and an hour and a half later, feeling fully refreshed and as fit as I was ever going to be, I made my first and only attempt.

Like all the best explorers, I had a plan, based on intuition, maybe, but a plan nonetheless. I reckoned that if I entered the river about one hundred yards upstream from where I wanted to be on the other side, all I would need to do, depth allowing, was to walk slowly across and with the flow of the river. I felt certain that as I was pushed toward the mouth of the river, where it widened to meet the sea, it would be shallower, wider and the current less strong. That was it then. In I went, wearing shorts and t-shirt, arms on head. I had seen this tactic in a Tarzan movie years ago, and it had worked then.

"Halfway across already," I remember thinking triumphantly, "no problem." The water was up to chest height, I was leaving a fair sized wake. One third of the way left to travel. One slow step at a time, shuffle, and feel the weight of water. Shuffle, and stop. No bottom. Unable to stop myself, the current took me. I couldn't stop. Tumbling over and over, under and around, until I finally surfaced, totally disorientated. I found I was moving at surprising speed out to sea.

"Hope I don't hit a rock." No sooner thought than done. My knee connected sharply, and my glasses, still miraculously clinging to my nose end, chose that moment to make their departure. "Ouch! Shit!" What else could I say? My rather expensive tinted varifocals lost, a damaged knee and a thorough soaking were all I had gained so far. Struggling to regain my feet, I resigned myself to wading back to the shore, the cafe, and worst of all, Queenie.

"Well, Jacky boy, that's another fine mess you've gotten me into." I muttered to myself as I struggled back up the beach. To cap it all, the hot sand burnt the soles of my feet, and I was more than a little aware of the ridiculous figure I cut as I danced across to reach the shade.

"Where's your glasses?" Asked Queenie, trying not to laugh. I jerked my thumb over my shoulder.

"And don't think I'm going back for them, either." I muttered, trying to smile.

"Soda and lime, please." I called to the waiter, who was hovering and grinning in the background.

'Too deep water sir. You must wait some hours." He said, as he brought the drinks.

"Yes, OK." I conceded, defeated for the moment.

Meanwhile, Queenie went off on a quest of her own, in search of an acceptable toilet, or so I thought. She took so long over it, I assumed she must have walked back to our starting point in disgust. "That's Queenie!" She finally turned up, grinning triumphantly.

"There's a bridge." She said breathlessly, between cooling slurps of soda.

"A what?"

"A bridge." She repeated calmly.

"Where's that waiter?" My blood pressure was rising a little, he could have said something.

"Oh, I paid him earlier." She said, struggling into her packs.

"I wasn't thinking of paying him," I said, "more of killin' 'im" However, he'd wisely disappeared into the back of the shack, so there was nothing for it but to shoulder my packs and follow Queenie to the old con-crete bridge which spanned the river. A mere two hun-dred yards away, behind trees and around a bend, but out of sight of where we had been sitting.

Crossing the river now with rucksacks, minus tin-ted varifocals, over the bridge, we passed a dozen or so attractive cottages set in small gardens then, following the path round to the right, we were on to the head-land proper. With the sea on our left, we trudged up the narrow, red rocky dusty goat tracks, open to the fierce sun. In no time at all we were lathered in sweat. We stumbled up and down the stony paths, until, hearts pumping, we crouched into the only available shade beneath a low growing tree.

Queenie almost took her bags apart in her frantic search for the bottle of water. "We surely must be nearly there." I wheezed. "It didn't seem anything like this far in the boat."

"I know." Gasped Queenie. "Come on, we'll have an-other go in a minute. Just let me get my breath." Queenie was now as wet as I had been in the water, she had sweat running from every pore.

"At least my hip isn't giving me any gyp today." She said bravely.

Bags back on, Queenie decided to try her luck by scrambling down the slope to sea level, to clamber around, rather than over, the headland. It seemed a better option to her than the switch back route we had been following. I soon found I was wrong to disagree with her. I went upwards with a view to getting to the top quickly and hoping for an easy ramble down the other side. "Not as easy as it seemed." I thought resignedly, as the dusty red rubble gave way and I slid painfully down the several yards back to the bush that had given us shelter. I followed Queenie.

Fifteen minutes later, and three and a half hours after we'd started the second leg of our trek, we rounded the headland, and spotted the beach, and better still, Pedro's beach hut cafe. Our spirits were given a boost, and yelling,

"Yes! Oh, yes! What are we like?" Queenie stubbed her toe on a rock, and tumbled over, laughing.

"Get me up, get me up! Don't leave me here all alone, Stanley!" She joked, as she struggled to right herself with the weight of her packs against her. Yes indeed. In our own small way, we had been "'trepid 'sploring", but we agreed later, boat trips were definitely easier.

Despite the hardness of the three-quarter inch of yet another biscuit thin mattress, and the energetically rattling fan, we slept well in our cow shed that night. We soon discovered that the shower did not work, but that the water butt did. The trick was, it transpired, that the butt had to be filled every other day, between five and seven thirty in the morning, when the government water was turned on otherwise, no water.

The facilities were in fact better than the food. Although cheap and filling, it always looked and tasted the same whatever we ordered, despite an apparently varied menu. It was always stewed cabbage, with tomato, carrot and onion in curry flavoured water, a kind of curry flavoured instant noodle without the noodle. No beer, either, the government men had seen to that on a surprise return visit. The only other thing on offer was,

"You smoke something? Very cheap price." we declined these kind offers.

Overall we had a good few days discovering new things, situations and people, and decided to spread our net further. We returned by boat to Calangut and then on to Mapusa, we said goodbye to Goa, with a wish that one day we may return.

Chapter 27

A trip to Hampi was next on our agenda, we reckoned we could do it in seven to ten days, then get back to Kerala, pick up our main packs which we'd left with our Kovalam landlady, before setting off east and north to 'do' some other bits of the country. We were becoming more and more confident about our ability to travel around in relative safety, using local, public transport and therefore much cheaper. We made our usual enquiries at the bus station, booked our tickets for the ten-hour trip to Hampi, and set off full of confidence. However, having said that, I will never get used to the hair-raising driving techniques on the subcontinent, and will never understand how a vehicle wreck per mile does not seem to influence the standard of driving here. Ah, well, "this is India, go with the flow" I repeated endlessly to myself. I also prayed a lot on journeys, and I found that closing one's eyes helps, too.

The bus to Hampi, scheduled to leave at six in the morning, finally left at nine thirty. It was not crowded, and everyone had a seat. We settled back, as far as was possible on the unyielding plastic seating, a most inappropriate material for this climate, easy to clean I suppose. I prepared to enjoy the journey.

We were a mixed bag of locals and tourists, with tourists in the minority, just us, a young French couple two seats in front, and a single German guy a few seats behind. That's what I discerned from the language at least.

There were lots of children, lots of baggage, and lots of noise. In fact, a normal, everyday bus ride in India. We never actually did collide with anything. However just two hours after we set off the driver did manage to pull into a garage just seconds before the engine burst into flames, which did give everyone time to get off. So I suppose it could have been much worse. We stood in a group, as the driver and several bystanders wrestled to put out the fire. The driver burnt his hands on a red-hot battery cable as he was trying to disconnect it from the engine.

There was very little shade, and the temperature felt like it was rising, aided by the flames from the bus. We were fairly confident that we wouldn't be finishing our journey on that particular vehicle. The driver and conductor disappeared for a while. The passengers stood about, talking quietly amongst themselves. The conductor reappeared, apparently having telephoned for instructions from his superiors. Some of the passengers, who had paid on the bus, were given refunds. We were told that we must apply to the ticket office for our refund, as we had purchased the tickets in advance, and the conductor did not have sufficient funds to cover these extra costs. We sat down on a wall under the little shade afforded by a tree. What now? We had no idea where we were. We did know we were about eight hours drive from Hospet, which was a further hour or so away from Hampi. There was no possibility of finishing our journey before dark or even today, even if we could get transport immediately.

Immediacy or a sense of urgency, as you may have gathered by now, are not concepts which easily spring to mind when considering India, so we waited. Our by now very apologetic conductor told us that another bus was on its way, and would be with us within the hour. The children played tag, or sat quietly with their mothers. The men lit cigarettes, or lay down in the shade. Queenie trotted off in the hope of finding someone by the roadside selling cold drinks, and returned in a very short time with a couple of bottles of ice-cold Limca. I can taste them now! There's nothing like being really hot and frustrated for the full appreciation of cooling drinks.

An hour passed, as did several buses. All of them were either full to overflowing, or not going our way, or both. As each bus approached, we rose as one and surged to the side of the road, only to be disappointed once again, and to hurry back to "our" patch of shade under the tree, before anyone could stage a take-over.

It was a full three hours before a bus finally stopped, and agreed to take us. The conductor insisted that our ticket was not valid for his bus, and so we paid again, but with little protest, as we were becoming quietly desperate.

The bus was incredibly crowded, and was only going as far as Hubli, which was certainly on the correct road. We hoped to find a hotel there for the night, and to continue on to Hampi the next day or even the day after.

I was crushed in the aisle, near the back of the bus, desperately trying to hang on to the back of a seat. My stomach was pressed embarrassingly into the face of the man occupying the seat. He didn't seem to mind at all, in fact he fell asleep, his head gently cushioned on my ample tum. Behind me, I could also feel a pressure on my backside, and twisting to see, was amused to find another bloke in the seat behind me, leaning cosily against my buttocks and also fast asleep.

I had been suffering from some form of stomach bug, which gave rise to cramps and phenomenal amounts of wind, but thankfully, not much else. I was also busting for a pee. I feared for the safety of these two unconscious passengers. The one in front was in danger of drowning and the one resting in blissful ignorance on my rear in danger of being gassed.

It wasn't long however, before I found a seat of sorts. Queenie had somehow squeezed down to the front of the bus, and was sharing one eighth of a seat with several young men. I wriggled down towards her, and was rewarded with one-quarter of a buttock's worth of suitcase in the aisle, courtesy of a kindly gentleman with a large family and much luggage.

There was little to see as we lurched along, the press of people, then nightfall blocked any good view of the landscape. So we crouched as comfortably as we could, took advantage of whatever short stops were made to stretch our legs, and endured. Even so, there's a real feeling of accomplishment when a difficult journey has been successfully completed.

To pass the time as we travelled, we consulted, with some difficulty in the cramped space, our trusty guide book. Several hotels were mentioned at Hubli as being cheap, clean and near the bus station. We decided to head straight for the nearest one when we arrived, taking into account the lateness of the hour, and with luck book in there.

We tried not to think too deeply about hotels being full of people, or worse, fleas and cockroaches. A positive approach at all times was the order of the day, backed up by the mantra "This is India, go with the flow." We went with the flow, there was no choice, and had one of those wonderful experiences which can suddenly burst upon one in India. The hotel we chose was opposite the bus station, and was a large modern structure. We were shown to a room on the fourth floor. It was a very small room, and bare but for two single beds, but clean, with a small bathroom off to the rear. There was also a balcony that was just large enough for the two plastic chairs which had been set there.

It was this balcony and the view from it which made our brief stay in Hubli so memorable. In the darkness, however, on this first night, there was little to see but the lights of the town. We slept well, due in large part to the cool refreshing breeze which blew through the open balcony doors, and which did away with the need for the rattly old fan.

Next morning, after a cheap and filling breakfast at a nearby eatery, we made our across the road to the bus station. The early bus for our next step of the journey had already left, and another was not scheduled until late in the afternoon. We didn't want to arrive at Hospet, our next destination after dark, again with no room booked. We might not be so lucky next time, we could find ourselves roaming around for hours looking for rooms. We decided to stay another night in Hubli, catch the early bus next day, and then make the final leg of our journey to Hampi from there.

The extra cost involved in our broken journey meant that we needed to change some money, so our next mission was to find the only bank in Hubli which would do this. We had a couple of false starts, banks with the same name but on different streets and not commercial banks, or banks that couldn't change foreign currency, but we eventually were directed to the correct place.

We thought we were used to the informality of the Indian banking system, but as always, there was another surprise up India's sleeve. Although the Indian banks we used did have high counters, similar to the ones we were used to in the UK, there the similarity ended. There were no bullet-proof glass partitions, and in fact, most people seemed to ignore the counters completely, and walked round them to join the staff, who were working in full public view.

Not only the bank counter clerks, but also the office staff all shared the same large space behind the counter. There were numerous large desks cluttered with books and papers, and small men who ran between the various departments, carrying papers for signature or filing. Confidentiality was non-existent, as I discovered as I idly picked a small ledger left lying on the desk where we were sitting. I flipped the paper file open merely to punctuate my boredom. It contained information about local businesses and individuals that would have surely been under lock and key at any western bank. Cheques, cash, and all sorts of paperwork were carelessly thrown about.

One worker, a woman, was searching frantically around her desk. She called to a colleague, in English, "Have you seen the packet of money I had just now?" Receiving a reply in the negative, she continued her search. Finally, she checked her handbag, which was lying on the floor near her seat. "Here it is!" She announced triumphantly, "I had put it into my bag for safety." And she withdrew a huge wad of large denomination notes from her handbag. Her companions smiled happily at her, and everyone continued with their work.

Queenie and I merely gazed at each other in silent amazement. It took a couple of hours to change our money, though there seemed to be no obvious reason for this, except that a junior clerk was instructed to go away with our passports and have them photocopied. We watched him leave the building with our precious passports with a sinking feeling. It seemed that the bank did not have photocopying facilities of its own. Would we ever see them again? We wondered, but then we settled back to watch the performance in the bank, and the next hour or so passed quite quickly.

We were finally handed our passports, a small brass token and some paperwork, which we were instructed to take up the stairs to the payment desk. Here our money was laboriously counted out, signed for, brass token exchanged for cash, and we were free to leave.

There wasn't much of the day left to do anything else, so we made our way back to the hotel. On the way, we passed a large stadium, which looked like some kind of sports arena. Through the open gates we could see preparations going on for some kind of entertainment. We had seen brightly coloured posters around the town, but none in English. This arena, however, seemed to be the venue for whatever entertainment was to take place, which, if the pictures on the posters could be believed, was to include fireworks and Gandhi. This arena was also directly below our room in the hotel.

"If the thing is on tonight, we should have a grand-stand view." Said Queenie, enthusiastically.

"Let's get some dinner, then grab a couple of beers and take them up to our room."

"Fine by me." By the time we'd finished dinner, and tracked down some beer — not easy in a "dry" state, people had already begun pouring into the arena below. A series of stages had been set up, and were spot lit in the now growing dark.

We hurried up to our room, opened our first beers, stepped onto the balcony, and prepared to be entertained. As we sat on the chairs, the lights went down, and the arena below us was plunged into darkness. But only for a moment. A fanfare, a roll of drums, a short display of fireworks, and the night's entertainment began.

As the story unfolded, it was obvious what it was about. It was about the struggle for freedom from British oppression. A spotlight would focus on one of the stages, and there the action would take place. A British army camp, a Maharajah's palace, a street scene. Long and incomprehensible dialogue, exploding cannon, banging, crashing musket fire, burning and fighting. This was revolution!

Even at our distance the scenes were clear and sharp, and we could almost see the expressions on the over painted faces of the actors. The grand finale came, with an unmistakable Gandhi leading his people to freedom. We stood and cheered and applauded with the rest. Without understanding a single word, we'd followed every twist and turn of the plot. We were impressed with the use of space and scenery, the lighting, the sound system, everything in fact. We were truly sorry when the spectacle ended, in a shower of fireworks and loud rattling tins and pans and sitar music. We watched until the last person had left the arena, and all the lights were extinguished, unwilling to give up the moment. We felt that this added more to our adventures on this journey, a touch of class, and went to bed well satisfied with the day, ready for an early start next morning.

Chapter 28

Full of expectation, we arrived at the bus station at six thirty next morning. The bus was scheduled to leave at seven. Our expectations were that it wouldn't. It didn't. It arrived at ten forty-five and left at eleven. This had given us lots of time to observe the comings and goings at each of the bus stands.

The place was full of people who were obviously off to some market or other in the out lying towns or villages. Men and women off to somewhere or returning from somewhere, bent double. Heads strained upwards under huge loads of vegetation, bulging sacks of vegetables, bags and boxes of household items piled on to their backs, rubbed elbows with people looking much more prosperous, who like us, we suspected, were on their way to Hospet and then on again to Hampi.

The guide book informed us that Hampi is a year round place of pilgrimage for Hindus, and judging by the numbers of people with luggage going in that direction, we were going to have to fight our way onto the bus when, or if, it arrived.

We watched and noted that as each bus pulled up at its designated stand, it was already swarming with people fighting their way on, throwing bags and other items through the windows in order to secure a seat, before they even got on the bus.

I knew I would have to overcome my British reserve if we were to get on the Hospet bus at all, let alone get a seat. Mantra time! Even if going with the flow meant elbowing, clawing and fighting my way on to the bus!

To gather our strength for the fray, we'd had breakfast. To pass the time and other things we used the toilets several times, chatted about life, the universe and everything to a Methodist minister who gave us his name and address and begged us to write to him, another lifelong friend! And swatted away the flies, and small beggars, who became more and more irritating as the morning wore on. All the while psyching ourselves up for the big moment. We knew we had only one chance.

We devised plans, scrapped them, and devised others. In the end, it was just a matter of going all out for it. Battered and bruised, but triumphant, we not only got on the bus, but with my blood well and truly up, wrested a seat for both of us from another contestant.

This man had stood on the wheel arch or some other protuberance outside the bus, and reaching through the window, spread a neat handkerchief on the seat, then fought his way on behind us hoping to claim his prize.

I considered this to be an unfair advantage, and, removing the small neatly pressed square of fabric, sat down. I then politely handed the disappointed man his hanky, and gestured for Queenie to join me. The man was distraught, and appealed to his fellow passengers, the gods, and the conductor.

We were mean, unremitting, and refused to move. Passengers, gods and conductor were all indifferent to his pleas, as they like everyone else knew he had not left the handkerchief to reserve a seat that he had been sat on before the bus had entered the station, but like others he was merely trying it on.

He finally withdrew, defeated. He appeared to bear us no malice, however, as he fought his way to another seat then settled down to sleep his way through the journey. We consoled ourselves with the thought that this was to be only a two hour ride, in daylight and with a seat. At least we'd see something more of the country we passed through!

What an amazing landscape it was! Once away from the dirt, noise and dust of the town, the plain stretched flat and featureless for miles, it seemed, until in the distance, a sudden outcrop of rocks would come into view, shaped like distant cities with high and low rise structures or giant creatures. As we drew closer, we could see the piles of red-brown rocks, some bigger than a good sized house, balanced precariously one on top of another, rising unexpectedly from the flat and featureless plain. They looked for the entire world as if they had been dropped only moments before from some giant, careless hand.

As we drew nearer to Hospet, these groups of huge boulders grew more and more common. It was a silent, eerie landscape, with few houses or settlements. We crossed several almost dry rivers, wispy streams flowing around rocky beds. The place had a desolate air, as if a long-forgotten tragedy had taken place, some huge disaster, a terrible war or an earthquake had left it devoid of life. It was barren.

In no time at all it seemed, we reached Hospet, a dry and dusty little town on the edge of this apparent nowhere. We easily found the bus to Hampi, and with very little delay or discomfort, were finally on the last leg of our journey to the famed ancient township and its splendid ruins. We drove between ever more precariously piled heaps of rock which dwarfed the bus, and turning a final bend and through a gateway, had our first view of Hampi.

It was late afternoon. The place looked deserted, but clean. A Western film set, just waiting for John Wayne to make his entrance from the prairie to the dusty street. We didn't pause to look around in any great detail, however, as we needed to concentrate on finding somewhere to stay, freshen up, and eat as our first priorities. Our trusty guide book came to the rescue again. We followed the map and its recommendation and secured a large room with a balcony and air conditioning on the first floor of a pretty little guest house just off the main street.

Clearly seen from the balcony and the bathroom window, the Gopuram of the Virupaksha temple rose in the distance, gleaming creamy white against the blue of the sky, towering above the rooftops, dwarfing the trees.

By the time we had unpacked, worked out the mysteries of the air conditioning and showered, and "lent" the young man who had carried our bags up the stairs two hundred rupees, the small town was beginning to stir into life. Without more ado, we clattered down the stairs to make our first inspection of the place we'd heard so much about.

Our rooms were situated on a narrow lane, which ran parallel to the main street, and were about midway along it. As we stepped out from a narrow alleyway into the main street, to our left rose the temple we had seen from our balcony. To the right, the road led to some ruined buildings at the foot of another heap of those enormous rock formations.

There was a quality and clarity of light we had not noticed anywhere else we'd been, in India or the Mediterranean. The sun was going down, and in the ruins which bordered each side of the long straight road, small yellow squares of light glowed in the open doorways of the dwellings that had been built within the magnificent buildings from another age.

We walked slowly down the street toward the temple, looking to right and left as we went. The street was clean and well swept. Dogs, chickens, goats and children scratched and played in the dust.

Simply-made bedsteads of poles and leather straps stood outside many of the white painted buildings, while the soft yellow lights from within gave the scene an unreal air.

It was like walking into a medieval painting. Further down the street were rows of shops and restaurants all hidden within the confines of antiquity.

Choosing one at random, we sat down facing outwards onto the street, ordered a meal, and spent the next few hours drinking lemon tea, eating, swatting mosquitoes and small black flies and chatting to others.

As we made our way to our room we could hardly wait for the next day, and for a thorough daylight investigation of this enchanting and unusual city.

We planned to go on one of the state bus tours leaving at nine thirty the next morning to get an overview of the place, before setting off later on for more interactive and detailed explorations on foot.

The tourist bus left promptly at nine thirty from outside the tiny tourist office on the main street. Our guide, a look-alike for the late Peter Sellers, regaled us with humorous tales of past glories and battles won as we sweated our way around the ruins. After each mini tour we dived for the cover of the tour bus, sinking gratefully into the seats and consuming vast amounts of bottled water to combat the dehydrating effects of the midday sun.

The buildings, the ruins were stupendous, the sheer size of the site meant that the bus tour was certainly the correct way to see as much as possible of this vast ruined city and all its temples, palaces, baths and pleasure houses in the time available. The trip inspired us to try as far as a couple of novices could, to discover more.

We planned to spend the next couple of days exploring on foot, before returning first to Goa, then back to Kerala to prepare for our long-overdue tour of other parts of India. Our first port of call was to the main temple at the end of the long village street. We left our shoes outside and walked under the huge archway and into the inner courtyard.

A young elephant stood next to his trainer with a small crowd around him. As each person presented him with a small coin, the elephant took it in his trunk, handed it carefully to his keeper, and then finally blessed the giver with a tap on the head from his trunk. We watched for a while and I decided that I'd like to be blessed by the elephant too.

The elephant regarded me with his small, dark-lashed, intelligent eyes, waiting for my donation. I offered a small coin. This was accepted gracefully, handed to the keeper, and the blessing given. Far from the gentle touch I'd been expecting, the sudden blow to the crown of my head buckled my knees for a second.

Recovering myself and laughing, I felt I'd been truly blessed by the young beast. We hoped the little elephant was well cared for in return for his long hours of labour with the tourists and pilgrims. As far as we could tell, he looked well fed and content.

I remember Hampi for things other than ancient ruins, temple elephants and incredibly detailed carvings. I remember the wildlife, too. Much of it seemed to have set up residence in our rooms. There was definitely a large family of termites living in the wall by the bathroom window. The preferred route for this group from home to school, supermarket, doctor's surgery or wherever it is that termites go, started from the bathroom window ledge, continued in a neat horizontal line to the right, as far as the water heater. The line then made a ninety-degree turn downwards, and carried on in another neat vertical line to the floor, where it disappeared. I was never quite sure whether the termites using this route were always the same termites, continually going round and round on some obscure mission; or whether in fact there were so many termites in that line, that in all the time we were there, they never actually came to the end of their procession. Another family of termites — or maybe the same termites but reappearing at some distance from the bathroom — lived in the bedroom. They also preferred a window entrance, but they differed from their bathroom brethren in that as they came in through the microscopic hole in the window frame, they followed an immediate vertical line down towards the floor. As the bed was pushed up against this wall, they made their way onto the floor via the length of the bed. I discovered this fact early on the first morning of our stay, as I sleepily opened my eyes and came face to antenna with a termite which was strolling across my pillow. I shot out of bed giving vent to what Queenie later described as a blood-curdling shriek. I maintain that it was not blood-curdling, merely a gentle cry of dismay and alarm. Be that as it may, Queenie did wake up, and throwing back her covers, was not a little surprised to observe the line of termites neatly bisecting the bed. We were not particularly happy about sleeping with a termite highway passing so close, so on the second night we moved the bed away from the wall, and shook out those termites that appeared in danger of setting up permanent residence there. Past experiences in Goa and Kerala had taught us that to attempt to divert these termite roads was useless. We learned to ignore them, avoid placing furniture near them, and to step over those lines which crossed our own paths.

We watched with great amusement as whole families of langur monkeys, from babes in arms to grandparents, leapt and scrambled over the roof tops, swung from the electric cables, and swooped down to steal titbits from the restaurants.

Chattering and gesturing, they would retire to the safety of the trees with their prizes, followed by the angry curses of the shopkeepers and the excited laughter and chatter of the children. The pretty little striped chipmunks were a delight to watch and seemed harmless, and prolific.

Outdoors, we saw large lizards with attractive yellow and black markings, plus the occasional snake. Local people are big into snake denial, "There's a snake!" we'd cry, full of excitement. "Look, look, a snake!" Large brown eyes would regard us sadly.

With a waggle of the head (I think we were being admonished), the nearest local would reply,

"No, no, sir, madam. There are no snakes here. Do not worry no snakes!"

It was always useless to protest that we had just seen one and though excited, we were not unduly worried by the occurrence.

Presumably snakes are bad for business. We know we saw real live, unconfined snakes, so there!

Despite and including these minor diversions, we were enchanted with Hampi and the surrounding villages. Stone chariots the size of large detached houses, musical stone pillars that surrounded a temple, rang out when struck by a designated small boy. Doe, ray, me, far, so, la, tee, doe, and then on to the next eight pillars, that rang out the same scale all around the perimeter of the ancient temple. They were extraordinary.

We made full use of the next couple of days exploring on foot.

An ancient air conditioning system consisted of a large square tower with a roof held up, as is the norm, by lots of stone pillars. The top flat surface maybe two hundred feet square, similar to the musical one. This complemented by a large, semi-restored but presently dysfunctional waterwheel, that would in its useful days scoop water out of the large stone open channel that surrounded the whole town, lift and drop the water into a chute onto the top of the roof, which in turn had smaller channels carved into it, each of which led to a series of small holes through which the water dropped.

The whole tower structure being built in an appropriate, well thought-out position, allowed the quite strong breeze to pass between the pillars through the water and thereby give off a cooling mist and breeze. What a fantastic piece of engineering.

The layout of Hampi was vast, in fact much more than a village, in the past a grand city more like, however most of the structures had eroded away or had fallen through the ages and been buried. Excavation is an on-going feature with an encampment in place for those who practice.

I suppose it may be that these air conditioning systems were once prolific, cooling down a number of dwellings at once. This being the only one being restored and left standing in something like its original condition. I could not help but ponder why it might be, that modern people do not appear to have learnt from, or why perhaps have rejected these life enhancing and health improving developments. What a huge enhancement an air conditioning system similar to this would be in many a city, here in India and worldwide.

We were intrigued by the number of people who had constructed their homes within total ruins, in a way that compromised themselves, rather than improving facilities for themselves, they had allowed their environs to slip into acute disrepair and dereliction, consequently making life more difficult for themselves than it needed to be. On a more positive note, the agriculture on the river valley bottom, and the tiny fields between the huge boulders, patch work like, pretty, every patch of soil, however small, seemed to be under cultivation of one kind or another.

We played with a group of children outside a small tea room, which was perched on the edge of a low cliff overlooking the river. These children had made themselves a rope swing which hung precariously from the branches of a large tree. This in turn overhung the edge of the cliff. Hearts in mouths, we watched as the children swung crazily out over the sheer drop, laughing at our horrified expressions, and posing cheerfully for the camera.

The coffee was good, too.

We enjoyed looking at the stars on those bright clear nights, when we couldn't sleep. Standing on the narrow balcony, wrapped from head to foot in sheets in order to foil the attentions of passing mosquitoes, like a couple of lost souls we gazed enraptured at the sky. We tracked the bright moving specks that denoted yet another piece of space junk orbiting the earth. So nice to be able to see it so clearly we agreed, between yawns. We grew used to standing on the balcony at night, and looking across the road to the flat roof of the school opposite, where an entire family slept huddled in blankets on the bare concrete.

At the end of the street where we were living, an elderly couple had set up home in a large steel box, which had been, in another life a shipping container.

This windowless box must have been suffocating to sleep in, as each evening the two old people locked themselves in, after cooking their evening meal on small kerosene stove outside. I was convinced that one morning the little door would fail to open, the couple having asphyxiated themselves during the night.

But each morning, with a clang of metal on metal, the door was thrown open, and their inscrutable lives carried on as before.

The high-pitched chanting of the children was the first thing that we heard each morning, as they repeated their lessons. We could just see inside the gloom of the schoolroom from our balcony, and apart from a few benches, it appeared to have no furniture or apparatus one would usually expect to see in a school.

We had to make plans for our return to Kovalam all too soon it seemed, and on our final evening, we negotiated with a rickshaw driver to take us to Hospet in time for the early bus straight through to Hubli and the train station. So enthusiastic was our driver, and so determined not to lose his fare, that he parked his vehicle outside our rooms, and slept in it for what remained of the night.

We were driven to our bus stop through eerie, deserted early morning countryside. Our driver was barely awake, and spoke little. He dropped us off at the bus station, found the correct stand for us, and then drove away into the ever-lightening morning.

We waited for several hours for our bus. Scheduled to leave at six thirty. Ha! Why did we always fall for that one? We scrambled aboard at nine thirty, fell into our seats, and settled down for the hair-raising ride, as it would inevitably be. This time, we hoped, without any breakdowns.

Wrong again, we were deeply shocked at the behaviour of the driver. He appeared to be under the impression that there was some kind of Highway Code in operation. He did not rev his engine for all he was worth. He braked gently. He paused at junctions. He did not drive at all aggressively. Was he some kind of lunatic? We had been dreading the return trip over the Western Ghats. We had made the initial journey in a crush of bodies, and thankfully, had not been able to see too clearly. We had been all too aware, however, of the numbers of overturned vehicles, and the measured groaning and wheezing coming from our vehicle's engine made it all too plain just how steep, narrow and winding the road was.

Going up had the advantage of slowing the vehicle down; going down would mean that the driver was free to give full rein to his need for speed. The consequences of this sort of driving had littered both sides of the road with wrecked vehicles. Now it was our turn to undertake the hazardous downwards return journey. Gripping our water bottles, biscuits and peanuts, we prepared ourselves for the worst and were rewarded with the best. The safest and by far best driving we had so far encountered in India. The driver was an artist, and in our view, was deserving of a medal, and was to be held up as a shining example of how to drive. He seemed to know every rule in the driving handbook, and what's more, he actually followed them. Instead of painfully white knuckling for most of the journey, we were able to relax and enjoy some of the stunning but heart-stopping views as we passed over the mountains.

Chapter 29

We finally took the train back to Trivandrum, it was fairly uneventful. Strange isn't it, how easy it is to describe a situation as uneventful simply because there were no accidents, crises or dilemmas. It was actually a pleasant journey with all the interest of the first trip with the usual performers and vendors. There was no great number of people travelling back down to the Deep South. The extra space was very welcome.

We eventually arrived in Kovalam feeling sleepy but a little less stressed than when we'd left a couple of weeks earlier. "K" met us in one of our favourite haunts one day, positively beaming with pleasure. Not only had he a boat tour booked for the next day, but the tourists had agreed to a lunch too, which presumably he had had to sell.

We were very pleased for him, and responded for his request, "to come see" and to help him and Valsala. We would provide cutlery and a tablecloth for the big table on the roof, and make sure everything else was clean and ready while Valsala cooked the fish curry and prepared the salads and fruit. We all worked hard that day to make sure it was a success.

The Swiss tourists were delighted with the trip and the meal, and we began to feel that maybe we hadn't totally wasted our time, money and effort. That was our final contribution to the tourist home. From then on, we left it all to Kardy and his family. He had made a good effort in our absence, and it bode well for the future.

It occurred to me that our holiday away for those few days, plus the fact that we had moved out of his house earlier had in fact removed the stress from Kardy, and he had something to work towards without any interference from me. He was happy again.

We made an arrangement with Prabu, to visit his Ashram. He arranged to meet us outside our room at eight am. Sure enough, bright and early, there he was, and with him was another European. Prabu introduced the young man as Simon, and his strong north of England accent cheered me enormously. A touch of home. I asked where he was from, and he told me he was originally from a small village, New Mills in Derbyshire, where Queenie had also lived some years before. We were all soon chatting like old friends. He had a unique view of life, and became an entertaining companion on other days after this.

There are some people in the world who act as the "glue" for the rest of us. No matter what their own personal circumstances, they are unfailingly cheerful and caring in all their dealings with everyone. Without them, the rest of us would fall apart and sink into barbarism. Prabu is one such.

He was bubbling with enthusiasm today. Not only had he pleased two old friends by introducing them to a new friend who, by happy coincidence had been near neighbours in their home country, but he was also visiting his favourite place, his Ashram. He had told us that he went quite often in order to recharge his batteries, after the rigours of working as a masseur in one of the many Ayurvedic parlours near the beach. Prabu was a very educated man, it appeared. He assured us that he was much happier working at Kovalam than anywhere else because there, everyone was happy, simply because they were on holiday. He had taken to wearing a baseball hat, turned back to front. He had laughed at my raised eyebrows, and had explained that the unusual choice of headgear was to help him blend in with the tourists. And it was true. He would don the cap with a flourish, and instantly, would become the cheery tout, looking for business for the massage parlour.

The baseball cap was not in evidence today. He wore a spotless white lungi and long collarless shirt, and was every inch the educated Indian gentleman. He was an excellent guide. He chaperoned us around busy Trivandrum, ensuring that we bought a small gift of fruit to hand in at the Ashram, making sure we boarded the correct bus, and all the while smiling cheerfully, and chattering happily, enthusing us with tales of the many improvements made to the quality of life for the people in and around the geographical area of the Ashram site.

The Ashram was situated about two kilometres out of the village where we left the bus. We were all hungry, so stopped off for food at a cafe, where Prabu was obviously well known. Our plates were piled high with a combination of hot, savoury and sweet pastries. When we finally finished eating, Simon decided that he needed a tidy up, as he put it. We followed him into the local barber's shop, and waited for him to have his shave. With the aid of a cut-throat razor wielded by the laughing barber, he was stripped of his three-day growth. We laughed as Simon fought off the further attentions of the barber, who wanted to at least comb his long unruly hair. Simon would have none of it. Simon won, and paid up, amidst general laughter. Prabu was greeted as an old friend at the barbershop, too. He explained that many in the village were volunteers at the Ashram and had made lifelong commitments to it. Prabu's happiness was infectious, and in high good humour, we crammed ourselves into a rickshaw for the final leg of our journey.

On entering the Ashram proper, we were taken on a guided tour of the factories, hospital and workshops surrounding the central area. Everything was ordered and clean, the workers seemed happy and relaxed. We bought soap from the soap factory, and inspected the Ayurvedic medicines being produced and in their final bottled stage. We were very impressed at the size and scope of the operations, and the apparently democratic and collective way of working.

No job it appeared was too menial to be undertaken by any member of the Ashram. There appeared to be a comprehensive education system for everyone, regardless of caste. Caste divisions, we were told, were outlawed here. It is remarkable to see what can be done with the introduction of small ordered societies, with group self-interest as part of a bigger picture.

We were treated well, and spent some time talking to one of the teachers, who attempted to outline the philosophy of the Guru, and as a consequence the Ashram for us, which included the all things to all men, modern religious creed. At its core is an investment in the future for each and every one, or so we were invited to believe.

Apparently life was complicated by the early politics and interpretations of Hinduism, a kind of myth clashing with myth, supposed truths denied and asserted, most of which passed over our heads. Not that we weren't interested, we were, but the names of deities were so similar and there were so many, it really was difficult to grasp. A thing it seemed to have in common with other proselytising religions was the "great changes are afoot, and pretty soon too, and if only people would subscribe now to this ancient, yet new twist on belief, everything would definitely be alright on the day."

We had been told that the Guru would see us, and that we could ask him any question, and he would be able to answer it for us. This rather threw us. Neither I nor Queenie had any particular wish to see "the great man." What does one ask of a being who has access to all knowledge? It would have to be something of greater import than will I win the lottery, or when will

I marry, surely. None of us could think of a suitably deep philosophic question, except of course, "Well done mate, but how do you keep such a straight face?" We knew the probable answer, so we decided to keep mum, and hope that at the appropriate moment, some form of divine intervention would occur, and the really big question would ask itself.

We would then perhaps have the answer to life, the universe, and everything, not that we were unfamiliar with the Hitch-Hiker's Guide to the Galaxy or consequential arithmetical solution. We were obliged to wait in line to see the Guru, along with many hundreds of his followers. Each petitioner carried a gift of fruit, which was laid on a steel tray carried by one of a group of workers.

The Guru sat in a glass-fronted, stationary, large Popemobile-type box, a big man, very overweight, with, I thought, a rather disagreeable expression, a sickly smile of sorts. It might of course have been indigestion, probably was, especially if he was expected to eat the ocean of fruit offerings each day. Or maybe he was just trying to smile to keep up appearances and was utterly bored with it all. I was totally unimpressed. After we left the public viewing hall, we were informed that the Guru would grant us private audience, at about five o'clock.

We decided to wait, as Simon was quite interested in meeting the Guru so, in the meantime, we looked around the beautiful white, lotus shaped concrete building, which was being erected next to the temple. It looked like a smaller version of the famous Bahai temple in Madras, except of course it was, as you might expect, their own unique and original concept.

It was very near to completion, and had a ramp running around the outside edge, which we climbed. The view from the top was spectacular. Simon, being an enthusiastic rock climber at home, couldn't resist the sight of the rickety ladder leading up the outside of the dome, which served to form the centre stamen of the lotus. The ramps on which we stood were the petals which would, we were told, eventually be surrounded by water.

Up he went. Prabu barely hesitated, and then followed him to the top. There they sat, another sixty feet or so above us, marvelling at the view, while we stood below, marvelling at their daring and sheer foolhardiness. It was almost time for our audience with the Guru, so we watched with bated breath as the two daring climbers scrambled down the bamboo ladder, before going off for our appointment with destiny.

We waited outside the audience chamber for over two hours. Simon became increasingly irritable, and his demands to see the great man were largely ignored. We were getting restive too, aware of passing time.

We had thought of staying at the Ashram, but the sight of wooden beds without mattresses put us off the idea. I had visions of a totally sleepless night as I wrestled with arthritic hip and shoulders whilst lying on a plank in a room full of strangers. With only a little regret, we had to turn down their kind invitations to stay.

We promised to return, however, equipped with inflatable mattresses and lots of insect repellent. We were now needing and wanting to move on.

We never did get to see the Guru. By eight o'clock in the evening we were thoroughly fed up. For a man who was supposed to be very holy and humble, and plainly a great organiser, he certainly had no compunction about keeping people waiting, indeed like any rich and important man in the outside world.

It must be said that the commitment shown by the residents and outside volunteers at the Ashram was remarkable. They appeared to work happily together, slowly but effectively passing steel bowls full of earth and stones to each other up the long chain of people. The contents of these bowls were excavated out of a huge hole in the ground, at least the size of St Paul's Cathedral. They were building or perhaps sculpting an enormous reservoir. This one particular event had the feeling of a science fiction film, some kind of brave new world, as the ladies and gentlemen executing this monumental task appeared to be doing so joyfully, smiling and chatting as they worked, dressed in their glittering Sunday best. They had, it appeared been taken over by some greater celestial being or maybe an ideology they would gladly die for.

Prabu was disappointed, but we insisted on returning home. Simon was more amused than angry when he discovered that someone had made off with his extremely tatty rubber flip-flop shoes. He was quite prepared to return to Kovalam barefoot, but I finally persuaded him to wear the spare pair I had with me in my bag. All four of us somehow squeezed into a rickshaw, Simon standing all the way, at least half of his body exposed to the breeze. It was a tiny vehicle.

We ended the day at a beach café, and were joined by Simon's friend, the evening ended with a promise to Prabu that we would indeed return to the Ashram, very soon, and stay for at least a week or two, offering our services as volunteers. Prabu tottered happily with this off into the darkness to find his bed.

We had arranged to go back to the Ashram on the following Thursday, so eight thirty on that morning found us with all four of our packs as we were not returning to Kovalam. Prabu was happily trotting on ahead. We however walked much more slowly under our heavy packs. One section of the path was particularly narrow, as it ran between a shoulder-high wall and fence for several hundred yards. It got so narrow with our packs so swollen with our belongings that they rubbed and bounced sometimes from the wall on one side to the chain link fence on the other. Part way into this section, my front pack, which must not have been fastened properly, came undone and fell forward, unbalancing me and tripping me at the same time. Queenie was a few yards ahead, making good time, and although I called to her, she did not hear. I couldn't re-fix the pack myself, so decided to carry it in one hand, until we were out of the narrow confines of the path at least, where I could stop Queenie and ask her to help.

I didn't want to break her stride at this point, as I knew her two packs were nearly as heavy as mine, and there was very little room for manoeuvre. Suddenly something totally out of character happened, Queenie turned, and saw me struggling with the pack in my hand, which had brushed against the wall and was entangling my feet. She wanted to take it off me, but I felt it was not necessary at this point.

Her packs were extremely heavy, and I knew I could manage until we got out of the narrow bit of path. I began to say this but she interrupted me, more demanding now,

"Come on Jack, give me the bag."

"No, it's OK," I started to say — then she erupted.

I had wanted to finish, and explain what I intended to do, but she refused to hear it, and, screamed, "For Christ's sake."

I had decided to leave India at the end of March, at least for a while or let's say rest, mainly because of the past ill feeling surrounding Kadhikan, plus Queenie's ever increasing physical pains and consequent stress she had plainly endured well and without complaint, but now she was very understandably losing her nerve — in fact she was poorly. We had to surely go now irrespective of our two week Ashram commitment to Prabu. That's what I thought at the time.

I spent a great part of this second journey to the Ashram staring out of the bus window. Thinking and thinking about how all this had appeared to go wrong especially after such good initial intentions. I could not understand people's behaviour, my own either. India, I concluded, was not the place to try to understand anything much, as most things can easily appear to work against you. This country with its heat and chaos after a while does not so much grate against your nerve endings as scream from inside them. It is a process one has to go through I am told, then, after a year or so one accepts everything as it is.

As it was for us, for me, it was time to leave. We must leave, for the sake of both our mental health, and the sooner the better.

Prabu remained cheerful as ever, Queenie's anger had dissipated as quickly as it had appeared. We had decided to stay at a hotel in the village for the first night at least, and then to explore other possibilities at the Ashram on the next day. We booked into the Hotel City Lights, a large modernist structure, entirely incongruous, a large Odeon in this small village of mostly shacks and small houses. It was hot and uncomfortable so we stopped for a drink in the bar. While waiting, I was overcome by the most terrible feeling of impending disaster. I felt sick, and giddy, sure that some other terrible event was about to happen. I snapped, "Where's my bloody soda? I'm dehydrating!"

Queenie and Prabu looked at me in surprise, and I subsided into my seat, muttering my apologies. The drink came at last, and the feeling dissipated. I put it down to the heat, thirst, and our earlier exchange. A scuffle suddenly broke out at the bar, so we decided it was time to leave. We hoped the disturbance would be resolved long before we returned to the hotel to sleep.

Having dumped most of the contents of the packs in our room, we set off for the Ashram. I was still feeling a little uneasy and put it down, once again, to nightmares and misunderstandings.

At the gates of the Ashram, Prabu was recognised and welcomed. Unlike our first visit we were asked to wait in the reception area.

It transpired that a nightmare had come true. A "communication" was waiting for us, we were told. Prabu disappeared inside, to check on the contents. I tried to fool myself, "No It wasn't for Queenie". Who knew where we were, anyway? It's some mistake. But, deep down, I knew. I had an inexplicable black cloud pass over me. Queenie's mum had died. Somehow I knew the news was for her. Prabu's concerned expression confirmed my suspicions.

"There is bad news from your home." He said gently. He still wouldn't say, but I knew. So did Queenie.

She was taken to the office proper, in order to use the telephone. She tried to ring her mother's home first. If she answered, all would be well in her world at least. There was no reply. With a sinking heart, she rang her brother's number. Engaged. Of course, it would be. There is much to do following a death. After several unsuccessful attempts to contact any of her family in the UK, we returned to the village.

Prabu led us to a small travel agent's shop and she tried again to reach her brother's number. Mercifully, after only three attempts, she got through. Diana, her brother's wife answered. She was greatly distressed.

The original communication in the form of a telegram had gone to Kadhikan who had, for once, on the intelligence volunteered by me as to our likely whereabouts before we had left him, had acted swiftly and telephoned its contents through to the Ashram.

With Prabu interpreting for us, and the staff of the travel agent working and pulling strings on our behalf, seats were found on a flight home the next morning. We would be home within hours. Just one more night to try and sleep.

Prabu had again been the adherent that had held us together for the rest of that terrible day, preventing Queenie from collapsing into hysterical tears, supporting me in my efforts to comfort Queenie. He amused us, chattered endless nonsense to us, sang to us, fed us, got drunk with us, interpreted for us, refused to let us sink into grief and shock. And finally, at midnight, he had unrolled a blanket on the corridor outside our room, and guarded us through what was left of the night. As I lay down in an attempt to sleep, I could hear his voice, as he quietly recited prayers. The sound was oddly comforting, though the language was unintelligible to us, the intent was clear.

Queenie and I lay awake, gazing silently up at the ceiling. We had nothing to say. A movement on the ceiling caught my eye. "What's that?" I asked Queenie, I couldn't see properly without my glasses. She glanced up to where the light from the corridor shone brightly through an air vent above the door. She was silent for a moment. Then she chuckled, a little uncertainly. I reached for my glasses, to see more clearly what the movements were on the ceiling which had begun to amuse Queenie, who by now was giggling helplessly. I lay staring in open-mouthed amazement at the now clear shadow show enacting itself above me.

"Monsters?" I asked incredulously.

I began to giggle, too. I could feel hysteria rising. Queenie joined in, even more heartily, and soon we were gasping helplessly as we watched. Two small geckos, their shadows projected enormously across the ceiling, were moving about near the light, which was throwing their grossly magnified shadows across our ceiling. Their jerky movements reminded us of nothing more than an old film, or a badly photographed cartoon. It looked hilarious.

We watched until we became bored with the impromptu shadow show, and our laughter had become dangerously close to tears. I finally fell asleep, wondering sleepily what Prabu must have thought of the hysterical giggles emanating from our room.

The taxi duly appeared at four am. Thankfully Prabu accompanied us to the airport. After paying the taxi driver for a return trip, I turned every bit of Indian cash we had over to Prabu and thanked him sincerely. I was sad to say goodbye to this well-meaning, kindly man, and hugged him gratefully as we left him, assuring him that we would write, and that we would return someday. We have had three attempts to spend some time in the Ashram, I'm not confident that we'll ever actually get there. We flew off home. It was a relief, yet this place had still left us with a yearning to learn more.

We stayed in England for a few months after the funeral. May found us once more winging our way back to India, to finally see some more of this fascinating country. We headed for Goa again, where we were able to relax. I spent the rest of the monsoon very happily, Queenie helped me a great deal to write this, and as you now know has made her own contributions to this book. We watched the rain. The monsoon season is such a beautiful period in time.

Printed in Poland
by Amazon Fulfillment
Poland Sp. z o.o., Wrocław